ExamInsight For Designing a Microsoft Windows 2000 Network Infrastructure

Exam 70-221

Download practice exam provided by BeachFrontQuizzer, Inc., Friendswood, Texas

Author

Michael Yu Chak Tin

MCSE 4.0/2000, MCSD, MCDBA 4.0/ 2000, MOUS, CCNA, CCDA, CCSE, OCP, CSA

Published by TotalRecall Press

TotalRecall Publications, Inc.
1103 Middlecreek
Friendswood, TX 77546
281-992-3131

NOTE: THIS IS BOOK IS GUARANTEED:
See details at www.TotalRecallPress.com

TotalRecall Publications, Inc.

This Book is Sponsored by BeachFront Quizzer, Inc.

Printed in United States of America

Printed and bound by Data Duplicators of Houston Texas

Printed and bound by Lightning Source, Inc. in the USA and UK

ISBN: 1-59095-027-5

UPC: 6-43977-02221-9

The sponsoring editor is Bruce Moran and the production supervisor is Corby R. Tate.

Edited by Chad Bayer

Dedication

This book is dedicated to my parents John and Esther Yu for their support and encouragement.

Michael Yu Chak Tin

ExamInsight®
For

Designing a Microsoft® Windows® 2000 Network Infrastructure

BY

Michael Yu Chak Tin
MCSE 4.0/2000, MCSD, MCDBA 4.0/ 2000, MCSA, MOUS, CCNP, CCDP, CCSE, CISSP

About the Author

Born in Hong Kong and educated in the US, Michael has worked for Fortune 500 companies as well as small high-tech startups, both in Hong Kong and in the US.

During his stay in the Silicon Valley, Michael developed invaluable experience in internal process improvement applications that automated much of the company's operations. At Pacific Rim Networks Ltd, Michael has participated in the management of technology projects, and the evaluation of new technologies for business applications. For years, Michael has been providing content and writing exam study guides for the leading IT Certification sites worldwide.

Michael has been working extensively on new Internet venture development. His experience and knowledge in shaping strategic framework is a valuable asset essential to the success of a venture.

Michael has been an active member and winner of high school Swimming and Volley Ball teams. Michael loves Volley Ball and Jet Skiing.

About the Book

Part of the TotalRecall: IT ExamInsight Certification Book Series, this new Self Help and Interactive Exam Study Aid with Download Practice testing material is now available for candidate's preparing to sit the Microsoft 70-221 Designing a Microsoft® Windows® 2000 Network Infrastructure Certification exam. The book covers the information associated with each of the exam topics in detail and includes information found in no other book.

Using the book will help readers determine if they are ready for the 70-221 Designing a Microsoft® Windows® 2000 Network Infrastructure certification exam. Each chapter in this book includes pre- and post-assessment questions to assess your comprehension of each topic. This book explains the concepts in a clear and easy-to-understand manner to help you not only pass the exam, but to apply the knowledge later in a real-world situation. Chapter summaries encapsulate the important areas of each chapter in a short review. The large glossary at the end of the book provides a review of essential exam-related terms and concepts that will prove invaluable just before taking the exam. Helpful tips and time management techniques will alleviate pre-exam jitters and put you in control. For implementing ISA Server in a production environment, tips on pre-installation, workstation tuning, application tuning, registry hacks, and maintenance techniques are included.

NOTE: THIS IS BOOK IS GUARANTEED:
See details at **www.TotalRecallPress.com**

Chapter Overview

Table of Contents

Introduction

This book is organized to follow Microsoft's published exam objectives for the 70-221 certification exam. In addition to using this book for exam preparation, you are encouraged to use the enclosed Beachfront Quizzer test modules to constantly assess your study progress.

Michael Yu Chak Tin

Foreword

The world is changing at an incredible pace. It has been many years since computers have entered the mainstream. Now, it is not just the government or a university that possesses them, most of us has at least one of them, in one form or another. Today, we carry around computers with more power then ENIAC had on our wrists or in our pockets. The sheer amount of raw computing power grows at tremendous rates daily. Of course, to make these all work, they need a program or set of guidelines in which to function. Moreover, that brings us to Microsoft Windows® 2000 Enterprise Networking.

Through the many years of experience working with various operating systems, applications and, of course, games, I have found my share of quirks & problems. However, I have also found a lot of potential in them as well. Windows® 2000 Enterprise Networking, in my honest opinion, brings together a new face to enterprise networking. Microsoft has done a remarkable job on improving the stability and reliability to Windows® 2000 Operating System line. Windows NT 3.51 and Windows NT 4.0 were powerful in their respectful days, but now, in the new millennium, we have processors reaching 2300 MHz and better in speed, hard drives revving over 10,000 RPM, and networks running at gigabit speeds, we need the OS to be as quick and possible.

This may sound a lot like a sales pitch, but it isn't. I am no sales person; I couldn't sell ice in the desert. I am a tech; I work with this stuff everyday and love it. I love the problems, the solutions, and staying up till the crack of dawn (my wife, however, is not to keen on that one).

Ultimately, the decision to use or not use any piece of software is up to you (or at least your IT department). I just hope that you give Windows® 2000 Enterprise Networking its fullest chance. Install it on your desktop and your laptop, try some of the new features (offline shares is one of my favorites), and truly put it thru its paces. Don't uninstall it to quickly, like most people do when they first get a problem, there are plenty of resources available to assist you when something doesn't work.

Michael Yu Chak Tin

70-221 Exam Preparation Guide

Designing a Microsoft Windows 2000 Network Infrastructure

You will find the Microsoft Windows 2000 Exam 70-221 guide located at their web site.

http://www.microsoft.com/traincert/exams/70-221.asp

Note: **Exam subject matter and skills being measured are subject to change at any time without prior notice and at Microsoft's sole discretion**

Information you will find in their document will include the following.

Certification Credit

Upon successful completion of this exam, you will achieve Microsoft Certified Professional status. This exam also provides credit toward Microsoft Certified Systems Engineer on Microsoft Windows 2000 certification.

http://www.microsoft.com/traincert/mcp/mcse/

Exam Audience

Exam candidates are those individuals that operate in medium to very large computing environments that use Windows 2000 Server Operating System. Candidates should have a minimum of one year's experience designing network infrastructures in environments that have the following characteristics:

Physical locations 5-150+ and supporting 200-26,000+ users

Typical network services and applications include file and print, database, messaging, proxy server or firewall, dial-in server, desktop management, and Web hosting.

Connectivity needs include connecting individual offices and users at remote locations to the corporate network and connecting corporate networks to the Internet.

Job Skills Needed

This certification exam measures your ability to install, manage, monitor, configure, and troubleshoot DNS, DHCP, Remote Access, Network Protocols, IP Routing, and WINS in a Windows 2000 network infrastructure. In addition, this test measures the skills required to manage, monitor, and troubleshoot Network Address Translation and Certificate Services. Before taking the exam, you should be proficient in the listed job skills.

Skills Being Measured

This certification exam tests the skills required to analyze the business requirements for a network infrastructure and design a network infrastructure that meets business requirements. Network infrastructure elements include:

Network topology

Routing

IP addressing

Name resolution such as WINS and DNS

Virtual private networks

Remote access

Telephony solutions

Analyzing Business Requirements

Analyze the existing and planned business models.

Analyze the company model and the geographical scope. Models include regional, national, international, subsidiary, and branch offices.

Analyze company processes. Processes include information flow, communication flow, service and product life cycles, and decision-making.

Analyze the existing and planned organizational structures. Considerations include management model; company organization; vendor, partner, and customer relationships; and acquisition plans.

Analyze factors that influence company strategies.

Identify company priorities.

Identify the projected growth and growth strategy.

Identify relevant laws and regulations.

Identify the company's tolerance for risk.

Identify the total cost of operations.

Analyze the structure of IT management. Considerations include type of administration, such as centralized or decentralized; funding model; outsourcing; decision-making process, and change-management process.

Analyzing Technical Requirements

Evaluate the company's existing and planned technical environment and goals.

Analyze company size and user and resource distribution.

Assess the available connectivity between the geographic location of worksites and remote sites.

Assess net available bandwidth and latency issues.

Analyze performance, availability, and scalability requirements of services.

Analyze data and system access patterns.

Analyze network roles and responsibilities.

Analyze security considerations.

Analyze the impact of infrastructure design on the existing and planned technical environment.

Assess current applications.

Analyze network infrastructure, protocols, and hosts.

Evaluate network services.

Analyze TCP/IP infrastructure.

Assess current hardware.

Identify existing and planned upgrades and rollouts.

Analyze technical support structure.

Analyze existing and planned network and systems management.

Analyze the network requirements for client computer access.

Analyze end-user work needs.

Analyze end-user usage patterns.

Analyze the existing disaster recovery strategy for client computers, servers, and the network.

Designing a Windows 2000 Network Infrastructure

Modify and design a network topology.

Design a TCP/IP networking strategy.

- Analyze IP subnet requirements.
- Design a TCP/IP addressing and implementation plan.
- Measure and optimize a TCP/IP infrastructure design.
- Integrate software routing into existing networks.
- Integrate TCP/IP with existing WAN requirements.

Design a DHCP strategy.

- Integrate DHCP into a routed environment.
- Integrate DHCP with Windows 2000.
- Design a DHCP service for remote locations.
- Measure and optimize a DHCP infrastructure design.

Design name resolution services.

- Create an integrated DNS design.
- Create a secure DNS design.
- Create a highly available DNS design.
- Measure and optimize a DNS infrastructure design.
- Design a DNS deployment strategy.
- Create a WINS design.
- Create a secure WINS design.
- Measure and optimize a WINS infrastructure design.
- Design a WINS deployment strategy.

Design a multi-protocol strategy. Protocols include IPX/SPX and SNA.

Design a Distributed file system (Dfs) strategy.

- Design the placement of a Dfs root.
- Design a Dfs root replica strategy.

Designing for Internet Connectivity

Design an Internet and extranet access solution. Components of the solution could include proxy server, firewall, routing and remote access, Network Address Translation (NAT), connection sharing, Web server, or mail server.

Design a load-balancing strategy.

Designing a Wide Area Network Infrastructure

Design an implementation strategy for dial-up remote access.

- Design a remote access solution that uses Routing and Remote Access.
- Integrate authentication with Remote Authentication Dial-In User Service (RADIUS).

Design a virtual private network (VPN) strategy.

Design a Routing and Remote Access routing solution to connect locations.

- Design a demand-dial routing strategy.

Designing a Management and Implementation Strategy for Windows 2000 Networking

Design a strategy for monitoring and managing Windows 2000 network services. Services include global catalog, Lightweight Directory Access Protocol (LDAP) services, Certificate Services, DNS, DHCP, WINS, Routing and Remote Access, Proxy Server, and Dfs.

Design network services that support application architecture.

Design a plan for the interaction of Windows 2000 network services such as WINS, DHCP, and DNS.

Design a resource strategy.

- Plan for the placement and management of resources.
- Plan for growth.
- Plan for Decentralized resources or centralized resources.

Total Recall

Chapter 1: Overview of Exam 70-221

The objective of this chapter is to provide the reader with an understanding of the following:

1. The Focus of the 70-221 Exam.
2. The study path of the 70-221 Exam.
3. The Knowledge and skills required to proceed with this book.
4. The Infrastructure Elements to be covered.
5. An overview of the various Microsoft Server products.

Getting Ready (Questions)

1) What is Network Infrastructure?
2) What are the prerequisites of taking this exam?
3) What is the role of Active Directory in this exam?
4) Windows 2000 uses what protocol for authentication in LAN?
5) What is one of the most common methods for securing data traffic to and from your IIS web site?

Getting Ready (Answers)

1) The backbone functions of the network that keep all the network applications and services running.

2) Solid understanding on the topics presented in 70-215 and 70-216.

3) Active Directory is not the focus of this exam. However, since Microsoft expects that all Windows 2000 networks run Active Directory, you must be familiar with it. Going through the topics of 70-216 is definitely helpful.

4) Kerberos is used for security authentication in Windows 2000.

5) SSL is a common method for securing data transmission.

I Introduction

Exam 70-221 Designing a Microsoft Windows 2000 Network Infrastructure is a case centric exam. The exam consists of multiple cases, each includes so-called the "new types of questions". These questions, rather than being traditional theory or skill based, focus on testing your ability to pinpoint problems and introduce solutions.

Scope

The reason why this exam exists comes from the fact that IT professionals tend to focus their efforts entirely on the technical considerations and ignore the business elements. This often disallow them to create designs that deliver results in an efficiently and cost effective manner.

This exam tests your skills in large environment that spans multiple regions. As stated in Microsoft's Audience Profile for the exam, "Candidates for this exam operate in medium to very large computing environments that use the Windows 2000 network operating system". The cases are based on environments that have the following characteristics:

Supported users range from 200-26,000+
Physical locations range from 5-150+
A wide variety of typical network services and applications
Connectivity between multiple sites

Since the exam is about "Network Infrastructure", your focus will be on the foundation services of the network as specified by Microsoft in its exam prep guide:

Network topology
Routing
IP addressing
Name resolution
Virtual private networks
Remote access
Telephony solutions

These foundation services are the backbone of the Active Directory network. You will not be exposed to questions regarding the administration of the Windows 2000 Active Directory network. Instead, you will need to "start from scratch". That is, from learning a particular problem, planning the infrastructure, to the actual implementation of your design.

It is worth to note that, while "Telephony solutions" is listed in the official exam information as one of the skills being tested, this topic has never been introduced in any official training material nor has never been tested in the real exam. You may safely interpret it as "using dial up telephone lines for remote access".

In fact, there is one important topic in the exam that is often ignored. This is compatibility – compatibility with UNIX systems and legacy applications. Almost every scenario case requires that your design be friendly with these "dinosaurs". So, keep this in mind.

Modern Infrastructure

What is meant by network infrastructure in this context? Whether you're building, deploying, or maintaining a solution, it is not possible to ignore its foundation - the network. From the ground up, solutions regardless of any vendor specific favorites must be constructed with the network infrastructure in mind. In fact, this "requirement" unites IT management and Network design efforts under the common goal of developing a scalable and reliable Windows 2000 enterprise solution.

In the past, when everything was simple, a network design job could be very straight forward, in a sense that you only need to ensure that "things work". As the users demand for more and more, simply making things work is no longer enough. You will need to ensure that things work efficiently and reliably. And, with the wide spread use of the internet, we need to further fine tune our solutions so that they can run cost effectively without sacrificing security.

The modern network infrastructure is getting more and more complex, especially when Internet becomes part of the equation. As a collection of networks based on IP, Internet enabled services and protocols have dramatically grown in popularity and have become the de facto standards for heterogeneous enterprise networks.

Modern Application Services

We do not worry about how the entire Internet operates. However, we need to make use of it and its related technology to enhance productivity and produce values. For example, we have intranets, which are the IP networks used by corporations for their own businesses. From a technical point of view, an Intranet is no different than the public Internet except that it is small and private. Applications that run on the public Internet can also run on the Intranets smoothly, making it possible for companies to use WWW technologies on their Intranets for internal applications.

The concept of private intranet has been expanded into the Business-to-Business context in the form of Extranets. These IP based networks are used for business-to-business activities, and are enjoying better and more secure control. In fact, many commerce applications are beginning to use Extranets. The existence of these applications simply makes our job more challenging and at the same time gives us more headaches.

Below are some of the most popular application protocols that run on almost every serious corporate network:

DNS – for resolution of host names
FTP – for transferring files between hosts
HTTP – for WWW browsing
Kerberos - for security authentication
RPC – for programs to execute subroutines remotely
SMTP – for exchanging emails
SNMP - for monitoring and controlling networks
SSL – for secure transmission of data
Telnet – for remote terminal access to hosts

There are many different types of servers to support the above applications. We have Application Servers to serve applications to users, Database Servers to sustain database-intensive operations, AV Servers to deliver streaming multimedia content over the network, Chat Servers to provide real-time online discussions, Fax Servers to send and receive faxes, Web Servers to provide contents on the net, EBusiness Servers to handle online transactions, and Mail Servers to handle message exchanges.

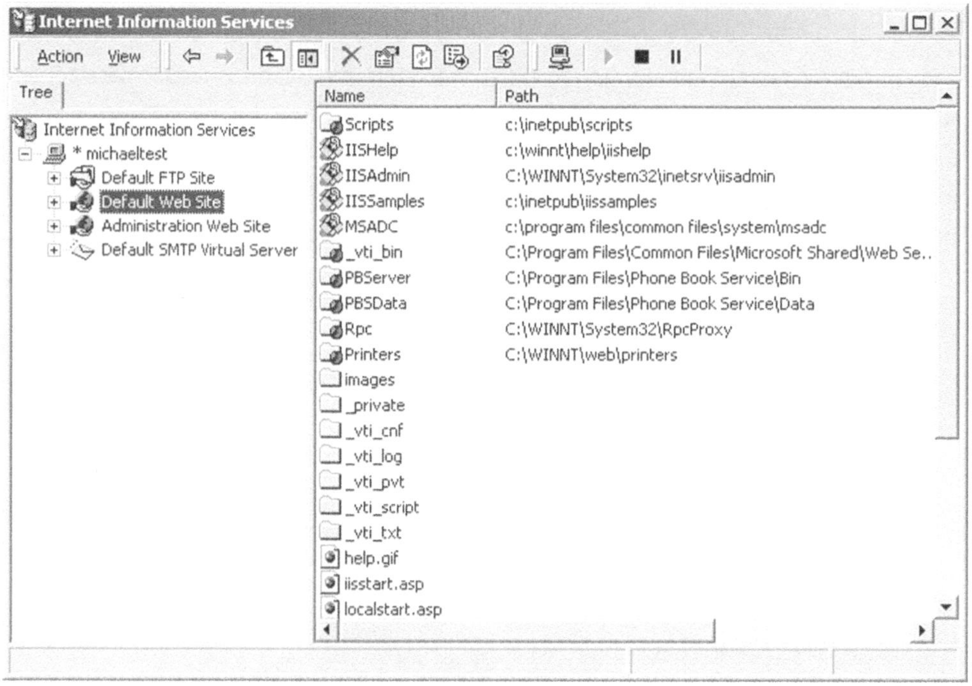

Internet Information Services

Windows 2000 comes with IIS5 for hosting web sites and FTP sites.

In a real world organization, the number of applications may be two to three times more than what we have listed here. The point is, different functions of the organization rely on these applications to exchange information and share resources. Our job is to design an infrastructure, most likely IP based, to support the information and resource flows within (and possibly beyond) the organization. In order for you to do so, solid understanding of the above mentioned services and protocols is necessary. They are out of the scope of this book, but are covered in depth in the TotalRecall Press Inside Scoop series for 70-215 and 70-216.

The Supporting Mechanisms

As mentioned earlier, there are many different types of applications running on the network nowadays. And since most of them are IP based, we need a series of IP related technologies to sustain the entire infrastructure. For the purpose of supporting a Windows 2000 based network, the components below are critical:

Network topology:

- LAN
- WAN
- Connection methods

Routing:

- RRAS
- CIDR

IP addressing:

- NAT
- Subnetting

Name resolution:

- WINS
- DNS

Virtual private networks:

- CA
- IPSec

Remote access:

- Terminal services
- Dial on demand

Compatibility:

- Unix
- Legacy applications

These components together form the entire infrastructure. In fact, on every case scenario you will need to have them applied towards your design selectively, carefully and smartly.

Pop Quiz 1.1

Pop Quiz 1.1 *Questions*

HTTPS uses what technology for security?

True or False: For performance reason, you should tell your browser to not use SSL when making e-transactions.

True or False: Network Infrastructure is a term used for Windows 2000 network only.

Give one example of a legacy application.

Pop Quiz 1.1

Pop Quiz 1.1 *Answers*

1) SSL
2) False. SSL is needed for security.
3) False. Network infrastructure is OS independent.
4) A text base application running on an early release of OS/2.

II Your Preparation Path

In this book, a framework consisting of the above components will be used for examining the case scenarios. We will focus on the WHAT, WHY, WHEN aspects (which are exactly what this exam is for) and will not cover the technical KNOW-HOW (which is the focus of 70-215 and 70-216). So, before proceeding with this book, make sure you are solidly familiar with the above technologies by going through the TotalRecall Press Inside Scoop series for 70-215 and 70-216 (or other books covering the 215 and the 216 exams, although books from TotalRecall Press are always highly recommended). In addition, know all the server products Microsoft provides. These server products include:

Exchange Server
Proxy Server (now replaced by ISA Server)
SMS Server
SNA Server
SQL Server

Note: The new Application Server and the BizTalk Server are too new to be covered in the actual exam, and are not to be included in the curriculum.

Pop Quiz 1.2

Pop Quiz 1.2 *Questions*

Refer to the list of Microsoft server applications in this chapter.

1) SMTP is mostly related to:
2) SNMP is mostly related to:
3) DLC is mostly related to:
4) NAT is mostly related to:

Pop Quiz 1.2

Pop Quiz 1.2 *Answers*

1) Exchange Server
2) SMS Server
3) SNA Server
4) Proxy Server

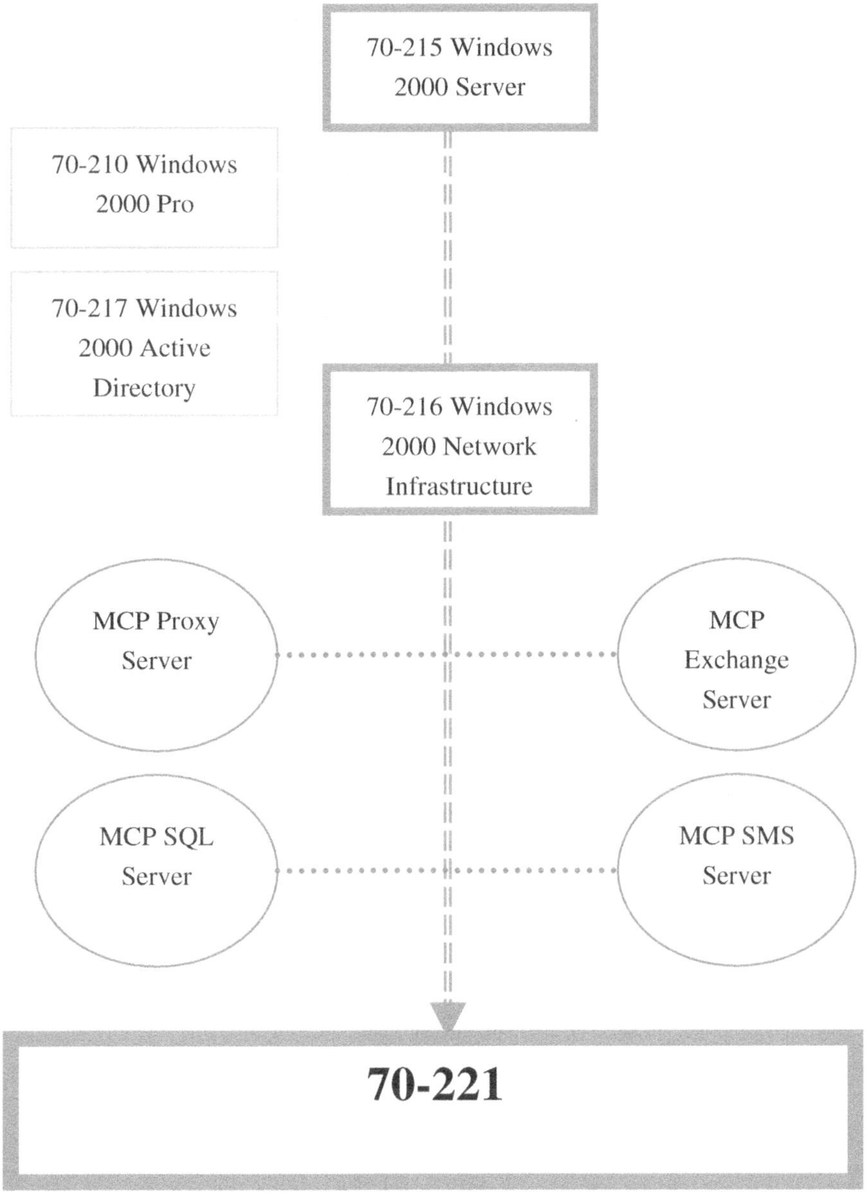

Suggested exam preparation path

III Technology Overview

Overview of Active Directory

Active Directory is the directory service that stores information about objects on a network and makes this information available to users and network administrators. It gives network users access to permitted resources anywhere on the network without the need for multiple logons, and provides network administrators with a single point of administration for all network objects.

Active Directory is made up of one or more domains. A domain is a collection of computers defined by the administrator that shares a common directory database and optionally spans more than one physical location. It has a unique name among the network, as well as its own security policies and security relationships with other domains. It provides access to the centralized user accounts and group accounts maintained, and acts as the maximum administrative boundary of the administrator.

A trust relationship is a logical relationship established between different domains, allowing pass-through authentication in which a trusting domain honors the logon authentications of a trusted domain.

DNS domains should not be confused with Active Directory networking domains. In the context of the Domain Name System (DNS), a domain is any subtree within the DNS namespace, and most often the names for these DNS domains are designed to correspond to the corresponding Active Directory domains.

Global catalog is a domain controller that contains the following:

- a partial replica of every domain directory partition in the forest
- a full replica of its own domain directory partition
- a full replica of its schema and configuration directory partitions
- a replica of every object in Active Directory, each with a limited number of attributes

Active Directory builds the global catalog automatically by its replication system. Although not straightly necessary, you can specify additional properties to meet the needs of your network.

Overview of Exchange Server

With Exchange 2000, network users can take advantage of Outlook Web Access client, full-text indexing, and instant messaging.

By leveraging Active Directory, mailboxes, contacts and distribution groups are stored and maintained in an entirely unified infrastructure. In fact, Exchange extends the Active Directory schema and provides additional options for Exchange management tasks.

Exchange 2000 can operate in Active Directory under the following two modes: mixed and native. Only in mixed mode can Exchange 2000 coexist in the same Exchange site as a server running Exchange 5.5.

Exchange 2000 operates under a distributed and extensible architecture, meaning it is possible to install additional servers running Exchange 2000 to the organization to accommodate extra load. An Exchange 2000 front-end server is a computer that redirects and proxies traffic to a back-end server hosting the Exchange 2000 store.

Replication is an important part of your Exchange 2000 operations. This probably is most relevant to the connectivity aspect of your infrastructure design.

Overview of ISA Server

ISA Server is a replacement upgrade of Proxy Server, with added firewall capabilities.

ISA Server caching features include:

Distributed caching with Cache Array Routing Protocol (CARP)

Hierarchical caching through the chaining of arrays of ISA Server computers

Reverse caching of HTTP and FTP content of publishing servers:

- Secure Web publishing allows secure access to internal Web servers.
- Secure application server publishing makes internal servers accessible to specific clients.

Scheduled caching for automatic content refreshment

In addition to caching, ISA Server provides the following firewall and security features:

- Configure site and content rules and protocol rules to control how your internal clients access the Internet
- Configure intrusion detection mechanisms to alert you should an attack occur.
- Centrally secure your Windows 2000 installations by setting the appropriate level of security via predefined templates.
- Analyzes and controls application-specific traffic via different application-aware filters.
- Deploy standards-based, secure remote access with the Windows 2000 virtual private network services.

Overview of SMS Server

Systems Management Server (SMS) delivers scalable and cost-effective configuration management for Windows–based desktop and server systems in your network. Through the use of the industry-standard management protocol SNMP, it can work with complementary management tools from Microsoft and other companies, and can integrate with other Microsoft Server products.

SMS can help you perform the following:

- Distribution of applications, software updates, and operating systems over simple or advanced enterprise networks
- Discovers and tracks the distributed Windows-based software as well as the hardware assets in your network
- Remote troubleshooting of Windows-based systems from a central location

Overview of SNA Server

SNA Server is a server gateway application that connects PC-based local area networks to:

IBM System/390 mainframe

AS/400 midrange systems

Its enables users of the leading desktop systems to share resources on mainframes and AS/400s without the need for installing SNA protocols on the PC or deploying any specific client software on the host.

Desktop clients supported include:

Windows 2000 Professional

Windows NT Workstation

Windows 95/98

Windows 3.x

Macintosh

UNIX

MS-DOS

IBM OS/2

The SNA Server gateway handles protocol translation and allows each machine to run its native protocols, thus minimizing resource requirements on each PC and on the host system.

On the LAN side, protocols supported include:

TCP/IP

Banyan VINES

Novell IPX/SPX

NetBEUI

AppleTalk

Overview of SQL Server

SQL Server 2000 is the database solution provided by Microsoft on the server side of the network. Apart from the regular database access functionalities, it includes the following facilities and supports:

Data Transformation Services
Data Mining
Analysis (OLAP) Services
Indexed Views
Meta Data Services
Office 2000 Integration
Data Warehousing Alliance
Web-Enabled Analysis
English Query
Rich XML Support
Web Access to Data
Distributed Partitioned Views
High Availability
Web and Application Hosting
Security
Clickstream Analysis
Developer Productivity Tools
Virtual system area network (VI SAN).
Full Text Search

SQL Server 2000 enables database access from within the internet using a Uniform Resource Locator (URL). This adds flexibility towards your network infrastructure design, as clients can use web browsers as their standardized access interfaces.

Replication and redundancy are the important parts of your SQL Server 2000 operations. This probably is most relevant to the connectivity and fault tolerance aspects of your infrastructure design.

What's Next

In subsequent chapters will be look at the each of the above elements one by one. As mentioned earlier, we will focus on the WHAT, WHY, WHEN aspects. To be precise, we will, based on the published Exam Objectives, examine the cases and make the following decisions:

WHAT infrastructure technology to deploy for a specific scenario

WHY a particular infrastructure technology is preferred for a specific scenario

WHEN is the best time (and what is the order of implementation) for deploying a particular infrastructure technology

IV Chapter 1: Review Questions

1. Draw a line between the protocols on the left to the descriptions on the right:

DNS		Programs to execute subroutines remotely
FTP		Resolution of host names
HTTP		Secure transmission of data
Kerberos		Remote terminal access to hosts
RPC		Transferring files between hosts
SMTP		WWW browsing
SNMP		Exchanging emails
SSL		Monitoring and controlling networks
Telnet		Security authentication

2. For a DNS server to work in a Windows 2000 Active Directory network, what three types of zone records must be supported?

---

3. What is the preferred name resolution method in a pure Windows 2000 network?

---

4. What Microsoft software product can be used to enhance client web browsing performance?

---

5. What Microsoft software product can be used to protect your intranet from malicious attacks originated from the outside world?

---

6. What Microsoft software product can be used to centrally manage all the network components within your enterprise network?

---

7. SNA Server connects your PC-based local area networks to what systems?

---

8. With ISA Server, distributed caching is made possible with what protocol?

Chapter 1: Review Answers

1. DNS---------------- Resolution of host names

FTP ------------------- Transferring files between hosts

HTTP----------------- WWW browsing

Kerberos------------- Security authentication

RPC------------------- Programs to execute subroutines remotely

SMTP ---------------- Exchanging emails

SNMP ---------------- Monitoring and controlling networks

SSL ------------------- Secure transmission of data

Telnet----------------- Remote terminal access to hosts

---

2. For a DNS server to work in a Windows 2000 Active Directory network, what three types of zone records must be supported?

Answer: SRV, A, and PTR are the records that a DNS server must support in order to run in an Active Directory network.

---

3. What is the preferred name resolution method in a pure Windows 2000 network?

Answer: DNS is always the preferred name resolution method in a pure Windows 2000 network.

4. What Microsoft software product can be used to enhance client web browsing performance?

Answer: Proxy Server provides caching functionalities so that requests can be served locally for better performance.

---

5. What Microsoft software product can be used to protect your intranet from malicious attacks originated from the outside world?

Answer: ISA Internet Security and Acceleration Server is the next generation firewall and proxy server designed for use with Windows 2000.

---

6. What Microsoft software product can be used to centrally manage all the network components within your enterprise network?

Answer: System Management Server uses SNMP to manage the entire network.

---

7. SNA Server connects your PC-based local area networks to what systems?

Answer: SNA Server is a server gateway application that connects PC-based local area networks to IBM System/390 mainframe and AS/400 midrange systems.

---

8. With ISA Server, distributed caching is made possible with what protocol?

Answer: ISA supports distributed caching with Cache Array Routing Protocol (CARP).

Total Recall

Chapter 2: Overview for Infrastructure Components

The objective of this chapter is to provide the reader with an understanding of the following:

1. Network topology
2. IP addressing
3. Name resolution
4. Routing and Remote access
5. NAT and Proxying
6. Security Measures and Virtual private networks

Getting Ready (Questions)

1) What is the most common WAN topology in use today?
2) What is the most common LAN topology in use today?
3) Why do you need to perform subnetting?
4) What name resolution method is used to support the legacy Windows 3.11 clients?
5) How do we improve web browsing performance?

Getting Ready (Answers)

1) Mesh is the most common type of WAN topology if redundancy is critical.

2) Star topology is most common among LANs.

3. Subnetting can be used to improve network performance and enhance security. It is a required measure if you are to segment your network.

4) WINS is the choice of name resolution method if legacy support is required.

5) Proxy Server provides advanced caching functionalities to resolve requests locally whenever possible.

I Introduction

To establish our infrastructure framework, let's go through the critical infrastructure components first. Remember, our focus will be on:

- Network topology
- IP addressing
- Protocols
- Name resolution
- Routing and Remote access
- Security Measures and Virtual private networks

In fact, many of these are mutually related, and they have all been covered in exam 215 and 216. We will briefly recap them here.

II LAN

A topology is the "shape" of a network. In the world of LAN, there are four principal topologies:

1. Bus topology: All devices are connected to a central backbone.

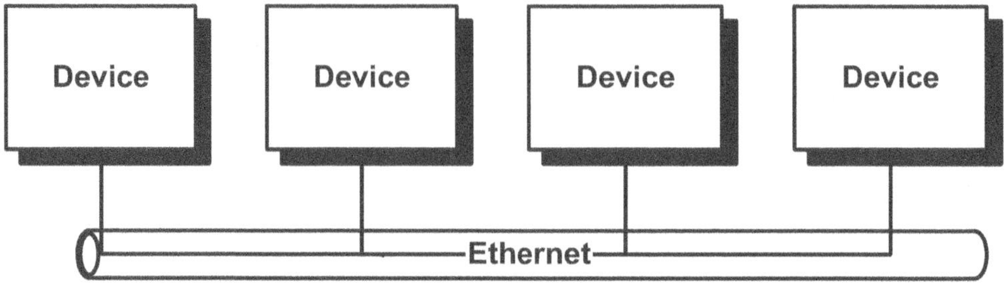

Figure 2.1 Ethernet

2. Ring topology: All devices are connected to one another in the form of a closed loop.

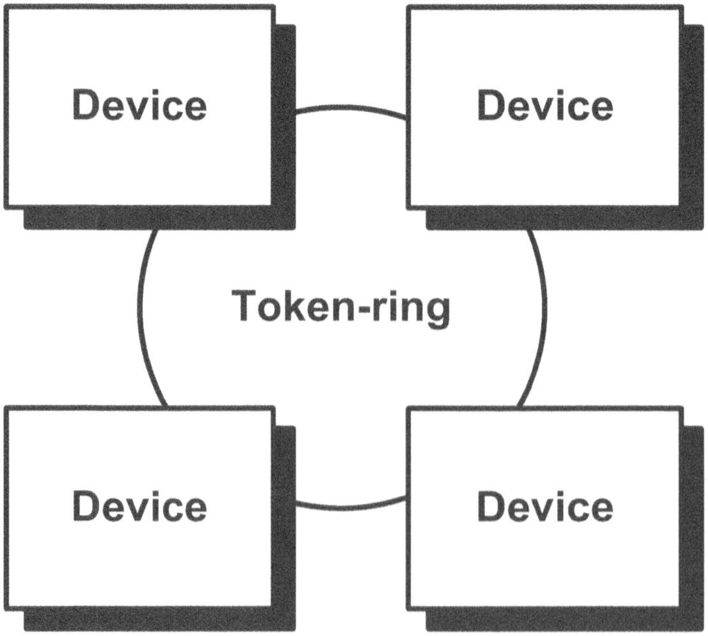

Figure 2.2 Token Ring

3. Star topology: All devices are connected to a central device, such as a hub.

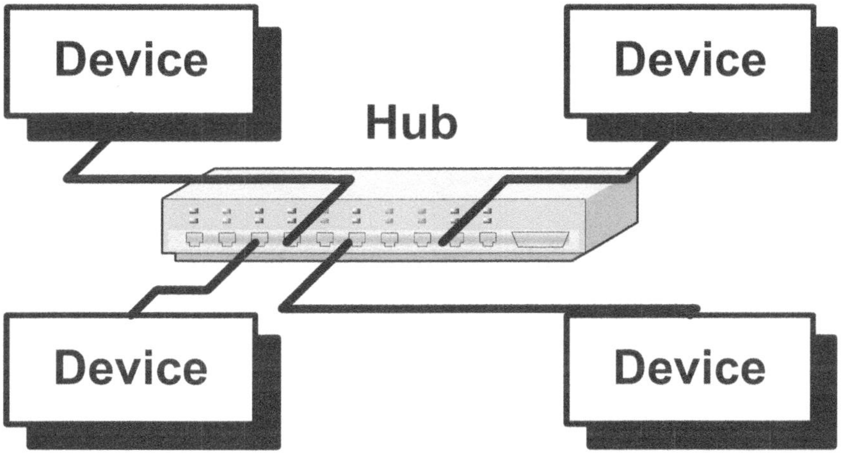

Figure 2.3 Star Topology

4. Tree topology: A combination of bus and star topologies.

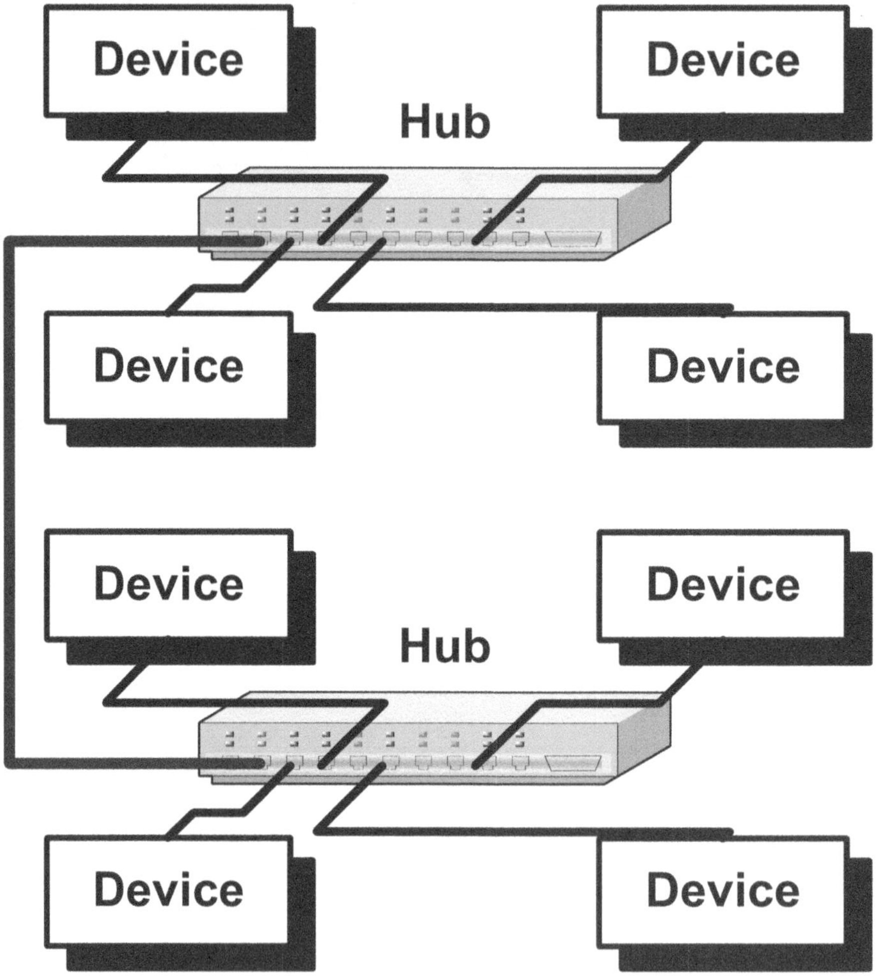

Figure 2.4 Combination bus and star topology

There are many different types of LANs. For example, we have Ethernet, which is regarded as the most common LAN type for PCs. On the other hand, most Apple Macintosh networks are based on the Apple's AppleTalk network system, which is an entirely different animal. What differentiates one LAN from another are the topologies, the protocols and the media used.

The 70-221 exam do not test your knowledge on LAN heavily. In fact, all modern LANs use the Star topology anyway. However, be expected to see scenarios with LANs of different types involved: some being the legacy IBM Token Ring, some running Novell Netware, and some running AppleTalk. Windows 2000 provides services to serve these needs, as introduced in exam 70-215.

Pop Quiz 2.1

Pop Quiz 2.1 *Questions*

1) What LAN topology is the most common in today's LAN?
2) What LAN topology uses only coaxial cable for connection?
3) What LAN topologies require the use of hubs or LAN switches?

Pop Quiz 2.1

Pop Quiz 2.1 *Answers*

1) Star
2) Bus
3) Star and Tree

III WAN

In the context of WAN, we have one common form of topology – the Mesh topology.

A WAN is a computer network that spans a multiple geographical areas. Typically, it consists of multiple LANs. Computers on the LANs are connected to a WAN mostly through public networks like the Internet or the telephone system for cost reasons. More stable performance can be obtained through the use of dedicated connections, assuming the company has a deep pocket.

Dedicated connections can be in the form of ISDN, leased lines, Frame Relays or ATM.

ISDN

ISDN - abbreviation of integrated services digital network, it is an aging international communications standard for sending voice, video, and data over digital telephone lines. It supports data transfer rates of 64 Kbps per channel. A basic rate ISDN solution allows you to use two channels for data communication, and is ideal for use by small remote branch offices. Its cost is charged based on actual usage, and is a viable choice for on demand backup connection (in case the primary connection method fails).

Leased Lines

Leased Line - a rather "permanent" connection between two points. Unlike dial-up connections, a leased line is always active, and fee is charged on a fixed monthly basis - the longer the distance between the end points the higher the cost it will incur. If your company has relative few points, that there is a high volume of data transfer on a daily basis, or that internet connection is essential, a T-1 channel with a maximum transmission speed of 1.544 Mbps is the ideal choice. If you need to establish a mesh topology among multiple points, leased lines may be way too costly though.

Packet Services

X.25 was a popular standard for packet-switching networks which connect multiple devices on a Wide Area Network. It is effectively a mesh mechanism. Frame Relay is a faster and more popular alternative nowadays, and is capable of supporting data transfer rates of 1.544 Mbps and 45 Mbps. For the best possible quality of service and performance, ATM is the most preferred choice.

Short for Asynchronous Transfer Mode, ATM works based on transferring data in cells of a fixed size. The constant cell size allows ATM equipment to transmit multimedia content and data over the same network smoothly without being hogged by any particular type of packet.

Mesh Topology

Regardless of the "medium" used, mesh seems to be the choice for multi–sites setup. A mesh network deploys a topology in which devices are connected with many redundant interconnections between network nodes. There are two types of mesh topologies: Full and Partial.

In a full mesh setup, every node has a circuit connecting it to every other node in the entire network.

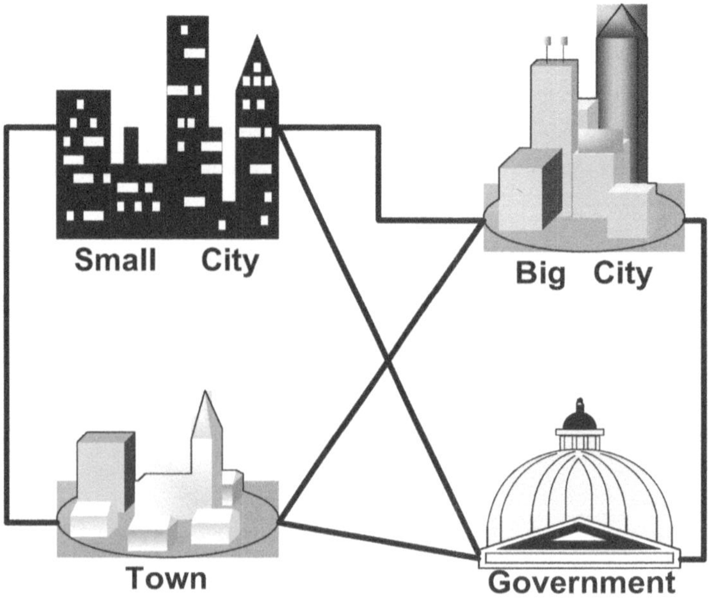

Figure 2.5 Mesh Topology

With partial mesh, only some but not all nodes are organized in a full mesh scheme.

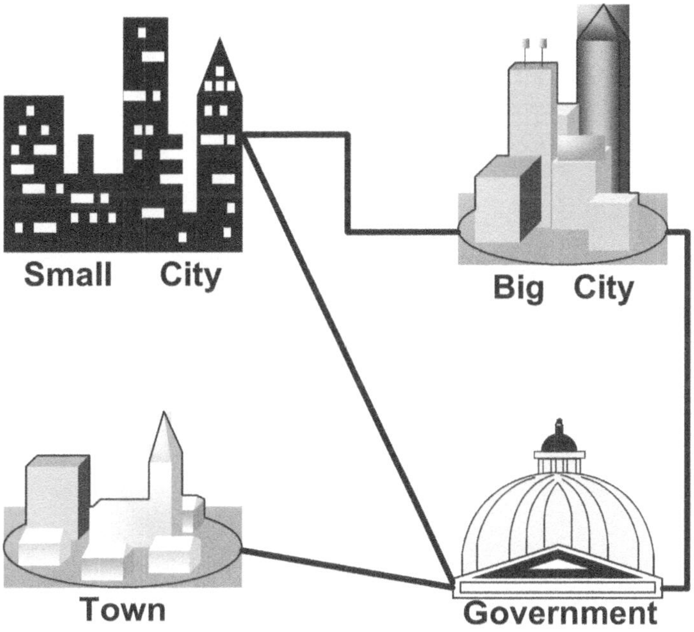

Figure 2.6 Partial Mesh Topology

A network that uses partial mesh as its topology is less expensive to build. However, if 100% redundancy is required, full mesh will be more preferable. Put it this way, for critical networks like the backbones, by all means go ahead with full mesh.

Pop Quiz 2.2

Pop Quiz 2.2 *Questions*

1) 2B + D is a term used in what WAN technology?
2) True or False: T1 has a higher data transfer rate than E1.
3) What WAN technology uses 53-bytes cells for data transmission?
4) True or False: ATM is ideal for connection from country to country.

Pop Quiz 2.2

Pop Quiz 2.2 *Answers*

1) ISDN
2) False. E1is used in Europe, and has a rate of 2MBPS.
3) ATM
4) False. ATM is ideal for connection within a Metropolitan area.

IV IP Infrastructure

An IP address is an identifier for a network device. The TCP/IP protocol relies on the IP address of the destination for routing messages. In version 4 of TCP/IP, the format of an IP address is a 32-bit numeric address written as four numbers separated by periods.

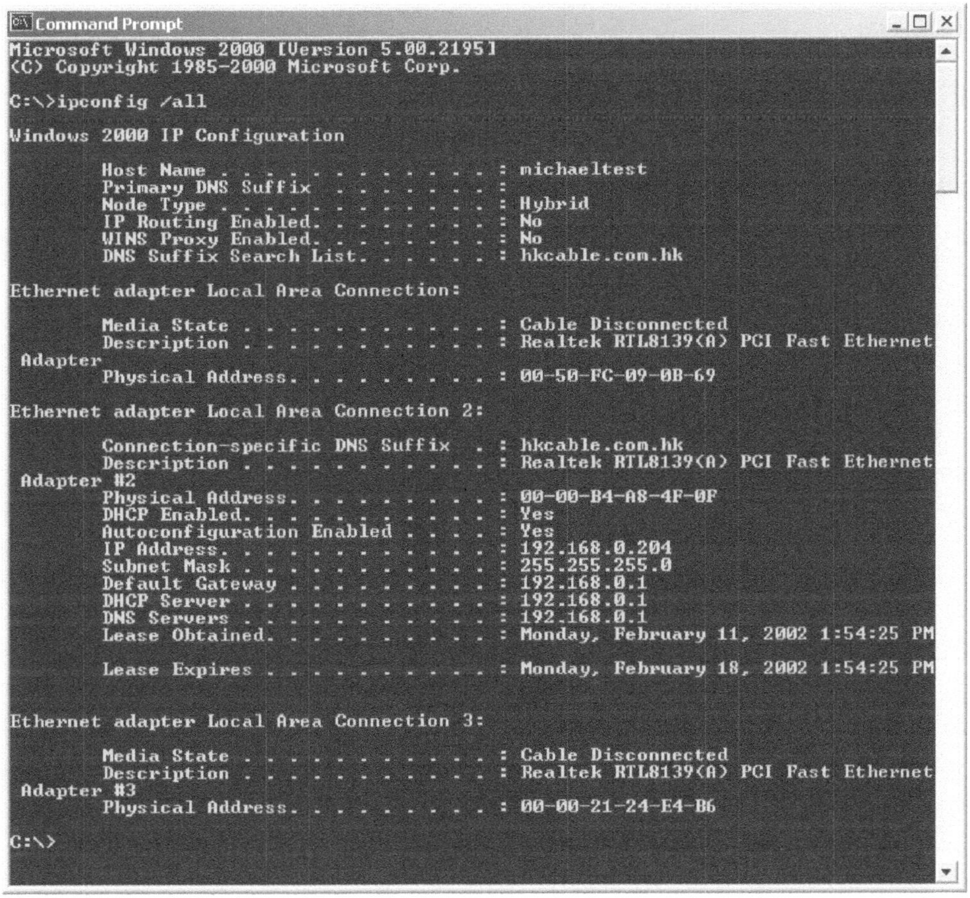

```
Command Prompt
Microsoft Windows 2000 [Version 5.00.2195]
(C) Copyright 1985-2000 Microsoft Corp.

C:\>ipconfig /all

Windows 2000 IP Configuration

        Host Name . . . . . . . . . . . . : michaeltest
        Primary DNS Suffix  . . . . . . . :
        Node Type . . . . . . . . . . . . : Hybrid
        IP Routing Enabled. . . . . . . . : No
        WINS Proxy Enabled. . . . . . . . : No
        DNS Suffix Search List. . . . . . : hkcable.com.hk

Ethernet adapter Local Area Connection:

        Media State . . . . . . . . . . . : Cable Disconnected
        Description . . . . . . . . . . . : Realtek RTL8139(A) PCI Fast Ethernet
 Adapter
        Physical Address. . . . . . . . . : 00-50-FC-09-0B-69

Ethernet adapter Local Area Connection 2:

        Connection-specific DNS Suffix  . : hkcable.com.hk
        Description . . . . . . . . . . . : Realtek RTL8139(A) PCI Fast Ethernet
 Adapter #2
        Physical Address. . . . . . . . . : 00-00-B4-A8-4F-0F
        DHCP Enabled. . . . . . . . . . . : Yes
        Autoconfiguration Enabled . . . . : Yes
        IP Address. . . . . . . . . . . . : 192.168.0.204
        Subnet Mask . . . . . . . . . . . : 255.255.255.0
        Default Gateway . . . . . . . . . : 192.168.0.1
        DHCP Server . . . . . . . . . . . : 192.168.0.1
        DNS Servers . . . . . . . . . . . : 192.168.0.1
        Lease Obtained. . . . . . . . . . : Monday, February 11, 2002 1:54:25 PM

        Lease Expires . . . . . . . . . . : Monday, February 18, 2002 1:54:25 PM


Ethernet adapter Local Area Connection 3:

        Media State . . . . . . . . . . . : Cable Disconnected
        Description . . . . . . . . . . . : Realtek RTL8139(A) PCI Fast Ethernet
 Adapter #3
        Physical Address. . . . . . . . . : 00-00-21-24-E4-B6

C:\>
```

Figure 2.7 Command Prompt

You may type ipconfig /all on a Windows 2000 computer to show all the IP address settings.

IP Address Classes

There are a total of five classes, with three of them being widely in use. The Class A address range supports 16 million hosts on each of 127 networks, the Class B range supports 65.000 hosts on each of 16.000 networks, and the Class C ranges supports 254 hosts on each of 2 million networks. On the internet, address assignments are coordinated by IANA.

Figure 2.8 IANA' web site is at http://www.iana.org .

Subnetting

To probably segment your network and to allow future expansion, you often have to deal with sub-netting. A subnet is a portion of a network that shares a common address component, i.e. uses the same IP address prefix. Sub-netting is useful for both security and performance reasons.

IP sub-netting is done via the subnet mask. As you know, every IP address has two components, the network address and the host address. A subnet mask determines what subnet an IP address belongs to by comparing the network part of the addresses.

Sub-netting requires that you further divide the host part of the addresses such that a part of the host address is reserved to identify the particular subnet.

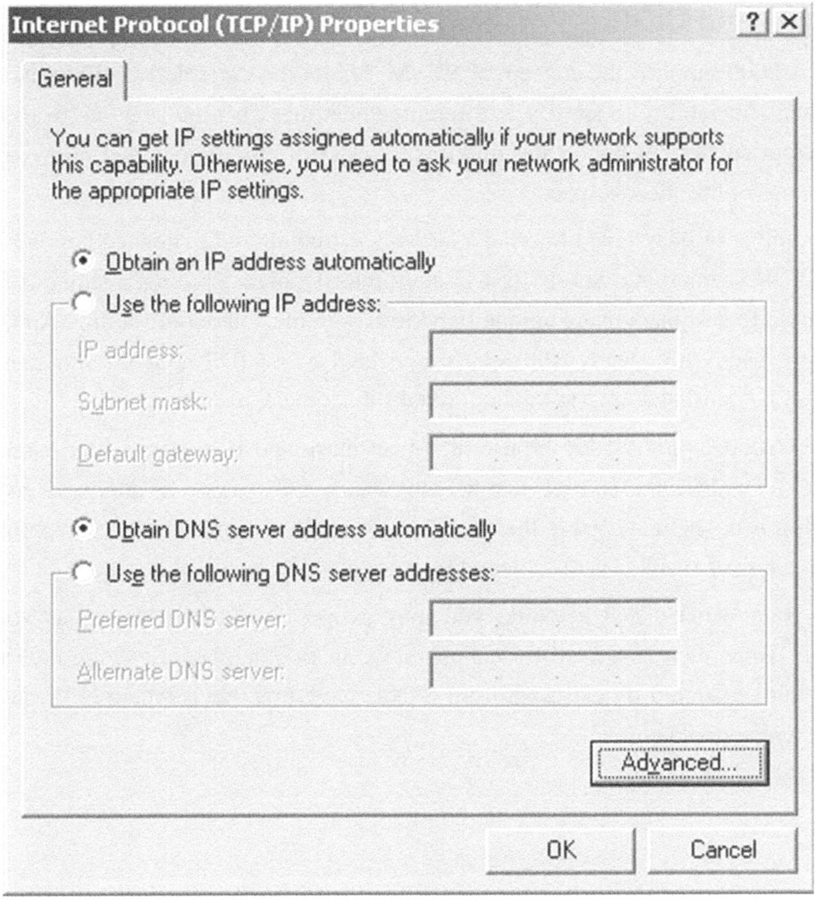

Figure 2.9 Internet Protocol Properties Options

You may configure the client subnet settings manually on each client, or have DHCP configure the settings centrally and automatically.

VLSM and CIDR

Windows 2000 supports the concept of VLSM. Shorts for Variable-Length Subnet Mask, it represents the ability to specify a different subnet mask for the same network number on different subnets. It breaks the traditional "classful" limitations and allow for more efficient use of the address space.

As the number of unassigned Internet addresses is running out, a new addressing scheme called CIDR is emerging. Shorts for Classless Inter-Domain Routing, a single IP address can be used to designate many unique IP addresses in the context of routing. An IP prefix is used to specify how many addresses are covered by a CIDR address, although such a prefix can be translated back to the traditional subnet mask format.

Windows 2000 supports both the use of subnet mask and IP prefix. CIDR addresses in practice can reduce the size of routing tables and make more IP addresses available, although it is not being tested in the 70-221 exam at all. As long as you can appropriately devise the proper IP subnets (as covered in exam 70-215), you will do fine.

Within your own isolated network, you may assign IP addresses freely as you wish. However, when there is a need for connecting your private network to the Internet, you must obtain registered IP addresses from IANA. Note that this is where NAT and Proxy Server come into play.

Pop Quiz 2.3

Pop Quiz 2.3 *Questions*

1) Which organization is in charge of allocating IP addresses for internet use?
2) Which organization is in charge of allocating IP addresses for internal network use?
3) CIDR reduces the workload of what device?
4) IP sub-netting is done via:

Pop Quiz 2.3

Pop Quiz 2.3 *Answers*

1) IANA
2) Your internal administrator.
3) Router
4) subnet mask.

DHCP

Static IP configuration is never desirable except for the dedicated servers. Dedicated serves should not use dynamic configuration. Clients, however, should have their addressing done dynamically via DHCP.

Shorts for Dynamic Host Configuration Protocol, DHCP is a protocol for assigning dynamic IP addresses to the network devices entirely automatically. It simplifies network administration because you do not need to manually keep track of the IP address assignments. DHCP client support is built into Windows 95. 98. ME, NT and 2000. Windows 2000 and NT Servers provide DHCP server side functionalities.

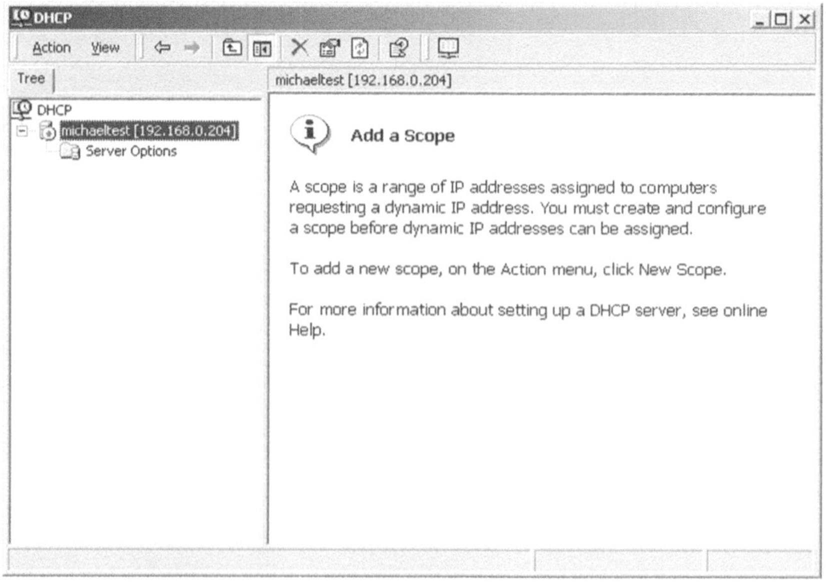

Figure 2.10 DHCP

The DHCP Snap-In allows you to configure your Windows 2000 Server to provide DHCP service to the clients.

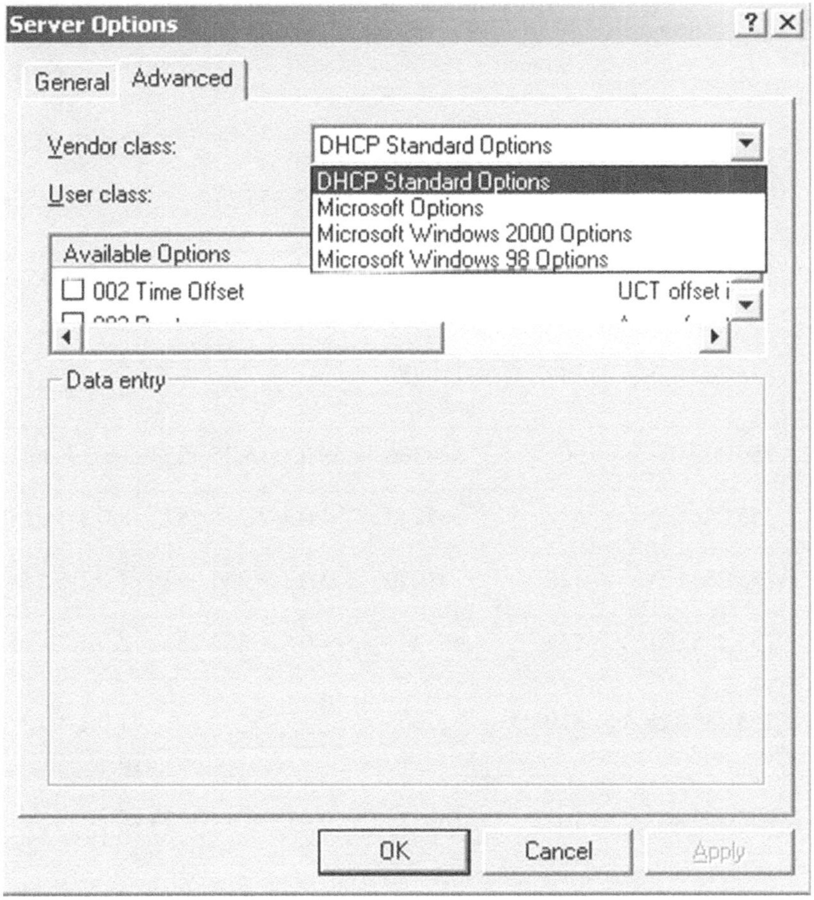

Figure 2.11 Server options

You may configure different DHCP options for different types of clients, or use the standard options for all clients.

For your convenience, enclosed are the IP address tables for Class A, B and C addresses:

IP Address Table (Class A)

Number of Subnet bits	Subnet Mask	Number of Subnets	Number of Hosts	The first Subnet Address Range	The second Subnet Address Range
2	255.192.0.0	2	4194302	64.0.1-127.255.254	128.0.1-191.255.254
3	255.224.0.0	6	2097150	32.0.1-63.255.254	64.0.1-95.0.254
4	255.240.0.0	14	1048574	16.0.1-31.255.254	32.0.1-47.255.254
5	255.248.0.0	30	524286	8.0.1-15.255.254	16.0.1-23.255.254
6	255.252.0.0	62	262142	4.0.1-7.255.254	8.0.1-11.255.254
7	255.254.0.0	126	131070	2.0.1-3.255.254	4.0.1-5.255.254
8	255.255.0.0	254	65534	1.0.1-1.255.254	2.0.1-2.255.254
9	255.255.128.0	510	32766	0.128.1-0.255.254	1.0.1-1.127.254
10	255.255.192.0	1022	16382	0.64.1-0.127.254	0.128.1-0.191.254
11	255.255.224.0	2046	8190	0.32.1-0.63.254	0.64.1-0.95.254
12	255.255.240.0	4094	4094	0.16.1-0.31.254	0.32.1-0.47.254
13	255.255.248.0	8190	2046	0.8.1-0.15.254	0.16.1-0.23.254
14	255.255.252.0	16382	1022	0.4.1-0.7.254	0.8.1-0.11.254
15	255.255.254.0	32766	510	0.2.1-0.3.254	0.4.1-0.5.254
16	255.255.255.0	65534	254	0.1.1-0.1.254	0.2.1-0.2.254
17	255.255.255.128	131070	126	0.0.129-0.0.254	0.1.1-0.1.126

Number of Subnet bits	Subnet Mask	Number of Subnets	Number of Hosts	The first Subnet Address Range	The second Subnet Address Range
18	255.255.255.192	262142	62	0.0.65-0.0.126	0.0.129-0.0.190
19	255.255.255.224	524286	30	0.0.33-0.0.62	0.0.65-0.0.94
20	255.255.255.240	1048574	14	0.0.17-0.0.30	0.0.33-0.0.46
21	255.255.255.248	2097150	6	0.0.9-0.0.14	0.0.17-0.0.22
22	255.255.255.252	4194302	2	0.0.5-0.0.6	0.0.9-0.0.10

Table 1 Class A IP Address Table

IP Address Table (Class B)

Number of Subnet bits	Subnet Mask	Number of Subnets	Number of Hosts	The first Subnet Address Range	The second Subnet Address Range
2	255.255.192.0	2	16382	64.1-127.254	128.1-191.254
3	255.255.224.0	6	8190	32.1-63.254	64.1-95.254
4	255.255.240.0	14	4094	16.1-31.254	32.1-47.254
5	255.255.248.0	30	2046	8.1-15.254	16.1-23.254
6	255.255.252.0	62	1022	4.1-7.254	8.1-11.254
7	255.255.254.0	126	510	2.1-3.254	4.1-5.254
8	255.255.255.0	254	254	1.1-254	2.1-2.254
9	255.255.255.128	510	126	0.129-0.254	1.1-1.126
10	255.255.255.192	1022	62	0.65-0.126	0.129-0.190
11	255.255.255.224	2046	30	0.33-0.62	0.65-0.94
12	255.255.255.240	4094	14	0.17-0.30	0.33-0.46
13	255.255.255.248	8190	6	0.9-0.14	0.17-0.22
14	255.255.255.252	16382	2	0.5-0.6	0.9-0.10

Table 2 Class B IP Address Table

IP Address Table (Class C)

Number of Subnet bits	Subnet Mask	Number of Subnets	Number of Hosts	The first Subnet Address Range	The second Subnet Address Range
2	255.255.255.192	2	62	65-126	129-190
3	255.255.255.224	6	30	33-62	65-94
4	255.255.255.240	14	14	17-30	33-46
5	255.255.255.248	30	6	9-14	17-22
6	255.255.255.252	62	2	5-6	9-10

Table 3 Class C IP Address Table

V Routing and Remote Access

Routing

When a router receives a packet, whether it is an IP packet, an IPX packet or any other routable packet, it makes a routing decision based on the destination address portion that comes with the packet. It then looks up the destination address in its routing table and make the following decisions:

If the destination address is known, the router forwards the packet to the next hop gateway for that destination network. Once the packet leaves the router, it is the responsibility of the next hop gateway to forward the packet to the next stop.

If the destination address is NOT known, the router may forward the packet to a predetermined default gateway and have the default gateway take care of the rest.

If the default gateway has no idea on who to handle the packet, the packet will be dropped.

The routing table includes a list of networks known to the router. It can learn these routes by the following means:

a routing protocol

a manually set static route

by being directly connected

For routing to be successful, all of the routers must know of a way to reach each other, and the receiving host must know how to reply back to the sending host in order for data to pass.

In Windows 2000. routing between subnets or networks is done via the RRAS service. It allows routing via dial up or dedicated connections. It also supports static routing through the use of the ROUTE command, or dynamic routing through RIP or OSPF.

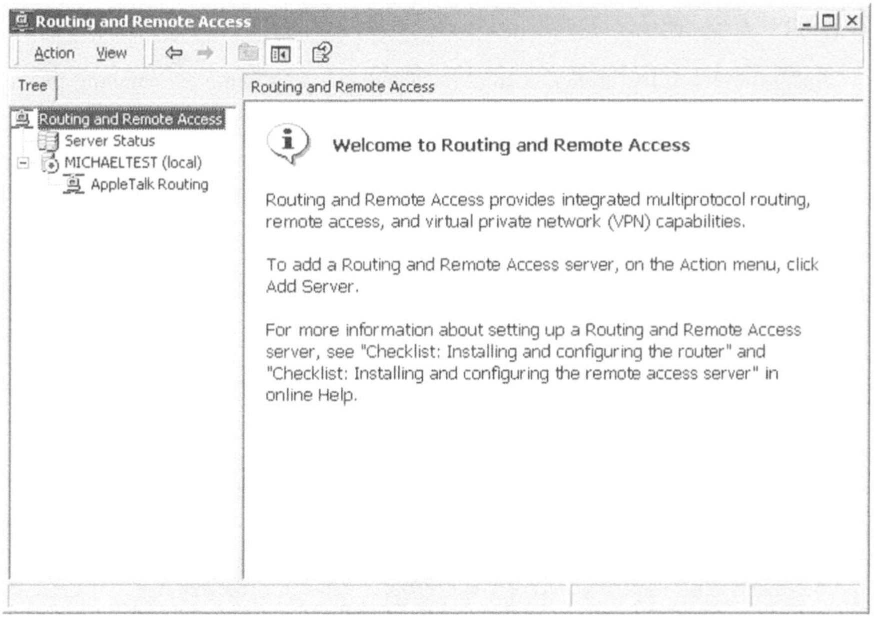

Figure 2.12 Routing and Remote Access

You may configure routing and RAS via the RRAS Snap-In.

RIP shorts for Routing Information Protocol. It is a protocol defined by RFC 1058 for specifying how routers exchange routing table information automatically. There are multiple versions of RIP.

OSPF shorts for Open Shortest Path First. It is a routing protocol based on the link-state algorithm, which is known to be more efficient at the expense of heavy processing power consumption.

The advantage of OSPF is that the network will have smaller but more frequent updates everywhere. Convergence is quick, thus preventing problems as routing loops and Count-to-Infinity. The network overall will be more stable, and will involve less bandwidth overhead than any deviation of RIP. However, the routing server that runs OSPF must be very powerful, as the link state computation is extremely processor intensive.

Remote Access

Remote Access refers to the ability of logging onto a network remotely, making the remote computer a full-fledged host on the network. Windows 2000 Server provides remote access support via RAS. Client on one hand dials in directly to the RAS server, typically through the use of modems.

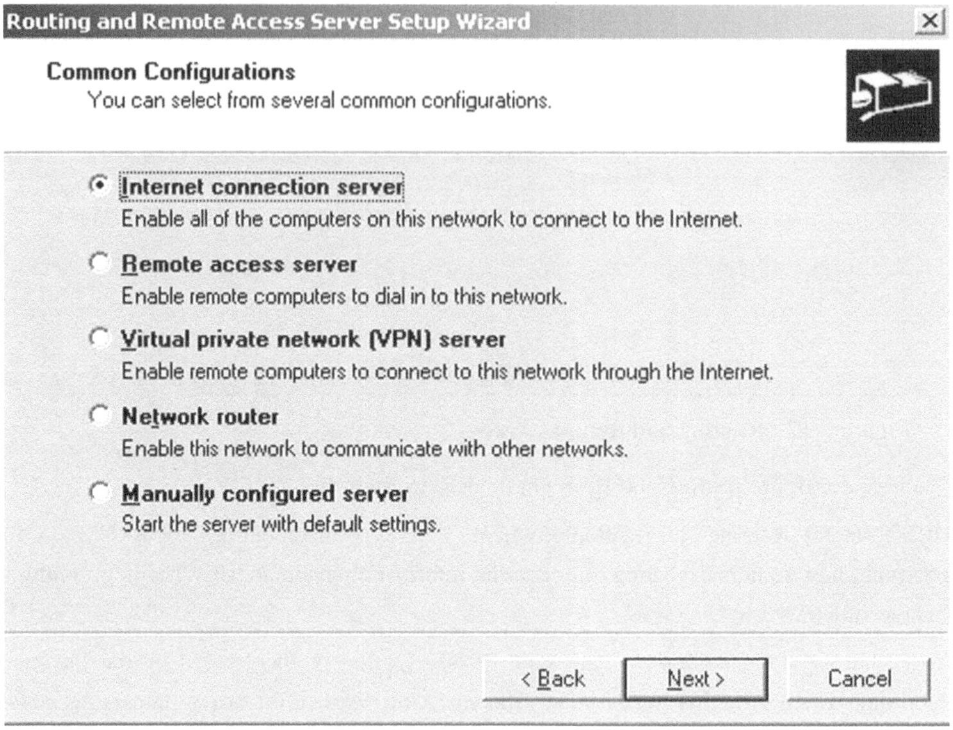

Figure 2.13 RRAS Setup Wizard

Different types of RRAS service can be created by using the RRAS Setup Wizard.

PPP is the dominant protocol in any remote access service. Shorts for Point-to-Point Protocol, it is more reliable and efficient than the older SLIP protocol.

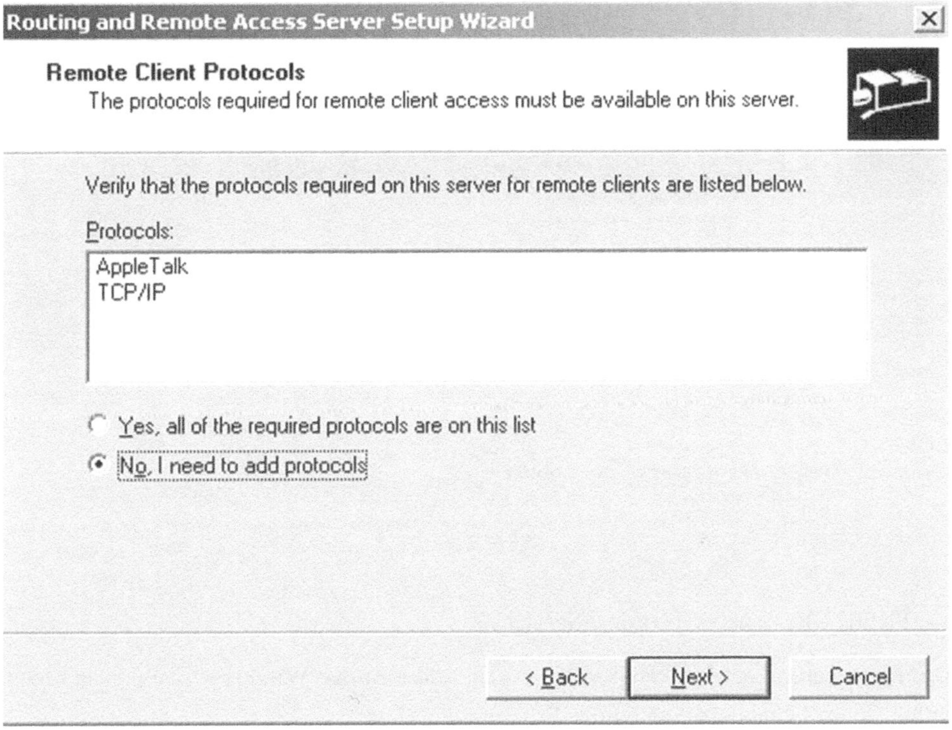

Figure 2.14 Remote Client Protocol Setup

For RAS to work, the protocols on the server and the clients must match.

In Windows 2000. you can configure the RAS service to work with the DHCP service to provide your remote access clients with dynamic addresses. Again, the technical detail is covered in exam 216.

Terminal Service allows you to remotely connect to a Windows 2000 computer for running applications or perform administration duties. The RDP protocol is used for this purpose.

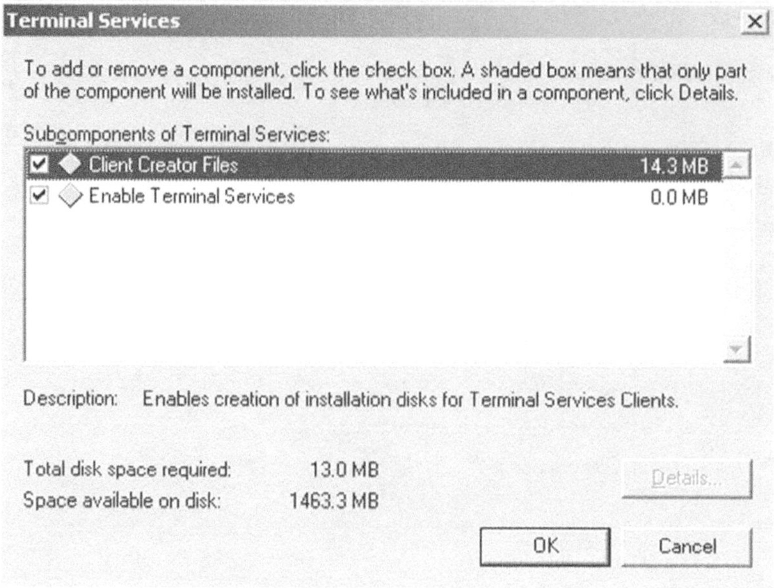

Figure 2.15 Enable Terminal Services

You may enable Terminal Services from the Add/Remove Windows Components menu within Control Panel – Add/Remove Programs.

Telnet allows for simple text based remote operation. Due to its insecure nature, its use is not recommended.

Figure 2.16 Telnet Session

Windows 2000 provides a text based interface for administrating telnet sessions. >

To ensure that remote access attempts are legitimate, we have to come up with a way to authenticate the users. RADIUS (shorts for Remote Authentication Dial-In User Service) is a popular authentication and accounting system used in the marketplace. When an user dial in to your remote access server, his/her username and password are passed to a RADIUS server for verification and recording. Windows 2000 provides the Internet Authentication Service, allowing you to run the Windows 2000 Server as a RADIUS server.

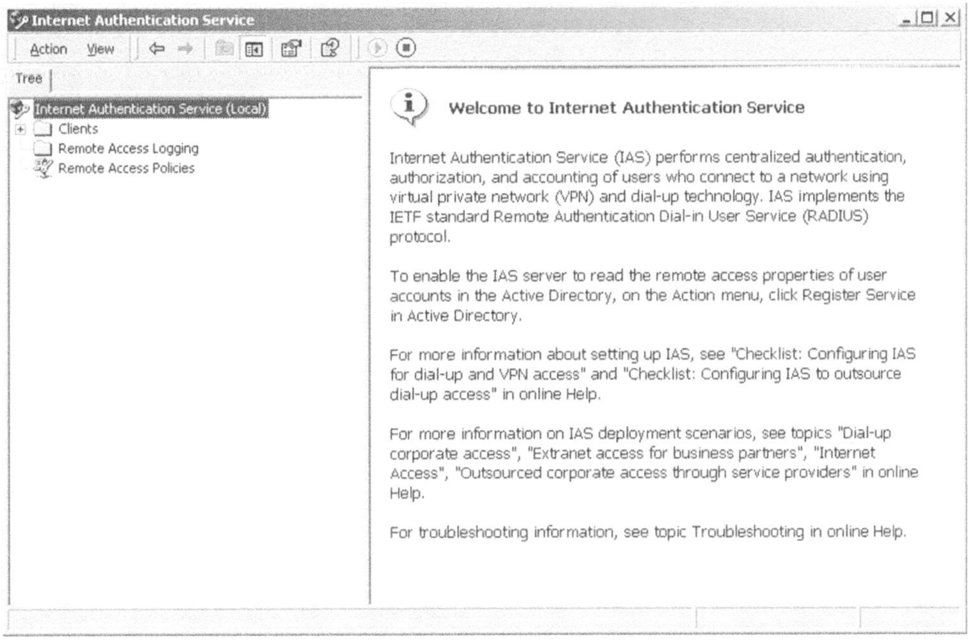

Figure 2.17 RADIUS Server

The IAS Snap-In allows you to configure your Windows 2000 Server as a RADIUS Server.

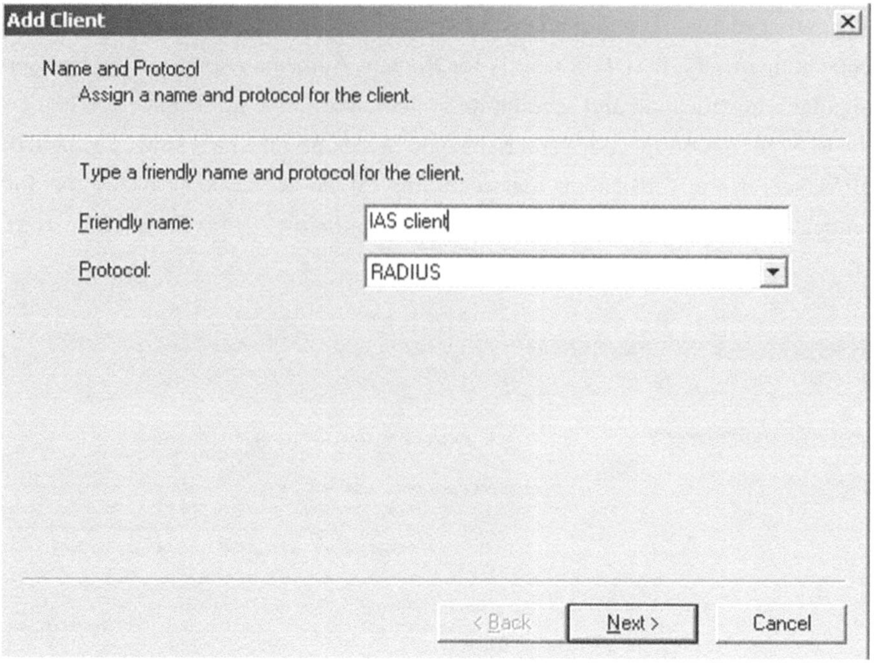

Figure 2.18 RADIUS Client

From the IAS Snap-In you can configure different RADIUS clients.

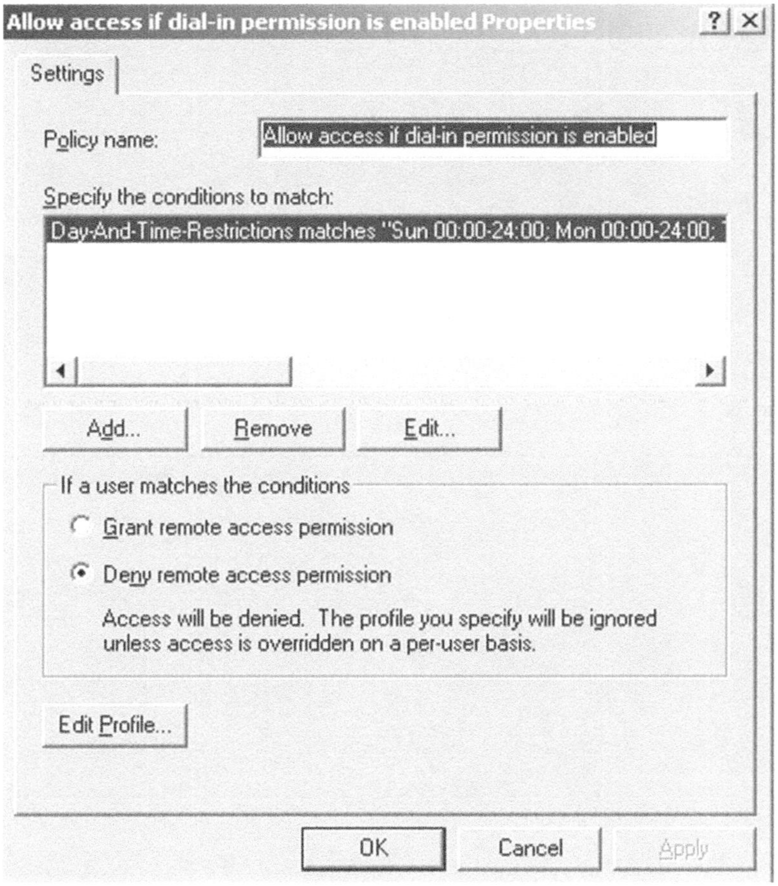

Figure 2.19 Remote Access Permissions

You may grant or deny remote access for different clients. >

Pop Quiz 2.4

Pop Quiz 2.4 *Questions*

1) True or false: RAS is strictly IP based.
2) True or false: Call back security can be deployed for T1 connection.
3) The primary function of RADIUS is:
4) RIP is based on what routing technology?
5) OSPF is based on what routing technology?

Pop Quiz 2.4

Pop Quiz 2.4 *Answers*

1) False. RAS allows different LAN protocols to be tunneled through the connection.
2) False. Call back security can be deployed for modem dial or ISDN connections only.
3) authentication.
4) distance vector.
5) link state.

VI NAT and Proxying

NAT

NAT shorts for Network Address Translation. It is a technique that allows a LAN to use one set of IP addresses for internal traffic and another set of addresses for external traffic. A Windows 2000 Server that performs the NAT function should be located at the point where the LAN meets the Internet. In fact, a Windows 2000 server with NAT enabled can protect the LAN by hiding the internal IP addresses in addition to allowing the use of more internal IP addresses

Proxying

A Proxy Server is a server that sits between a client application and the destination server. It intercepts all requests to the destination server and tries its best to fulfill the requests itself through advanced caching mechanism. By doing so, network performance can be dramatically improved, and requests can be filtered to prevent internal users from accessing specific destinations.

VII DNS and WINS

Name Resolution with DNS

A domain name is a name that identifies one or more IP addresses. Every domain name includes a suffix to indicate which top level domain it belongs to. On the internet, there are a limited number of such domains (although the list is growing):

com - represents commercial businesses

edu - represents educational institutions

gov – represents government agencies

mil - represents the US military

net - represents network organizations

org - represents organizations that are of nonprofit nature

Since the Internet is based on IP addresses, we rely on name resolution mechanism such as the Domain Name System to map these names to the corresponding IP addresses.

DNS is the abbreviation for Domain Name System. It translates domain names into IP addresses. If a DNS server doesn't know how to translate a particular domain name, it will seek help from its peer until the correct answer (or an error) is obtained.

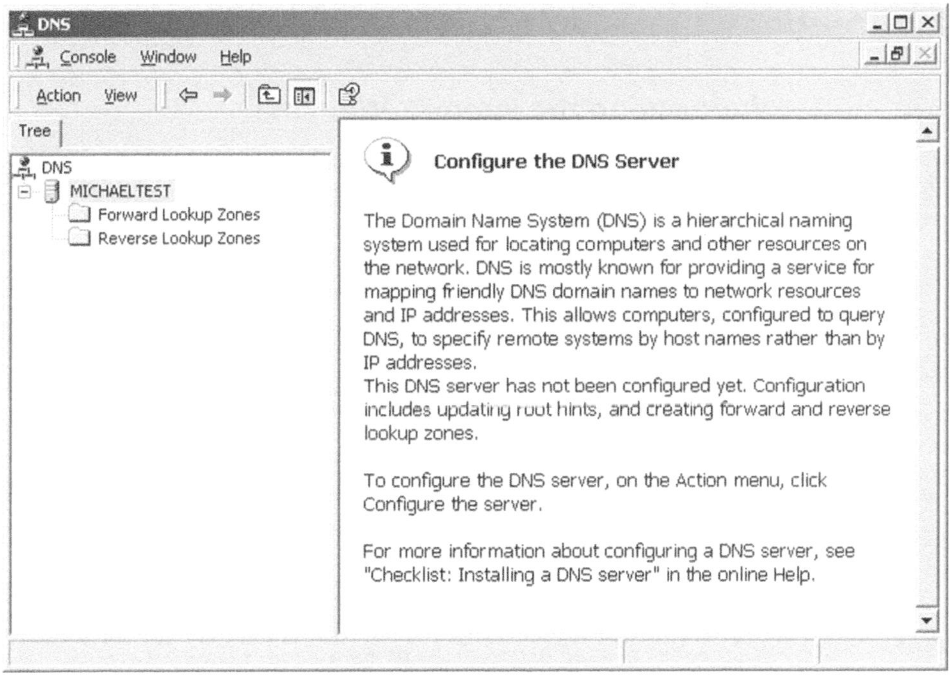

Figure 2.20 DNS Snap-In

The DNS Snap-In allows you to configure DNS service on your Windows 2000 server.

To obtain a domain name, you can register directly with InterNIC at www.internic.net. In fact, your Windows 2000 domain tree should have a root that is based on your registered domain name.

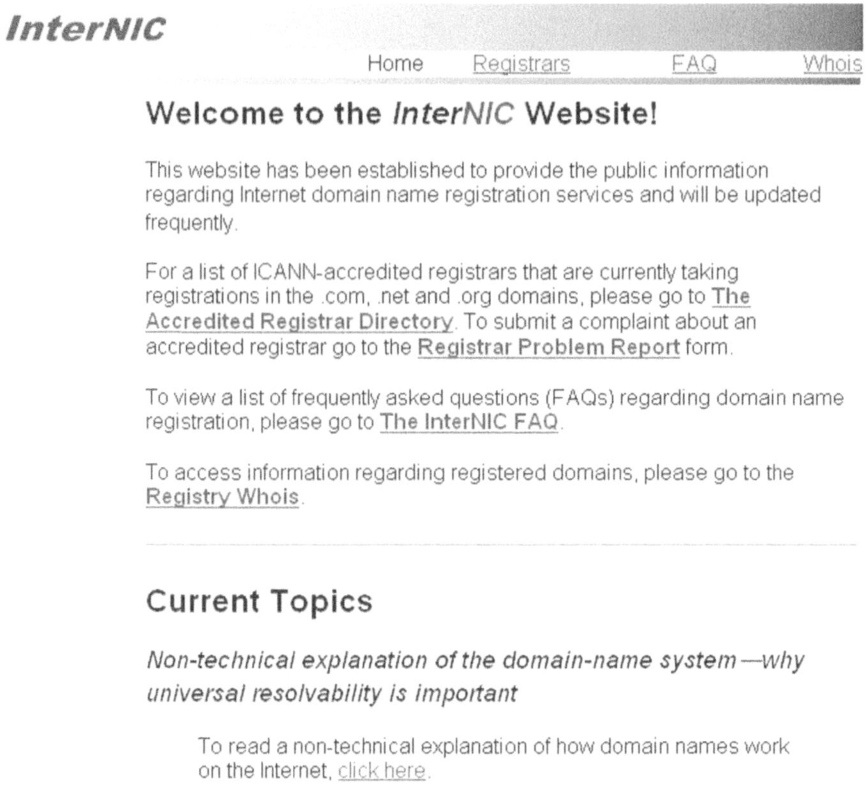

Figure 2.21 InterNIC

All domain name registration requests can be sent directly to InterNIC for processing. In many cases, your ISP can do the work for you though.

Name Resolution with WINS

DNS is the standard used on the Internet and on most of the Windows 2000 network, while WINS is only used for backward compatibility in Windows-based networks. Short for Windows Internet Naming Service, it is a system that determines the IP address associated with a particular network computer. It is different than DNS because it maps the computers' NETBIOS names to their IP addresses. NETBIOS (shorts for Network Basic Input Output System) is an application programming interface that augments the PC BIOS by adding certain network functions into it. Since it is a Microsoft only feature, it prohibits WINS from being deployed openly. It does not mean that WINS can never provide name resolution for other computers. In fact, it is possible to do so given special but troublesome arrangements such as static WINS entries.

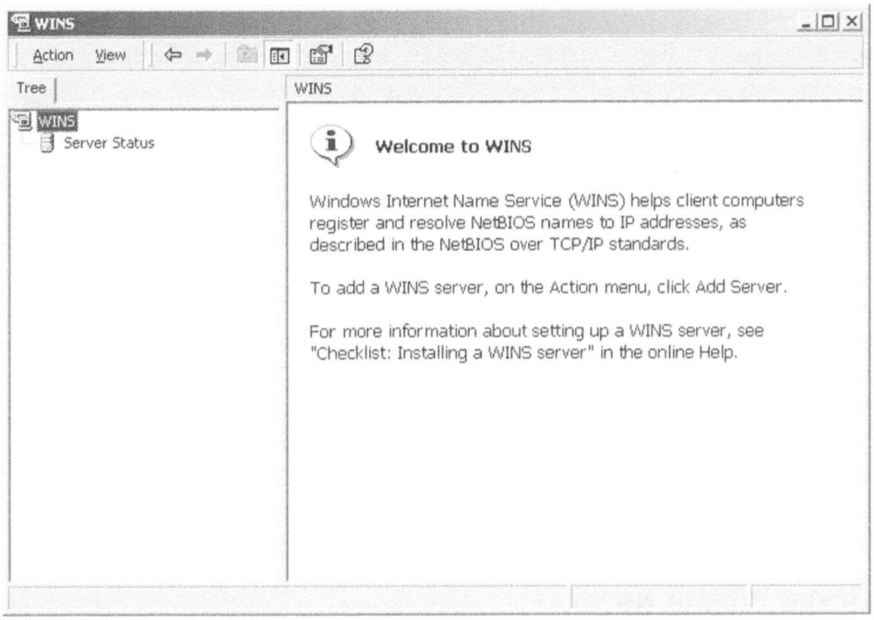

Figure 2.22 WINS Snap-In

You configure WINS through the WINS Snap-In.

Note that in the NT4 era all DNS entries must be manually entered. With Windows 2000. DNS becomes dynamic. It works with the DHCP function to automatically keep track of all the IP address to names mapping. WINS is always dynamic and automatic, although often being regarded as a measure primarily for supporting the legacy Windows clients.

VIII Firewall and VPN

Firewall

A firewall is the first line of defense in protecting your private network. It is a system designed specifically for preventing unauthorized access to or from your private network. Generally speaking, Firewalls can be implemented in both hardware and software (or a combination of both), although from Microsoft's point of view it will be the best if you use Windows 2000 Server together with ISA Server (covered in exam 70-227) to do the job.

For a firewall solution to work, all messages entering or leaving the internal network must pass through it. It will examine each packet and block those that do not meet the security criteria you specified.

Proxy server is considered to "firewall capable", because it is responsible for intercepting all messages entering and leaving the network. A router with simple filtering capabilities can be seen as a weak form of firewall too.

Virtual Private Network

VPN shorts for virtual private network. It is constructed by using the Internet as the medium for transporting data between systems. Encryption and other security mechanisms are used to ensure that only authorized users can access the network and that the data cannot be wiretapped.

For VPN to work, a reliable encryption mechanism must be in place. Windows 2000 supports IPSec in this regard. Shorts for IP Security, it is a set of protocols developed by the IETF to support the secure exchange of IP packets in VPN.

IPSec supports two encryption modes, with the Transport mode encrypting only the payload of each packet and the Tunnel mode encrypting both the header and the payload. For IPSec to work, both the sending and receiving devices must share a public key.

Certificates

Digital certificate serves as the authentication mechanism in VPN. It is an attachment to an electronic message for verifying the identity of the message sender. An individual or organization wishing to send an encrypted message must apply for a digital certificate from a Certificate Authority (CA). This CA can be internal or external, depending on the context of use. An encrypted

digital certificate containing the applicant's public key and other identification information will be issued once the application is evaluated.

A Certificate Authority, in theory, is a trusted third-party organization that issues digital certificates used to create digital signatures and public-private key pairs. With the involvement of a CA, you can guarantee that the individual entity granted the unique certificate is in fact who he/she or it claims to be.

On your own enterprise network you can use the Certificate Service of Windows 2000 to establish internal CA. Transactions with outside parties on the internet will typically require the use of an "outside" third party CA though.

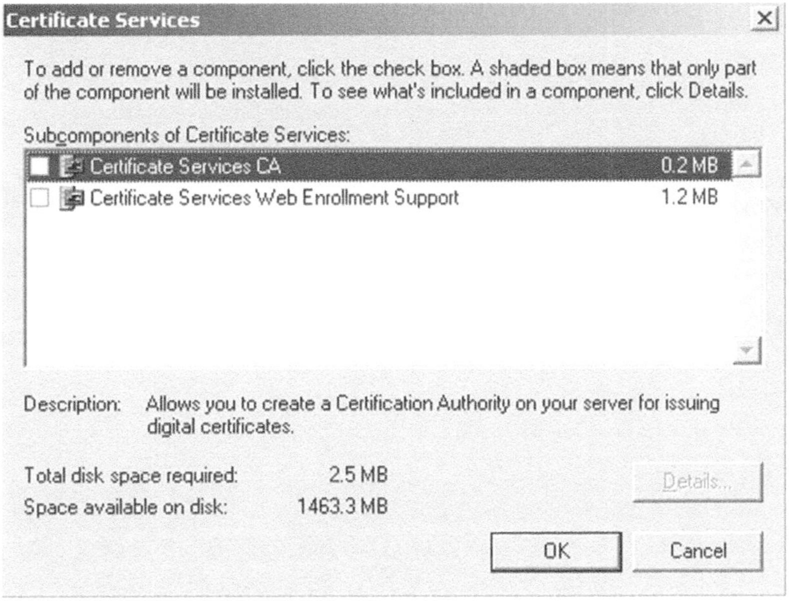

Figure 2.23 Certificate Service

You may enable the Certificate Services from the Add/Remove Windows Components menu within Control Panel – Add/Remove Programs.

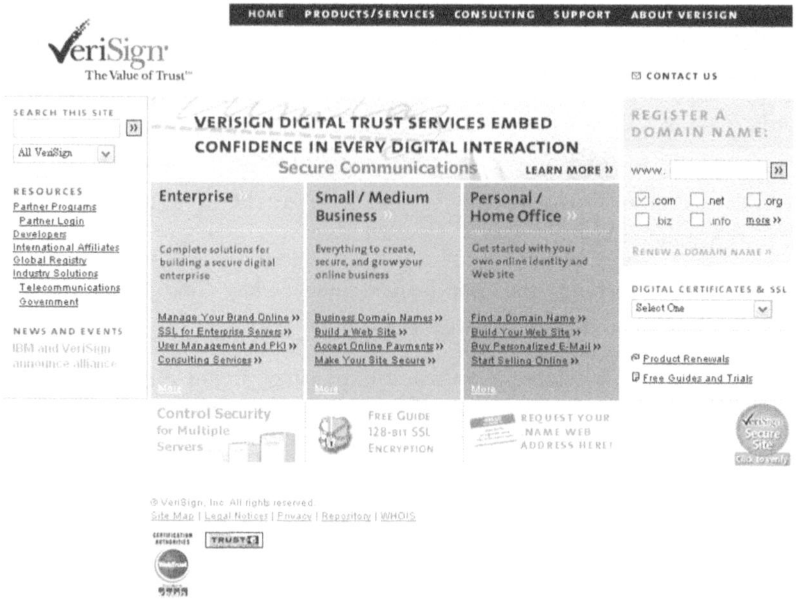

Figure 2.24 VeriSign

Revising is one of the most famous third-party CA in the marketplace.

Figure 2.25 THAWTE

THAWTE is another reputable CA competing directly with Revising. >

Pop Quiz 2.5

Pop Quiz 2.5 *Questions*

1) What is known as the first line of defense in a network?
2) VPN uses what as the connection medium?
3) DNS replaces the function of what local file?
4) WINS replaces the function of what local file?

Pop Quiz 2.5

Pop Quiz 2.5 *Answers*

1) Firewall.
2) Internet.
3) hosts.
4) lmhosts.

IX Other Protocols

Special Topic: A Brief Overview of The IPX Protocol

According to the Novell IPX addressing scheme, each host on a Novell IPX network has a unique 80-bit logical address. This address is grouped in a typical NETWORK.NODE format, and is divided into two main parts:

the Network Number consisting of up to 32-bits

the Host Number that represents the MAC address of the interface card.

The Network Number is a hex number between 1 and FFFFFFFD. It is the first 32-bits. The remaining 48-bits represent the Host Number.

Examples of IPX Address:

C15C0.0000.0000.0001

There are many different Novell encapsulations. Encapsulation type is a very important issue in an IPX environment, as two devices using different encapsulation methods on the same medium will fail to communicate. Although Novell clients are generally able to adapt to the encapsulation available, sometimes you must manually configure the encapsulation type on both sides.

The available IPX encapsulation types:

Ethernet_802.3 (raw)

Ethernet_II

Ethernet_802.2

Ethernet_SNAP

FDDI_SNAP

FDDI_802.2

Token Ring

Token Ring_SNAP

IPX uses SAP and RIP broadcasts to build a list of available services and routes. SAPs, (Service Advertisement Protocol) carry information on:

the type of service available

the name of the server

the corresponding IPX address

RIPs (Routing Information Protocol) on the other hand carry information on the route to take to reach the destination.

Windows 2000 supports communication and routing with IPX. However, unless you are running Netware services heavily, there is really no need to configure IPX support on your hosts.

Special Topic: A Brief Overview of The SNA Protocol

SNA shorts for IBM's Systems Network Architecture, and is often being referred to as the legacy SNA. In fact, it was one of the first networking protocols in the world, and is still widely deployed.

SNA was designed around the host-to-terminal communication model that IBM's mainframes use in the good old days. As time passes, IBM expanded the SNA protocol to support peer-to-peer networking with the introduction of Advanced Peer-to-Peer Networking (APPN) and Advanced Program-to-Program Communication (APPC).

SNA has a number of components that map closely to the OSI reference model:

Data link control (DLC)

Path control

Transmission control

Data flow control

Presentation services

Transaction services

The DLC layer of the SNA model supports a number of media that provide access to devices and users with different requirements. These medias include (and not limited) to:

SDLC

X.25

Token Ring

Mainframe channels

X Chapter 2: Review Questions

1. IPSec supports which two encryption modes?

---

2. What is regarded as the first line of defense in protecting your private network?

---

3. WINS is a system that maps the computers' ___________ names to their IP addresses.

---

4. What is used to cache internet contents and improve web browsing performance?

---

5. What is the dominant protocol used in RAS?

---

6. What represents the ability to specify a different subnet mask for the same network number on different subnets?

---

7. What technology transports multimedia data with cells of a fixed size?

---

8. What are the four commonly used (or once commonly used) LAN topologies?

Chapter 2: Review Answers

1. IPSec supports two encryption modes: Transport mode and Tunnel mode.

---

2. A firewall is the first line of defense in protecting your private network.

---

3. The Windows Internet Naming Service a system that maps the computers' NETBIOS names to their IP addresses.

---

4. A Proxy Server intercepts all requests to the destination server and tries its best to fulfill the requests itself through advanced caching mechanism.

---

5. PPP is the dominant protocol in any remote access service. It is more reliable and efficient than the older SLIP protocol.

---

6. Variable-Length Subnet Mask represents the ability to specify a different subnet mask for the same network number on different subnets.

---

7. ATM works based on transferring data in cells of a fixed size. The constant cell size allows ATM equipment to transmit multimedia content and data over the same network smoothly and reliably.

---

8. In the world of LAN, there are four principal topologies: Bus, Ring, Star and Tree.

Total Recall

Chapter 3: Analyzing Business Requirements

The objective of this chapter is to provide the reader with an understanding of the following:

1. Business Model
2. Company Processes
3. Organization Structure
4. Company Priorities
5. Product Life Cycles
6. TCO and ROI

Getting Ready (Questions)

1) What are the two most popular management models?
2) What is one major issue to face when a multi-national corporation sets up an overseas operation?
3) A small branch office usually uses what type of remote connection method?
4) Who is the decision maker in a company responsible for setting enterprise level strategic decision?
5) Who is the person in the company responsible for identifying resource constraints and making the appropriate arrangements in response?
6) What is the business term of measuring the monetary return generated by an investment?

Getting Ready (Answers)

1) Centralized and decentralized.

2) Law and regulations.

3) Dial up.

4) The CEO.

5) The CFO.

6) ROI – Return On Investment.

I Introduction

Half of the 70-221 exam actually tests your reading comprehension skills! You are asked to read through a couple pages long case and then determine the following:

The existing and planned business models.

The company model and the geographical scope. Models include regional, national, international, subsidiary, and branch offices.

The company processes. Processes include information flow, communication flow, service and product life cycles, and decision-making.

The existing and planned organizational structures. Considerations include management model; company organization; vendor, partner, and customer relationships; and acquisition plans.

To proceed further, you will need to analyze factors that influence the company strategies, such as:

Company priorities.

The projected growth and growth strategy.

Relevant laws and regulations.

The company's tolerance for risk.

The total cost of operations.

The structure of IT management. Considerations include type of administration, such as centralized or decentralized; funding model; outsourcing; decision-making process, and change-management process.

Are we taking an MBA class here? Well, don't be scared. These business issues exist to serve a single purpose: to confuse you! That is it. To confuse you, and nothing else. We can break them down one by one easily, using the following rules:

II Company Models

You are NOT asked to decide what to be achieved. You are hired to design a network that accomplishes what your client wants. That means, you only make decisions on what to use or what to deploy to achieve what they want! Keep in mind, the existing business model does not really matter. It is only a background story. What matters the most is the planned business model, as this is what your clients want!

There are different "models" mentioned by Microsoft, including regional, national, international, subsidiary, and branch offices. Do they matter? YES!

A Regional Business

A regional business is one that has its activities in certain local regions only. This kind of business usually gives fewer headaches, because:

- You do not need to consider the issue of foreign languages
- You do not need to worry about the laws that restrict the "export" of certain technologies, such as 128bit encryption.
- WAN connection within a region is usually cheaper
- CENTRALIZED administration is easier, although NOT mandatory

In most cases, small business like this does not require separate domain trees in Active Directory

Example Case – Rocky Mountain School of Music – Part 1

You are recently requested by the Rocky Mountain School of Music to design the Windows 2000 network for the entire school.

The mission of the Rocky Mountain School of Music is to advance the art of music and its related disciplines. It seeks to educate students in the various fields of the profession and to promote an understanding of music. The School endeavors to preserve diverse repertories and cultural traditions while also creating opportunities for artistic, intellectual, and scholarly innovation in the realm of music. The School is dedicated to excellence in research, performance, composition, and teacher education, undertaken in a spirit of collaboration among its own constituents.

Currently the school has the following buildings:

Rocky Band Building
Computer-Assisted Music Lab
Music Project Lab
Experimental Music Lab
Performing Arts Lab
Music Library Building
School of Piano Building
Jeff Memorial Hall

Comments:

As you can see here, the school is a regional organization. All of its buildings are located in the same campus area, at least for the time being.

A National Business

A national business has its operations spanned over many different regions of the country. You may have offices in many different states, that these offices are physically far away from each others, making face to face contacts and centralized administration difficult. However, you do not yet have to worry about the language issue. The main concerns in this kind of business are:

- WAN connectivity
- DECENTRALIZED administration
- The Active Directory domain name structure: whether the different offices should be under the same tree or be separated into different trees.

Example Case – Rocky Mountain School of Music – Part 2

Future Vision:

The school plans to open a branch in Austin, Texas. The management is willing to pay for a high speed 128K dedicated connection between the main campus and the new location. This new location will mainly be used to teach Music History and Music Appreciation.

Comments:

Here we go. The school plans to open a branch in Texas. Rocky Mountain School originates from Canada, so a branch in Texas can be seen as a "cross border" expansion. However, the tie between Canada and the US is so close, that from a business point of view they are usually seen as an entity within North America. There is no need to worry about any export restriction nor any multi-lingual issues.

An International Business

An international business is the most complicated business type.

First of all, it is almost for certain that management is entirely decentralized. In fact, overseas operations may run entirely independent of the head-office.

Due to the need for localization, different language versions of Windows 2000 and business applications are deployed. You must ensure that the data to be shared can be accessed by both sides.

Dedicated connection to overseas destination is too costly to be considered. Internet will be the only choice, indicating the need for VPN.

In terms of Active Directory domain structure, entirely different forests may be used.

Example Case – Rocky Mountain School of Music – Part 3

The school will also open up a branch in London. This new location will use dial up modem to connect to the main office. This new location will mainly be a marketing office to promote the school's "Student Exchange" program.

Comments:

A new office in London is a different story. UK is part of the EU, and certainly there are legal, social and economical issues that need specific attentions. This is why Microsoft includes "relevant laws and regulations" as part of the exam objective list.

One important point to illustrate here: what is in place at present does not really matter. What matters is what is going to happen. In the Rocky Mountain case, your network infrastructure must take into consideration these future expansion moves.

When your client is an international business, pay serious attention to the technology export controls that were established in 1949 to prevent "potentially devastating" technology from reaching the Soviet bloc countries from outside. Although the Soviet bloc countries no longer exist in their previous form, similar restrictions still exist and are applied towards other parts of the world.

Subsidiary and Branch Office

The issue with a subsidiary or a branch office is usually management related. That is, whether administration should be done in the head-office or locally. You do not have any authority to make such decision. You simply have to go with the decision made by your client.

A Subsidiary model can be though of as a child company, with internal company politics being an important concern. On the other hand, a branch office is the smallest possible business model that usually has specific functions to perform.

A Branch Office usually resides in some sort of relatively rural areas. The number of users is usually small, and dedicated connection is likely to be too much. Dial up access via phone line or ISDN seems to be more appropriate.

Example Case – Rocky Mountain School of Music – Part 4

Risk Management:

In the past the school was once in difficulties due to a problem in funding. There had been a situation where the salaries of the teachers were not distributed on time, leading to a strike and a delay in the class progresses. Although this situation is not likely to happen again, the management insists on carry out a risk management process.

Comments:

Again, take the future London office of Rocky Mountain School as an example. It is going to be a small marketing office, so it does not really make sense to give them 24 x 7 dedicated connections. As an exam objective, you want to reduce the "total cost of operation" for the school. So, it is for the interest of the school if you suggest that they use dial up connections for the London branch.

With regards to "the company's tolerance for risk" (which is part of the Microsoft exam objective list), from the track record we can see that the school is never too solid financially, although initiative is to be taken to address the issue of risk management.

The thing is, whether the school will bankrupt or not is not under our control, and there is really nothing we can do in this regard. So, the term "risk" as implied by Microsoft must mean something else. I suggest that you think about this "risk" in terms of the project itself. Is this project risky during its implementation? Will it lead to a 2 weeks downtime during the network upgrade? Will a 2 weeks downtime cause a deadly consequence towards the school? The answers to these questions will have impacts on the method you choose for the upgrade. The upgrade has to be done (you do not have the authority to say no to the client's request), and you have to do it in a smart way to minimize disruptions.

Pop Quiz 3.1

Pop Quiz 3.1 *Questions*

1) Which company model requires consideration on the part of export laws?
2) Dial up ISDN connection is best suited for which company model?
3) In an internal business, the use of what technology must be carefully considered in order to avoid legal problems?

Pop Quiz 3.1

Pop Quiz 3.1 *Answers*

1) International Business
2) Remote branch office
3) Encryption

III Product Life Cycles

The concept of product life cycle acknowledges the fact that every product or system goes through a series of steps between the time it is first conceived and the time the manufactured product is retired.

Every product starts with a need in the market. For example,

the need to reduce cost

the need to increase functionality

Once a need is defined, a concept for a product is created to address the business model of the company, and the product and manufacturing process are designed. Upon completion of the design process, the product is produced and deployed.

After the product is deployed, it is supported and maintained throughout its lifespan. The need for upgrades varies, largely depending on the life expectancy and usage of the product. At the low end, some products are completely disposable, if:

the repair/upgrade labor is more expensive than the product

technology is evolving quickly and the product is obsolete

Eventually, the product is retired and replaced by the next generation counterparts.

The product life cycles in a sense reflects the status of the company. If the company's core product is at its growth stage, scalability is to be seriously considered, as the company is likely to expand to cop with the growth. If the product is to be fade out soon, cost saving may be more desirable, as the company may have to cut spending in response to the declining market condition.

On the other hand, if the focus of the life cycle is on the systems the client company is currently using, you are effectively facing a series of decisions:

Keep the existing system intact?

Keep the existing system intact, but upgrade the underlying hardware to improve performance?

Discard the existing system entirely?

Migrate the current data from the existing system to a new system?

Upgrade the existing system to its latest version?

When making your decisions always take into account the cost involved with your decisions, as well as the benefits that will be brought.

Example Case – Supreme Manufacturing – Part 1

Supreme Manufacturing Company was established in the early 80s, with its root in Korea as a manufacturer of Photo Albums. Due to the strong predicted growth of its business in the coming years, it plans to develop at least 10 new types of albums in the foreseeable future.

Comments:

It is quite obvious that the album product line is at its growth stage. It implies that future growth is expected, that your infrastructure must be extremely scalable.

IV Other Factors

External Relationships

Relationships with vendors, partners, and customer means there is a need to share resources with external parties. Some resources are to be shared while some are not. Security in terms of authentication (using Digital Certificate) and encryption (using IPSec VPN) is a MUST HAVE.

When acquisition is to be made, your focus will be on the following topics:

- whether separate entities should be maintained
- the possibility for merging the different domains into one
- the possibility for consolidating all administrative works

Since these issues are more Active Directory related, they are more likely to be seen in exam 70-219.

Company Processes & Organizational Structure

Company processes are indicative of the way information is distributed throughout the organization. Before looking at the company processes, it will be helpful to first figure out the client's organization structure as well as its management model. In a centralized management model, most of the administrative works are done at the head-office. This indicates the need for frequent and reliable communication between the head-office and the offices.

Pop Quiz 3.2

Pop Quiz 3.2 *Questions*

1) When someone proposed to you the installation of a NT4.0 based application, what factor will you consider?
2) Centralization VS decentralization is an issue related to:
3) VPN is a technology essential to which aspect of a company?

Pop Quiz 3.2

Pop Quiz 3.2 *Answers*

1) Product life cycle
2) The organizational structure
3) External partner relationship

V A debate: Centralization V.S. De-Centralization

Why is centralization desirable in some circumstances? There are many text book reasons. To be right to the point, centralization allows for:

- tighter control over local operations
- more efficient resource coordination
- resource sharing among different divisions (with the coordination of the head office)
- standardization of operation processes among different divisions
- reduced complexity on local operations (allow them to focus on their core competency)

In the real world, centralization may not be practical if the organization is too big or its structure is too complex. Decentralization gives the local departments the authority to make many decisions, thus allowing faster responses to the changing market conditions.

A traditional organization structure emphasizes the concept of "division of labor". That is, different people focus on different areas of operations. This departmental or divisional structure certainly has its advantages, but if designed improperly, duplication of resource and efforts may result. A modern organization encourages collaboration and resource sharing among the different functions and offices.

If each office is totally independent from the others with no intention to share anything, a Star topology (with the head-office acting as the hub) is the best setup. If the staffs in these offices always have to work together, a mesh topology may be more appropriate in terms of performance and redundancy.

Example Case – Supreme Manufacturing – Part 2

Currently the production of each product category is under the supervision of its own divisional head. The logic behind this arrangement is that the production of each type of albums actually requires totally different types of expertise.

The president directly oversees the operations of the different divisions. Since the president himself owns the company, there is no board of directors. However, there is a position called Managing Director, which is at the top of the hierarchy. The law of Korea requires this. His wife took the position.

Supreme has three locations, one being the head office and the others being the factories. The president is located in the head office, while the divisional heads are completely mobile – they have to travel around the factories.

Comments:

It is quite clear that the organization structure of Supreme is flat. The divisions are mutually independent, and there is no hint on any possible collaboration between them. At this moment, you may safely assume that resource sharing among these divisions is not an issue, at least for now.

The president directly oversees every operation, although the divisional heads are responsible for managing the day-to-day activities. In a sense, this is more of a centralized management model with certain room for decentralized decision making. We have to live with the fact that there is no such thing as 100% centralized nor 100% decentralized management. Delegation is always needed, both in the case and in real life.

Anyway, this management issue is more relevant to Active Directory Administration than to the infrastructure. What we care is the daily flow of information required under this management model.

As stated in the case, the divisional heads are completely mobile. They need to report directly to the president, and it is likely they will do so through their laptop computers. RAS dial-in to the head quarter server seems to be a good strategy for them.

Sometimes we need to look at how practical a management model is. If centralized management is preferred, we must ensure that WAN connectivity is reliable and optimal (in terms of performance). This kind of guarantee is not always possible, especially when your offices are located in areas with poor communication infrastructure.

Keep in mind though, that the administrative model of a company is a rather "sensitive" issue for a company. If management insists on doing things in a particular way, your job will be to try your best to meet their needs rather than to argue for alternatives.

Example Case – Supreme Manufacturing – Part 3

Head office

Dokok-Dong, Gangnam-Gu, Seoul, Korea

Number Of Staff: 10

Korea Branch - Factory

Goori City Kyunggi-Do, Korea

Number Of Staff: 600

China Branch - Factory

Yang Hong, Jiangsu, China

Number Of Staff: 300

US Branch – Sales Office

Recently opened in San Francisco of California

Number Of Staff: 30

Comments:

Given the fact that the offices and the factories are geographically separated to the largest possible extent, it will be too expensive to have them connected through dedicated means. If cost is a constraint, you may assume that the links are slow and less stable.

Under such condition, does it make sense for you to place the domain controller and the file resources in the head office? Certainly no (not until faster connections are made available). Does it make sense to have network resource administration performed entirely in the head office? Well, due to the issues of languages and time difference around the globe, centralized resource administration may not be an optimal choice.

In a real world organization, company processes can be very complicated. It is not unusual to see situations where there are many different processes in conjunction with many different flows of information between different departments. In such a real world setup, in addition to the issue of connectivity, you must plan carefully on the placement of resources, how these resources are shared, who have the rights to do what on the resources, and who monitors resources usage.

VI IT Structure

The company's IT Infrastructure is another key factor to consider. If the management is committed to improving productivity and efficiency via technologies, we will most likely see a large budget reserved for the IT operations.

Traditionally, management sees the IT function as a supporting function, which is simply a cost center. As the importance of IT is recognized, the IT function gradually becomes a strategic component of the business (or even becomes a revenue center).

Given enough funding and resources, what was impossible in the past may become possible tomorrow.

Example Case – Supreme Manufacturing – Part 4

Currently only the head office has a LAN running NT 4.0. The domain model is a simple single domain model. They do not YET have dedicated connection to the factories. The factories are using Win95 as dial up clients to connect to the head office server running RAS. The factories also runs Netware 3.X as the NOS. In the coming months 256K dedicated connection will be installed. Currently, within all locations there are already 100MBPS LANs running smoothly.

The president recognizes the importance of IT, and is planning to spend 30% of its last year revenue on the complete re-design of the IT infrastructure.

Because of the growing importance of IT, the head office will house a new IT department. This department is further broken down into 4 smaller departments.

Comments:

Now we know that the communication infrastructure will be upgraded, and a whole team of IT experts will be available in the head office to provide tech support, centralized administration suddenly becomes more viable!

VII Company Priorities

We all live in an environment where resources are limited. In a real world business environment, all sorts of constraint exist, both resource-wise and time-wise. To ensure that your project is successful, priorities must be clearly identified.

If everything is stated clearly in a case, our life will be much easier. For example, if the case mentions specifically a project deadline of 10 days from today, that this project is about to generate half of the company's annual cash flow, we can of course allocate the necessary resources accordingly. However, in an attempt to confuse you, the exam will present scenarios that require careful judgment on what is to be done first. The sources of information are the management people, such as the CEO, the CFO, and the CIO.

Example Case – Excel Forwarder – Part 1

Excel Forwarder Corp, an international freight forwarder and Customs Broker, has been providing Logistics and Transportation services since 1929. Excel also provides logistics and distribution services as well as purchase order management and ancillary freight services in addition to freight forwarding and Customs Brokerage.

The company divides its operations into two main categories: Air and Ocean. The management structure is as follow:

Air – One director, directly reports to the CEO. Under the director are a group of managers responsible for running the different service departments.

Ocean – One director, directly reports to the CEO. Under the director are a group of managers responsible for running the different service departments.

The CEO admits that there are overlapping of activities and resources among Air and Ocean. However, he does not plan to modify this structure as of the time being.

Excel has recently become the partner of XSite, a web site that provides a central search engine for local, state and federal government agencies. This new site is useful in a sense that it eliminates the need to track down all the various agencies to locate available services. This partnership is expected to draw substantial new businesses to Excel. The CEO of Excel is looking into enhancing its existing IT structure in order to cope with the growing demand for its services.

Comments:

On the issue of duplication of activities and resources among Air and Ocean, the CEO does not plan to take any action as of the time being. The duplication is a problem, but not one that has to be fixed urgently.

On the other hand, we see that the CEO is looking into enhancing its existing IT structure in order to cope with the growing demand for services brought by the XSite partnership. The partnership has been formed, and "substantial new businesses" are expected to come very soon. So, it is natural to see this as an urgent issue - Excel Forwarder's IT function must be "upgraded" as soon as possible so that the increasing amount of business activities can be handled.

Sometimes things are further complicated when you receive different messages from the different management people. CEO may ask for something which is not known to the CIO, while the CFO will oppose to what the CIO has proposed due to resource constraints.

The CEO is the key man in the game. He is in a position to set the overall strategic objectives of the company, while the CIO is in a position to outline the problems and the expectations from an IT perspective. You must make both of them happy.

Your design must be geared towards completing the overall strategic objectives, while at the same time addressing the CIO's concerns at the operational level.

Always remember, what needs to be done has to be done regardless of the financial condition. When the CFO complains about resource shortage, what you can do is to push down the cost as much as possible.

Pop Quiz 3.3

Pop Quiz 3.3 *Questions*

1) Who in a company often poses restrictions on the money to spend for an infrastructure project?
2) Overall strategic direction of a company is set usually by:
3) IT infrastructure is the responsibility of:

Pop Quiz 3.3

Pop Quiz 3.3 *Answers*

1) The CFO
2) The CEO
3) The CIO

VIII Total Cost of Ownership

TCO is receiving increased attention today, as many organizations realize that modern computing operations are expensive and require a complex set of management processes, which in many cases do not justify the budget and staffing requirements incurred.

In fact, an organization will face eventual disaster and possible extinction if management does not have a clear understanding of the TCO concept.

It is vital to understand that TCO is NOT about technology, but about business philosophy. When judging the TCO of a platform, you must have its cost balanced against the potential return on investment. Then, when it comes to the time for you to implement a major operating system upgrade, you may start by evaluating tools and hardware that can help you cut costs and improve efficiency, which will eventually lower the TCO.

Think of cost in terms of TCO. TCO represents how much it actually costs to setup and run something. For example, under the TCO concept, the true cost of installing a new system can include:

Cost of the computer
Cost of the software
Cost of any upgrades
Cost of maintenance
Technical support cost
Training cost

When you design your network, always take into consideration the TCO. By doing so, you will be able to work out a truly cost effective solution.

IX Return on Investment

As an IT Professional, in addition to the technology works, you must be prepared to make your budget proposals in order to stake your career. You must be prepared to answer questions such as:

"How much value does our IT department produce?"

"What is the return on my IT investments (ROI)?"

In reality, management's view of the ROI on IT Investments can vary greatly. It would, however, be easier to quantify the differing perceptions of IT by deconstructing the IT budget and segmenting spending into discrete categories. In fact, such segmentation is often found to be the useful basis of the IT budgeting and reporting structure.

All business processes incur both maintenance and new investment expenses. While most of the budget is spent maintaining and operating existing infrastructure, this part of the budget segment is not perceived to be value-adding. And this is where most objections on IT spending come from.

Quoted from Microsoft's paper on its newly introduced REJ Framework: "Bottom line: IT Managers today must be able to show their CIO or CFO in hard numbers what kind of a return they can expect on their IT investment."

Traditionally, companies evaluate IT investments on the basis of cost improvements such as TCO. This method somehow makes it awkward to quantify IT's true value to the enterprise, as the payoffs from IT are not truly measured.

Rapid Economic Justification (REJ) is a framework introduced by Microsoft to "help IT professionals analyze and optimize the economic performance of IT investments, and appropriate optimal resources and capital for IT projects". With REJ, the focus is on business improvement - defining success for the business.

While such methodology may be foreign to a "technical person", it is recommended that you take a look at the REJ white paper and make yourself familiar with the Microsoft business terms. After all, to pass the 221 exam requires that you are "business-aware".

The REJ framework whitepaper can be obtained from the following URL:

http://www.microsoft.com/business/whitepapers/value/valuerejwp.asp

Pop Quiz 3.4

Pop Quiz 3.4 *Questions*

Which of the following should be included as part of the TCO equation?

Cost of the computer

Cost of the software

Cost of any upgrades

Cost of maintenance

Technical support cost

Training cost

Electricity cost

Server room cleaning cost

CIO's salary

Pop Quiz 3.4

Pop Quiz 3.4 *Answers*

The following should be included as part of the TCO equation?

Cost of the computer

Cost of the software

Cost of any upgrades

Cost of maintenance

Technical support cost

Training cost

The costs below are almost "fixed" and should not be in included in the TCO calculation:

Electricity cost

Server room cleaning cost

CIO's salary

X Chapter 3: Review Questions

You are a Network Consultant with specialized skills in designing Windows 2000 network infrastructure. You are recently requested by the Rocky Mountain School of Music to design the Windows 2000 network for the entire school.

School Mission

The mission of the Rocky Mountain School of Music is to advance the art of music and its related disciplines. It seeks to educate students in the various fields of the profession and to promote an understanding of music. The School endeavors to preserve diverse repertories and cultural traditions while also creating opportunities for artistic, intellectual, and scholarly innovation in the realm of music. The School is dedicated to excellence in research, performance, composition, and teacher education, undertaken in a spirit of collaboration among its own constituents.

School Background

The Rocky Mountain School of Music is consistently ranked among the strongest professional music schools in Canada. It attracts outstanding students and faculty in composition-theory, music education, musicology, and performance. The school is large enough to provide a wide variety of experience for students seeking degrees in music. At the same time, the atmosphere of a smaller school prevails with emphasis on individualized instruction in performance, comparatively small classes, and a faculty and staff that cares about its students. As a significant cultural resource, the School of Music serves the musical needs of the community, the region, the state, and the nation, and its influence is felt on an international level as well. One measure of a university's quality is the success of its graduates. Among the more than 10.000 alumni of the School of Music are 5 Pulitzer Prize winners in composition; members of major symphony orchestras, opera companies, jazz ensembles, and professional choral groups; and faculty members at many of the nation's most prestigious colleges and universities. Music education graduates direct some of the finest elementary and secondary music programs throughout Canada as well as in foreign countries. The school is proud of its record in assisting qualified graduates to assume leadership roles in the music profession through career counseling and professional advising.

Programs offered

The Rocky Mountain School of Music has two different degree programs available:

Bachelor of Music

Specializations available in:

- Applied Music
- Composition-Theory
- Music History
- Open Studies

Bachelor of Music Education

Specializations available in:

- Choral Music
- General Music
- Instrumental Music

Divisions

The school currently has the following divisions:

- Brass
- Composition-Theory
- Music Education
- Musicology
- String
- Woodwind
- Accompanying
- Jazz
- Organ
- Percussion
- Piano
- Piano Pedagogy
- Voice Divisions

Faculties

The strength of the school lies in its distinguished and internationally known faculty, who are committed to teaching and at the same time maintain active performance schedules, contribute substantially to research in all areas of music. The school is justifiably proud of the excellent facilities, nationally recognized degree programs, and enjoyable campus life, but these are secondary considerations when compared to the quality education provided by the faculty for the students.

The professional relationship between students and faculty is based upon mutual respect and a common interest in the quest for musical knowledge and artistry. There are nearly 100 full-time faculty members in music, which provides a student to faculty ratio of approximately 20 to 1. The wealth of experience the faculties bring to the classroom, studio, concert hall, or research facility, is supported by their continuous commitment to excellence.

Buildings and Facilities

Currently the school has the following buildings:

Rocky Band Building

Computer-Assisted Music Lab

Music Project Lab

Experimental Music Lab

Performing Arts Lab

Music Library Building

School of Piano Building

Jeff Memorial Hall

Admin Structure

The school has a Board of Directors for supervising the overall operations. The school president reports directly to the board. There are 2 vice presidents sharing the workload of administering the divisions of the school.

IT Infrastructure

There are currently 2 IT staffs in the school. The existing network is purely DOS-based with Netware 3.1 as the network OS. No special feature has been implemented. The registration office currently runs a 386PC with dBase3+ as the school registration system. The staffs generally use the old Geoworks software for designing flyers and other publications. Due to the availability of funding last year, the school managed to install a 100BaseFX network across the campus. In terms of bandwidth, the school has more than enough bandwidth for use.

Levels of Skills in IT

According to the IT Supervisor of the school, their students are very positive towards the use of IT in their learning process. Some students already uses computer to do the music composition. Others have uses notebooks to take notes during lectures.

Risk Management

In the past the school was once in difficulties due to a problem in funding. There had been a situation where the salaries of the teachers were not distributed on time, leading to a strike and a delay in the class progresses. Although this situation is not likely to happen again, the management insists on carry out a risk management process. It has been suggested that Microsoft's Risk Management process is the ideal methodology to use.

Future Vision

The school plans to open a branch in Austin, Texas. The management is willing to pay for a high speed 128K dedicated connection between the main campus and the new location. This new location will mainly be used to teach Music History and Music Appreciation.

The school will also open up a branch in London. This new location will use dial up modem to connect to the main office. This new location will mainly be a marketing office to promote the school's "Student Exchange" program.

Questions

1. Which of the following correctly describe the current company model of Rocky Mountain School?

A. regional
B. national
C. international
D. subsidiary
E. branch offices
F. None of the choices.

---

2. What company strategy is the school pursuing?

A. merger
B. growth
C. price leader
D. cost cutting
E. retention
F. None of the choices.

3.Which of the following will you see as an important element in your network infrastructure for the school?

A. connectivity with the new offices
B. connectivity within the campus
C. wireless environment
D. secure course content access
E. None of the choices.

4. To upgrade the network infrastructure for the school to Windows 2000. which of the following must be done first?

A. LAN connectivity
B. publishing software
C. routers
D. gateways
E. hardware
F. None of the choices.

5. The school encourages the students to use laptop computers to do their works. Which of the following network access technologies may be suitable for students who need to frequently move around inside the campus?

A. Infrared LAN
B. Satellite
C. Fiber Optics LAN
D. Wireless LAN
E. None of the choices.

6. Which of the following will you recommend as a way for the school teachers and students to share their latest music works?

A. a VPN hosted by Windows 2000
B. an online mall hosted by the Site Server
C. an intranet site hosted by IIS
D. a discussion group hosted by Microsoft Exchange
E. a collaboration group hosted by Microsoft Outlook
F. None of the choices.

7. What is the best way to migrate the current school registration system?

A. Export the data to a new 32bit application
B. Keep the existing system intact
C. Run the existing system using the DOS VM built into Windows 2000
D. rewrite the application to deploy a new GUI interface front end for running in Windows 2000
E. None of the choices.

---

8. You need to determine the following:

A. Estimated minimum figure of network usage
B. Estimated maximum figure of network usage
C. Estimated average figure of network usage

---

9. Network utilization data of the school can be collected by which of the following tools?

A. Sniffer
B. Perfmon
C. IIS
D. ISA
E. None of the choices

---

10. You need to draft the business objects within the school as well as the organization of these business objects. What type of diagram should you use?

A. Hierarchical Diagram
B. Horizontal Organizational Chart
C. Entity Relationships Diagram
D. PERT
E. None of the choices

---

11. Before you perform the Windows 2000 upgrade for the school, you are asked to determine what existing components in the network will meet the minimum requirement for the new Windows 2000 network. What type of analysis should you perform?

A. Upgrade Analysis
B. Installation Analysis
C. Optimization Analysis
D. Gap Analysis
E. None of the choices.

---

12. The school plans to implement video conferencing between the main campus and the London sales office. Which of the following connectivity option will you consider?

A. ISDN for the London office
B. Frame Relay for the London office
C. E1 for the London office
D. E3 for the London office
E. None of the choices

Chapter 3: Review Answers

1. A
2. B
3. A
4. E
5. D
6. C
7. A
8. A
9. A
10. A
11. D
12. A

Chapter 4: Analyzing Technical Requirements

The objective of this chapter is to provide the reader with an understanding of the following:

1. Connectivity Methods
2. Security Considerations
3. Network Applications and Protocols
4. TCP/IP infrastructure

Getting Ready (Questions)

1) What WAN connectivity method makes use of the existing telephone lines and networks to transmit multimedia data?
2) Frame Relay is regarded as what type of WAN connectivity service?
3) What security measure can you use against wiretapping?
4) Call back is a measure for protecting what type of WAN connection method?
5) What is the most common version of IP in use today?
6) What risk management strategy is always recommended?
7) What is known as the contract between an ISP and the customer for stipulating and committing the ISP to a required level of service?
8) What is the file sharing standard in the Unix world?
9) What is the directory standard in the world of Netware?

Getting Ready (Answers)

1) ISDN.
2) Packet switching.
3) Encryption.
4) RAS.
5) IPV4.
6) Proactive strategy.
7) SLA.
8) NFS.
9) NDS.

I Introduction

In the previous chapter we talked about the business requirements. Once the business requirements are identified, the next step is to look into the technical requirements and figure out the relationship between the two sets of requirements. Again, the one golden rule to follow: focus on the planned future structure. The current structure can give you hints in terms of what critical applications are being used at present and what have to be preserved. However, you must work towards the structure your client is expecting.

II Technical Factors

Existing and Planned Technical Environment and Goals

Let's take a look at the first set of objectives. Microsoft expects that you evaluate the company's existing and planned technical environment and goals:

Analyze company size and user and resource distribution.

Assess the available connectivity between the geographic location of worksites and remote sites.

Assess net available bandwidth and latency issues.

Analyze performance, availability, and scalability requirements of services.

Analyze data and system access patterns.

Analyze network roles and responsibilities.

Analyze security considerations.

Of the above items, most of them are related to what we have discussed in Chapter 3. These are the items raised by the CIO to echo the strategic objectives set by the CEO.

When the company size is large, it is more likely to see users and resources being allotted in a "distributed manner". Available connectivity between the geographic locations becomes an important issue, and you will be asked to evaluate the current options and find out if any upgrade is necessary.

During such an evaluation, you need to determine the so called "net available bandwidth" and latency.

Bandwidth Use

Bandwidth is the amount of data that can be transmitted in a fixed amount of time. Latency, on the other hand, means the amount of time it takes a packet to travel from source to destination. These two elements together define the speed and capacity of a network.

In the real world, we need to evaluate the truly available bandwidth, which is the "net available bandwidth". For example, when site A is connected to site B via a 512K link, in effect there is less than 512K available for the user applications. Factors limiting the net available bandwidth include:

- poor communication infrastructure provided by the service provider
- regular replication and synchronization traffics
- unnecessary user traffics (for example, employees browsing entertainment web site during work hours)
- other application overheads (such as data for control purpose)

In regards to the actual effective bandwidth, two terms deserve your attention. They are SLA and CIR.

A SLA is a Service Level Agreement contract between an ISP and the customer for stipulating and committing the ISP to a required level of service. When drafting such contract, the following are specified:

- Specific level of service
- Available support options
- Penalty provisions for services not provided
- Guaranteed level of uptime

CIR (shorts for committed information rate) represents the specified amount of guaranteed bandwidth on a packet switching service such as Frame Relay. With a CIR in place, the network vendor guarantees that frames not exceeding the specified level are guaranteed to be delivered. A higher CIR value usually incurs a higher service cost.

Latency is affected not only by the net available bandwidth, but also by the data and system access patterns. These patterns can be determined by:

- the type of applications used
- the way the applications are structured to access data
- the work hours

Simply put, different kinds of user may use different applications with different demand in different time frames throughout the day. You must collect information on this pattern and determine if bandwidth is actually enough.

Sniffer (such as Network Monitor) is a tool for capturing and analyzing network packets. The Microsoft Network Monitor tool to a certain extent reassembles such functionality. In practice, a sniffer can be used both for legitimate network management functions, such as the analysis of user traffic patterns, and for non-legitimate purposes, such as wiretapping. In any case, for a sniffer to capture network traffic, the NIC must be capable of running in promiscuous mode.

Pop Quiz 4.1

Pop Quiz 4.1 Questions

1) Network Monitor is an example of what application?
2) For sniffing to be possible, the NIC must be in what mode?
3) What is the agreement between an ISP and the customer for stipulating and committing the ISP to a required level of service?

Pop Quiz 4.1

Pop Quiz 4.1 *Answers*

1) Sniffer

2) Promiscuous mode

73) SLA

Example Case – Excel Forwarder – Part 2

The headquarters is running a NT4 network. The PDC of the single account domain is located in the headquarters. There are 5 BDCs for the account domain, and the BDC's are installed in the local offices. In addition, there are resource domains defined. All servers are running with dual 300mhz processors and 256M RAM.

Excel uses State of the Art software to insure that all documentation is prepared quickly and correctly. The software runs on NT Workstation that has TCP/IP configured.

The Excel Trade BBS allows the customers to receive email responses to the leads. This BBS runs on a standalone Linux server.

Excel is also in the process of finalizing the installation of new software that will enable its clients to track their shipments on the Internet.

Comments:

Excel uses a Single Master Domain structure. To speed up login, BDCs are placed in the local offices. Depending on the amount of changes to the account database as well as any modification to the default replication settings, you need to set aside certain capacity solely for the purpose of replication.

The case does not mention specifically where the resource domains are located. If resources are placed separately on the local offices, you must check and see if users have to frequently access resources across the WAN links.

If this happens to be the case, you should either upgrade the WAN link or consider the relocation of resources.

Excel has its BBS running separately on Linux, meaning authentication and authentication are likely to be done separately. Check and see what connectivity it runs on and determine its bandwidth usage.

Regarding the new software that enables its clients to track shipments on the Internet, you must work with management to come up with a forecast of the likely usage volume and demand. It is likely that you will have this internet application hosted on a Windows 2000 Server running IIS and SQL Server 2K, so you should also pay attention to the server system configuration: any fault tolerance necessary? How about load balancing? Ever consider to run a Windows 2000 cluster?

III Redundancy and Security

Redundancy

It is always important to consider the worst case scenario. What if the WAN link fails? You may consider the use of link backup methodologies such as DDR.

Shorts for Dial-on-Demand Routing, DDR is a routing technique that allows a site to utilize modem or ISDN connections on an on-demand basis should the primary link fails. This method is cost effective as a backup method because the connection becomes active only when data is actually sent across it.

When multiple WAN links are available to a site, you are often required to configure the routing cost (or metric) for each link. The link with a lower cost is always used first, and it is usually up to you as to how the cost is valued and assigned.

Connection Security

Security is another concern. Most security measures involve the use of data encryption techniques that translate data into unintelligible forms. Windows 2000 supports the three “A's” of security: Authentication, Authorization and Accounting.

Authentication is the process of identifying an individual user based on his/her supplied username and password. This process ensures that the individual is who he or she claims to be.

Authorization is the process of granting (or denying, if necessary) access to a network resource. This process takes place AFTER authentication.

Accounting is the process of logging user activities for future auditing.

Microsoft also mentions network roles and responsibilities. Simply put, who are in charge of the various IT functions? Where are the administrators located? Who do the maintenance? This is more an Active Directory arrangement than an infrastructure arrangement. Delegations are done via the use of OU, and the boundaries of administrative power are set by the domains. The only relevant infrastructure issue seems to be the “physical location” of the admin staffs. If all the administrators are on duty at the head office, most of the critical IT management tasks will have to be done centrally.

Critical servers are more likely to be placed close to the IT guys, and local system maintenance is likely to be done remotely via Terminal Services (if necessary, with a minimum degree of help from local staffs who have been granted a subset of the full administrative privileges). All these signal the need for stable and fast WAN links (both for remote resource access by users and remote management by administrators) as well as the need for backup links (should the primary WAN links fail).

Pop Quiz 4.2

Pop Quiz 4.2 *Questions*

1) DDR usually involves the use of what type of WAN connectivity?
2) What is the processing of granting user access to network resources?
3) What is the process of logging user activities for future auditing?
4) What are the elements of AAA?

Pop Quiz 4.2

Pop Quiz 4.2 *Answers*

1) Dial up connectivity such as ISDN
2) Authorization
3) Accounting
4) Authentication, Authorization, Accounting

Example Case – ABC Toys – Part 1

ABC Toys, formerly Supreme Hobbies and Toys, is owned and operated by people who have over 110 years of combined experience as retailers, hobbyists, and business professionals. The mission of the company is to introduce, support, and nurture the exciting world of model building and collecting.

The toys sold by ABC are known as family oriented - they offer product lines that introduce the youth to the excitement of toys. As introductory products, these lines also offer more advanced items for the rest of the family. To make sure that no rain check is ever needed, they keep stock of over 30,000 items in the stores.

The HQ is located in Hong Kong. The purchasing department is in Taiwan. The rest are run in Vietnam. The company has an IT team of 4 in Hong Kong. They have developed the NT 4 network using the multiple domain model. All remote offices can connect to the HQ server via the lease lines.

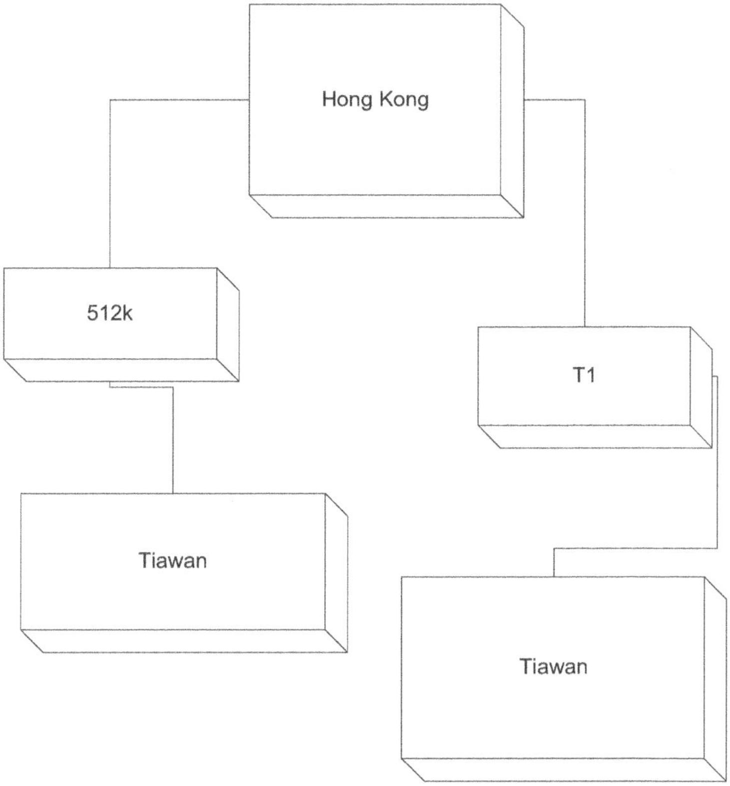

Figure 4.1 ABC Toys

Comments:

Based on the existing network structure, you may assume that there is almost no need for the staffs in Vietnam to access the resources in Taiwan, and vice versa. Although it is technically possible for the Vietnam staffs to access the Taiwan resources by passing through the Hong Kong office, such a setting can be very slow.

If there is really a need for the Vietnam office and the Taiwan office to share resources, the best way will be to host all the resources on the Hong Kong servers. Of course, you need to carefully design the domains and trust relationships so that access control can be properly implemented.

There are 4 IT staffs in Hong Kong. Nothing is said about the availability of IT staffs in the other offices. You may assume that centralized IT administration is the way to go. This somehow echoes the strategy of hosting all resources in Hong Kong: By having ALL these resources maintained in Hong Kong, they can be properly backed up handled correctly.

IV Compatibility Issues

Application Compatibility

Assessing current applications is one important aspect of your job. There are always some sorts of applications running in the company, with some of them being critical and some being less important. You always have to decide whether to upgrade these applications so that they can become "native", or to have them coexist with your new infrastructure.

When the applications were written for the earlier versions of 32 bit Windows, chances are that you have handful of upgrade paths. Win32 is the Windows API for developing 32-bit applications. It is built into Windows 95, 98 and NT, allowing applications that rely on the API to run equally well across these environments.

Compatibility for the older 16-bit Windows/DOS applications is less than optimal. For them to run, Virtual Machines acting as the 16 bit subsystem are to be relied on, at the expense of performance.

It is strongly advised that any older 16-bit applications be upgraded to the 32bit version. Keep in mind that Windows 2000 supports SMP (Symmetric Multiprocessing), a hardware architecture that make multiple CPUs available to complete individual processes simultaneously. You can take advantage of SMP only if your applications are written natively as 32-bit.

Example Case – MediAssociate – Part 1

Since 1986, MediAssociate has been conducting research for legal and health care professionals involved in medical malpractice, personal injury, product liability and workers' compensation cases. Target customers are those who are overwhelmed with complicated health care issues and baffling medical jargon. The founders of MediAssociate have been in the medical-legal consultant field for over ten years. They have been providing consulting services for attorneys, physicians and other legal nurse consultants.

The existing NT4 network was built with scalability in mind. There are 2 account domains together with 5 resource domains.

The CIO wants to upgrade the network to W2K. He is impressed by the stability of the new OS.

Comments:

The CIO said that he wants to have the network upgraded. You will have to plan for an upgrade. However, for certain specific critical services you may suggest that the existing platform be maintained, or that upgrade be done by incremental phrases. Remember, a truly successful upgrade does not introduce service interruption.

Always ensure that the server hardware is powerful enough to house Windows 2000. Windows 2000 is extremely demanding. If your budget is limited, re-consider the upgrade decision. Running Windows 2000 on slow systems will only make things worse.

Support for non-Microsoft Systems

Another area of concern is the so called legacy application – application designed to run on non-Microsoft operating systems, such as UNIX and Netware. UNIX has become the leading operating system for heavy duty servers and workstations due to its portability, flexibility, and power. Netware was a major network operating system in the marketplace that runs on a variety of different types of LANs.

Windows 2000 has a limited range of capabilities for dealing with "legacy" or "foreign" systems. For example, Gateway Service for NetWare (GSNW) can act as a redirector for a Windows 2000 Server and as a gateway for other client computers, allowing the NetWare resources to be shared as if they are located on the Windows 2000 server. Print services for UNIX allows UNIX client to print to the Windows 2000 print service. However, it is always the intention of Microsoft to get you into "migrating" these systems to Windows.

Due to the significance difference in architecture, technical complexity does exist to hinder the upgrade/migration process. In fact, unless strictly necessary, leave these systems alone.

Netware version 4.11 or later supports TCP/IP, while UNIX has been running on IP for decades. If these servers are for running web based services, there is no reason why you must replace them, as the nature of such services does not really require Active Directory integration.

If these servers are to host network resources, replacing them with Windows 2000 servers does allow for better control and management via Active Directory.

When co-existence is necessary, make sure your infrastructure can allow these systems to continue their works and at the same time allow them to communicate with your Windows 2000 systems.

Example Case – ProX Auditing Group – Part 1

ProX Auditing Group uses a logical sequence of steps to perform audits in the most efficient, effective, and timely manner possible. Its audits comply with the highest professional standards and lend credibility to client company's financial statements. Its experts can assist the clients in improving internal controls and operating efficiency, as well as recommend enhancements to make client companies more profitable.

Organization Structure

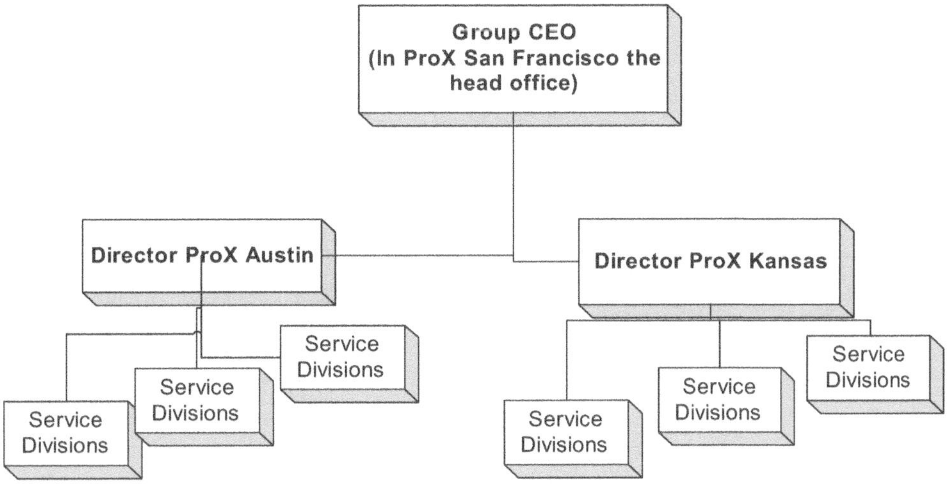

Figure 4.2 Group CEO

The SF office is the head office. All the offices share the same set of rules and standards.

The three ProX offices are interconnected with high speed T1 lines. Currently they are running on Netware 4.X. However, for file sharing, some NT servers are deployed as well. These NT servers are working together with the Netware 4.X servers on the same network. Clients are mainly Win98 based.

There is a special subnet called Sub09 configured in the head office that has purely UNIX servers. The servers are used as Intranet Web Servers, and the primary duty is to serve HTTP request only.

Comments:

There are Netware servers and UNIX servers running on the network. The Netware servers are "in charge of" the network, so a full scale upgrade seems to be required (this is what Microsoft prefers anyway).

On the other hand, the UNIX servers are placed in a specific subnet for serving HTTP requests and nothing else. The management does not mention any expected new functions on these servers. Active Directory integration does not seem to be necessary for these servers. You may leave them intact entirely.

Pop Quiz 4.3

Pop Quiz 4.3 *Questions*

1) How to you ensure that your Win16 applications can take advantage of SMP?
2) Which edition of Windows 98 supports SMP?
3) Which editions of Windows 2000 support SMP?
4) True or false: Under SMP, each processor has a separate pool of memory for use.

Pop Quiz 4.3

Pop Quiz 4.3 *Answers*

1) Upgrade them to the 32bit versions.
2) Windows 98 does not support SMP at all.
3) Windows 2000 Pro, all server versions of Windows 2000
4) False. The processors have to share memory.

V Co-existence with other platforms

Special Topic: Services For UNIX

Windows Services For UNIX (SFU) provides a set of additional features to Windows NT and Windows 2000 to allow for greater interoperability with existing UNIX-based systems in the enterprise through its ability to share network resources among Windows NT, Windows 2000, and UNIX.

The current version of SFU as of this writing is version 2.0 (although version 3.0 is in beta release stage). The following components are included:

Client for NFS – for Windows NT and Windows 2000 clients to mount exported file systems directly from UNIX NFS servers

Server for NFS – for sharing directories from Windows-NT based and Windows 2000-based servers

Gateway for NFS – for sharing UNIX NFS exports as Windows-based shared directories

Server for PCNFS – for enabling Windows 2000 to act as a PCNFS daemon server

NFS shorts for Network File System, which is a client/server application standard designed by Sun Microsystems (but publicly available and widely used) to allow all network users to access shared files stored on the UNIX computers. It provides access to shared files through the Virtual File System which runs on top of TCP/IP.

Special Topic: Windows Services for NetWare

Windows Services For NetWare (SFN) provides a set of additional features to Windows 2000 to allow for greater interoperability with existing NetWare-based systems in the enterprise by simplifying the introduction of Windows 2000 Server and its Active Directory service into a NetWare/NDS network environment.

NDS is the Novell Directory Services that complies with the X.500 standard and provides a logical tree-structure view of all resources on the network for user accesses. The key issue for the co-existence of Netware and Windows 2000 is to determine which directory service (NDS versus Active Directory) takes precedence.

The current version of SFN as of this writing is version 5.0 (although version 3.0 is in beta release stage). The following components and utilities are included:

Microsoft Directory Synchronization Services - for synchronizing the Active Directory and NDS with each other

Microsoft File Migration Utility - for migrating the files stored on the NetWare servers to the Windows 2000 Server

File and Print Services for NetWare 5 - for consolidating the file and print servers to Windows 2000 Server by having their Windows 2000 Server act like a NetWare file and print server to administrators, users and clients

Directory Service Manager for NetWare – for a Windows NT 4.0 Domain Controller to centrally manage multiple NetWare 2.x/3.x binderies

Special Topic: Services for Macintosh

Services for Macintosh is an integrated component of Windows 2000 Server that allows computers running the Windows and Macintosh operating systems to share files and printers. With this service, a Windows 2000 Server can function as a file server, remote access server, and print server for Macintosh client computers, in addition to performing the functions of an AppleTalk router.

Services for Macintosh includes the following components:

File Server for Macintosh

Print Server for Macintosh

Support for AppleTalk Protocol

Support for AppleTalk Control Protocol

Pop Quiz 4.4

Pop Quiz 4.4 *Questions*

1) Apple computers use what protocol for networking?
2) NFS is a networking standard used by what platform?
3) NDS is a networking standard used by what platform?
4) SAP is a networking protocol used in what environment?

Pop Quiz 4.4

Pop Quiz 4.4 *Answers*

1) AppleTalk
2) Unix
3) Netware
4) Netware

VI Migration and Upgrade

Migration

Below are the guidelines to follow when you are about to perform an upgrade or migration:

Check the hardware compatibility list (HCL).

Ensure that your hardware is sufficiently equipped to run Windows 2000.

Back things up before proceeding.

Perform the upgrade or migration only in non-office hours to avoid disruption.

If you plan to migrate from another system to Windows 2000, you must decide to go either with a gradual migration or a direct migration path. Gradual migration allows different services from different vendors to coexist for an extended period of time. This approach involves a higher cost because the work is to be carried out over a longer period of time, and thus requires multiple support and management resources expressly associated with a complex infrastructure. However, the risk is much lower as rollback can be performed easily should something go seriously wrong. Also, problems can be resolved given the long time frame, with little impact introduced on the production system. Direct migration, on the other hand, represents a quick way of migration with lower cost but higher risk.

Upgrade

Windows 2000 supports a variety of incremental deployment options.
Such options include:

1. Simple deployment of Windows 2000 Professional
2. Add new application servers in the existing environment
3. Deploy the advanced capabilities provided by Active Directory

A more gradual and incremental upgrade approach, as recommended by Microsoft, is as follow:

1. Start by upgrading desktops to Windows 2000 Professional
2. Move on to installing Windows 2000 Server in the existing Windows NT 4.0 domain environment, with focus on application servers and file and print servers
3. Upgrade Windows NT 4.0 domains to the new Windows 2000 domain architecture

All upgrade projects require that the following tasks be performed carefully:

1. Select the computers that are equipped for Windows 2000
2. Distribute the Windows 2000 source files to all the needed sites
3. Monitor the distribution of the Windows 2000 source files
4. Provide enough operating system rights to perform the upgrade
5. Initiate the installation of the software package (if possible, have it done automatically, with the option of allowing users to control the actual timing)
6. Resolve problems produced during distributions or installations

One best tool to use to perform the above is SMS System Management Server. Keep in mind though, that SMS provides tools ONLY for upgrading your current computers, not for installing new computers that do not have an operating system already installed.

Client Requirements

Sometimes you will see cases where specific clients are running, that you must ensure they can work fine in the new infrastructure. Although it is always possible to have the clients upgraded to Windows 2000, we do not normally recommend such because of the potential cost of doing so.

Remember, an enterprise can have thousands of clients. The cost for the upgrade and the subsequent support can be sky high.

When the infrastructure is upgraded to Windows 2000 Active Directory, certain upgrade on the client side may become necessary. As outlined in module 70-216 and 217:

- Windows 95 clients require special Active Directory client software to be installed.
- For your legacy Windows clients to live in an Active Directory network and make use of advanced features such as DDNS and DFS, special settings are necessary.

Refer to the BFQ Press Inside Scoop series on 70-216 and 70-217 for the technical details.

Project Risk

Project involves risks. This is unavoidable. Microsoft's famous MSF (Microsoft Solution Framework) provides a Risk Management Model that sets forth a discipline and environment of proactive decisions and actions to continuously assess risks.

According to MSF, risks are:

- inherent in every project
- neither intrinsically good nor bad
- not something to fear, but something to manage

Successful risk management the Microsoft way includes the following principles:

- Assess risks continuously throughout the project life cycle.
- Use risk-based decision making, meaning all decisions must be made within the context of their risk.
- Establish some level of formality for your team.
- Cover all key people and processes.
- Treat risk identification as a positive, without fear of punishment or criticism.

The best way to handle risk is to be proactive, that the project team has a visible, measurable, and repeatable process for managing risks.

The MSF approach advocates the carrying of risks forward - deal with them until the risk impact is reduced to zero. By identifying risks ahead of time, you can have multiple options at hand to prevent them. You may prevent risk through:

Reducing the likelihood that a risk will occur

Minimizing the impact if the risk does occur

Transfer the risk

Avoid the risk by doing something less risky

In any case, thoroughly assess the risks before proceeding with any project. Make sure you have disaster recovery plan ready before putting your hands on!

Disaster Recovery

Disaster recovery strategy for client computers, servers, and the network is an essential ingredient in your network infrastructure plan. Microsoft asks you to analyze the existing strategy, although most of the time your client companies will not have any plan of this kind available.

The ability to recover from disaster relies on multiple measures. First of all, regular backup is a MUST. Apart from this, you should consider the use of RAID or cluster.

Shorts for Redundant Array of Independent Disks, RAID employs multiple disk drives in combination for fault tolerance and performance.

There are many different RAID levels. Windows 2000 supports software based RAID level 1 and level 5 for fault tolerance. Level 1 provides disk mirroring while

Level 5 provides data striping with error correction at the byte level. Any failure of a single array member will not result in data loss.

A server cluster is a group of independent servers managed as a single system. The primary purpose of such cluster is higher availability: the ability to detect the failure of a server and quickly restart it on a surviving server. The minimum requirements for a Windows 2000 server cluster are:

two servers connected by a network

a method for each server to access the other's disk data

Windows 2000 Advanced Server or Data Center Server

Pop Quiz 4.5

Pop Quiz 4.5 *Questions*

1) What RAID levels are natively supported by Windows 2000 Server for fault tolerance?
2) True or false: Risks are inherent in every project.
3) True or false: Risks are neither intrinsically good nor bad.
4) Before upgrading a server to Windows 2000, what should be checked first?

Pop Quiz 4.5

Pop Quiz 4.5 *Answers*

1) RAID 1 and 5
2) True
3) True
4) Hardware compatibility

VII Chapter 4: Review Questions

You are a Network Consultant with specialized skills in designing Windows 2000 network. You are recently requested by the Supreme Manufacturing Company to design the Windows 2000 network for the entire company.

Company Background

Supreme Manufacturing Company was established in the early 80s, with its root in Korea as a manufacturer of Photo Albums. Due to the strong predicted growth of its business in the coming years, it plans to develop at least 10 new types of albums in the foreseeable future.

Divisions

Currently the production of each product category is under the supervision of its own divisional head. The logic behind this arrangement is that the production of each type of albums actually requires totally different types of expertise.

The president directly oversees the operations of the different divisions. Since the president himself owns the company, there is no board of directors. However, there is a position called Managing Director, which is at the top of the hierarchy. The law of Korea requires this. His wife took the position.

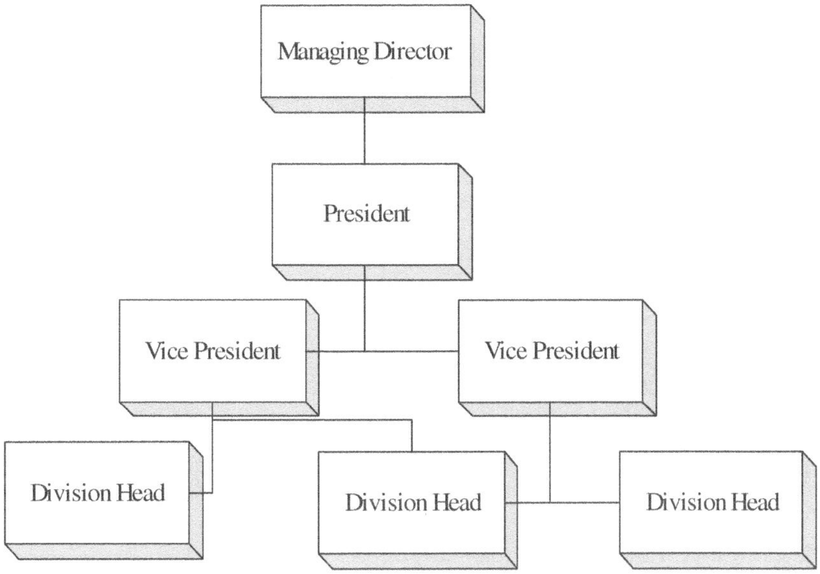

Figure 4.3 Divisions

Product offerings

Supreme's main products are photo albums. Products offering include:

Covered ring type albums:

Self-adhesive sheet albums.

P.V.C. slip in sheet albums

Memo type paper sheet albums.

Flip up type albums:

Single size cover albums.

Double sized cover albums.

Library style albums.

Slip in albums:

Soft transparent P.V.C cover albums.

Vinyl padded cover albums.

Minimax type albums.

Post bound type albums:

Self-adhesive sheet albums.

Slip in P.V.C sheet albums.

Binder type albums:

Self-adhesive sheet albums.

Slip in P.V.C. sheet albums.

Memo slip in albums:

Glue binding type albums.

Needlework binding albums.

Book bound type albums:

Wood free paper sheet classic type albums.

Self-adhesive sheet albums.

Wedding albums:

Hinge style joint albums

Bolt screw type albums. (Post bound type).

Due to the strong predicted growth of its business in the coming years, it plans to develop at least 10 new types of albums in the foreseeable future.

Supreme is manufacturing not only the finished goods, but also the separated parts of the photo albums, such as

Covers

Sheets

Labels

Apart from manufacturing products under their own brand, they also accept special orders in term of O.E.M.

Locations and Staffing

Supreme has three locations, one being the head office and the others being the factories. The president is located in the head office, while the divisional heads are completely mobile – they have to travel around the factories.

Head office

Dokok-Dong, Gangnam-Gu, Seoul, Korea

Number of Staff: 10

Korea Branch - Factory

Goori City Kyunggi-Do, Korea

Number of Staff: 600

China Branch - Factory

Yang Hong, Jiangsu, China

Number of Staff: 300

US Branch – Sales Office

Recently opened in San Francisco of California

Number of Staff: 30

IT Structure

Currently only the head office has a LAN running NT 4.0. The domain model is a simple single domain model. They do not YET have dedicated connection to the factories. The factories are using Win95 as dial up clients to connect to the head office server running RAS. The factories also run Netware 3.X as the NOS. In the coming months 256K dedicated connection will be installed. Currently, within all locations there are already 100MBPS LANs running smoothly.

The president recognizes the importance of IT, and is planning to spend 30% of its last year revenue on the complete re-design of the IT infrastructure.

Because of the growing importance of IT, the head office will house a new IT department.

Questions

1, Which of the following correctly describe the current company model of Supreme?

A. regional
B. national
C. international
D. merger
E. None of the choices.

2, What company strategy is Supreme pursuing?

A. merger
B. growth
C. vertical integration
D. cost cutting
E. retention
F. None of the choices.

3, Which of the following will you see as an important element in your network infrastructure for Supreme?

A. scalability
B. security
C. performance
D. cost savings
E. None of the choices.

4, What strategy should you use regarding the NOS of Supreme?

A. Leave the Netware systems "as is". Use Windows 2000 only for DHCP and DNS.
B. Have Windows 2000 running only in the head office. Install GSNW for coexistence with the Netware server
C. Leave all Netware installation intact. Install the TCP/IP patch for Netware.
D. Migrate to Windows 2000 completely
E. None of the choices.

5, What connectivity methods should you use for the US Sales office (Choose all that apply)?

A. ISDN for connecting to the head office
B. RAS for the sales staffs to dial back to the Sales office
C. 128k dedicated connections to the head office
D. ISDN for the sales staffs to dial back to the Sales office
E. RAS for the sales staffs to dial back directly to the head office
F. None of the choices.

6, Which of the following technologies, when being considered for deployment in Supreme's factory sites, deserve your special attention in terms of law and regulations?

A. compression
B. WAN link
C. encryption
D. LAN link
E. Windows 2000 migration
F. software license

7, You plan to upgrade the entire infrastructure of Supreme to Windows 2000. Which of the following issues should you pay the most attention to when proceeding with the upgrade?

A. The availability of the different language versions of Windows 2000
B. The migration path of the network topology
C. The cost of such upgrade
D. The availability of training staff in the local sites
E. None of the choices.

8, You need to prepare a diagram that represents the physical network infrastructure of Supreme. In addition to the Hubs and the Switches, what else must you include in the diagram (Choose all that apply)?

A. WAN connections
B. Routers
C. Users
D. Managers
E. None of the choices.

9,Before proceeding to analyze Supreme's technical requirement, which of the following processes should be completed first?

A. Information gathering
B. Action planning
C. Contingency planning
D. Training
E. None of the choices

10 Network Monitor can be used to gather information about:

A. the network traffic on the existing Supreme network
B. the estimated network traffic on the planned Supreme network
C. server performance
D. server Windows 2000 upgrade eligibility
E. None of the choices.

---

11 What is the primary protocol used by the factory in China?

A. IPX/SPX
B. NetBEUI
C. SNA
D. DLC
E. AppleTalk

---

12 You are told to look for an alternate WAN service provider for the Head Office. You need to ensure the minimum guaranteed bandwidth of the connection supplied. What specifically should you look for?

A. CIR
B. BSDN
C. ADSL
D. BDSL
E. ATM

13 You want to prepare two connections for the head office, with one as the backup. How would you ensure that the primary link is always used first?

A. Assign it with a lower metric
B. Assign it with a higher metric
C. Assign it with a metric of zero
D. Assign it with a metric identical to that of the backup link
E. None of the choices

---

14 Which of the following WAN connectivity option is ideal for use as backup and load sharing?

A. ISDN
B. Frame Relay
C. X.25
D. Modem
E. ATM

Chapter 4: Review Answers

1, C

2, B

3, A

4, D

5, A, B

6, C

7, A

8, A, B

9, A

10, A

11, A

12, A

13, A

14, A

Total Recall

Chapter 5: Designing a Windows 2000 Network Infrastructure

The objective of this chapter is to provide the reader with an understanding of the following:

1. IP Addressing
2. Routing
3. DHCP Integration
4. Name Resolution
5. Global Catalog
6. Dfs
7. LDAP

Getting Ready (Questions)

1) In Windows 2000, what service is responsible for routing TCP/IP?
2) For a Windows 2000 server to act as a router, how many NICs must it have?
3) DHCP servers and clients can register with DNS only if:
4) True or False: DHCP and static DNS service are compatible for keeping name-to-address mapping information synchronized.
5) A WINS client typically makes how many attempts to find the primary WINS server?
6) All WINS communications use directed datagrams over which port?
7) How many types of Dfs root can you create?
8) How many Dfs roots can a Windows 2000 server host?
9) What standard does Active Directory follow?

Getting Ready (Answers)

1) RRAS.
2) A minimum of two.
3) The server supports Dynamic DNS updates.
4) False.
5) Three attempts.
6) UDP port 137.
7) Two types: Domain based and standalone.
8) One per server.
9) LDAP.

I Introduction

This chapter talks about "Designing a Windows 2000 Network Infrastructure". To be precise, the following topics will be covered:

IP Addressing

Routing

DHCP Integration

Name Resolution

Global Catalog

Dfs

LDAP

This chapter is one of the heaviest chapters in this book, and is the foundation of the Microsoft Exam Objective "Designing a Management and Implementation Strategy for Windows 2000 Networking".

II IP Addressing

An IP address uniquely identifies a location on the network to which IP datagrams can be sent. Not all addresses are usable: some of them are reserved for special uses, as listed in the table below:

Class	Addresses / Ranges	Status
A	0.0.0.0 1.0.0.0 to 126.0.0.0 127.0.0.0	Reserved Available Reserved
B	128.0.0.0 to 191.254.0.0 191.255.0.0	Available Reserved
C	192.0.0.0 192.0.1.0 to 223.255.254 223.255.255.0	Reserved Available Reserved
D	224.0.0.0 to 239.255.255.255	Multicast
E	240.0.0.0 to 255.255.255.254 255.255.255.255	Reserved Broadcast

Table 4 IP Addressing

In TCP/IP V4, the IP address is 32-bit, and is grouped 8 bits at a time, with each group consisting of 8 bits in an octet. The four octets are separated by dots, and are mostly represented in decimal format. The minimum value for an octet is 0 when all bits are set to 0, while the maximum value for an octet is 255 when all bits are set to 1.

The network number component of an IP address identifies the network, and must be assigned by the Internet Network Information Center at www.InterNIC.net if the network is to be connected to the Internet. On the other hand, the host number is responsible for identifying a host in the network, and is mostly assigned by the local network administrator.

The class of an address can be easily determined by looking at its first octet. In fact, the left-most bits in the first octet indicate the network class:

- Class A address has the first octet as the network number and uses a subnet mask of 255.0.0.0.
- A Class B address has the first and second octets as the network number and uses a subnet mask of 255.255.0.0.
- A Class C address has the first, second, and third octet as the network number and uses a subnet mask of 255.255.255.0.

To calculate the subnet mask, you may set all bits to a value of 1 in the octets designated for the network number and all bits to a value of 0 in the octets designated for the host number.

Subnetting

IP Subnetting is one of the most important aspects of IP addressing. It is made possible by borrowing bits from the host field and have them designated as the subnet field. The number of bits to borrow is entirely up to you, although you must set the subnet mask accordingly for changes to be effective.

The scenarios you will face involve devising an addressing plan that covers:

the number of subnets to use

the IP address ranges

the subnet mask to use

In terms of the number of subnets to use, it depends entirely on the number of geographical locations as well as the number of divisions / departments. Remember to also count the number of router used.

To illustrate, take a look at the exhibit below:

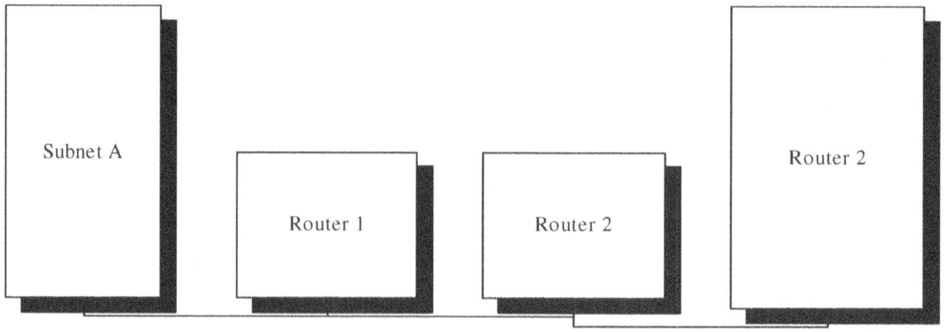

Figure 5.1 Subnet 1

How many subnets are required in the above exhibit? The answer is THREE, because two routers are in use. This type of setting is required when the connection is between remote locations:

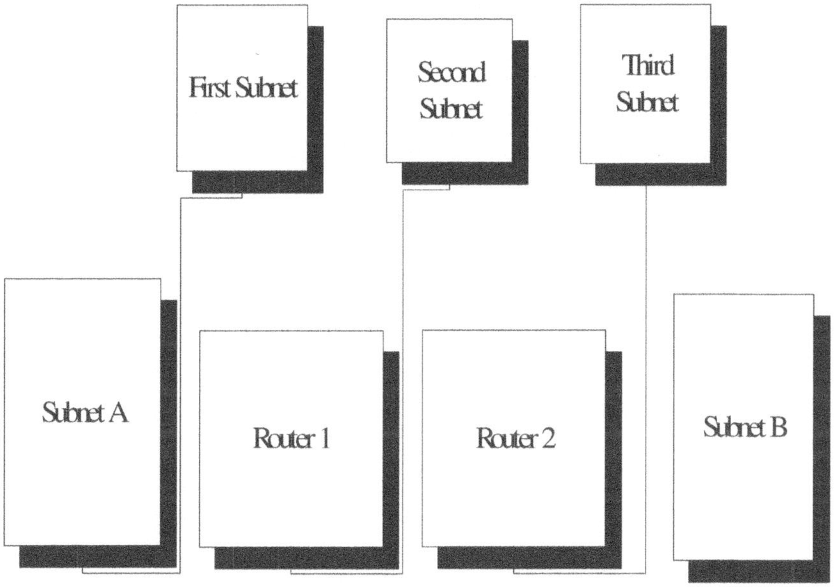

Figure 5.2 Subnet 2

On the other hand, if your network is setup as below, the number of subnet can be reduced by one. However, this type of connection is possible only in a LAN:

Example Case – ABC Toys – Part 2

The HQ is located in Hong Kong. The purchasing department is in Taiwan. The rest are run in Vietnam. The company has an IT team of 4 in Hong Kong. They have developed the NT 4 network using the multiple domain model. All remote offices can connect to the HQ server via the lease lines.

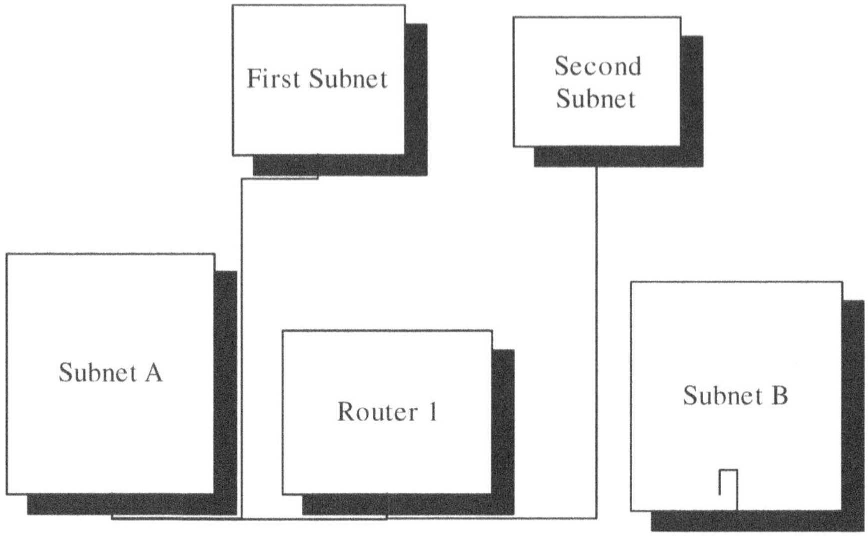

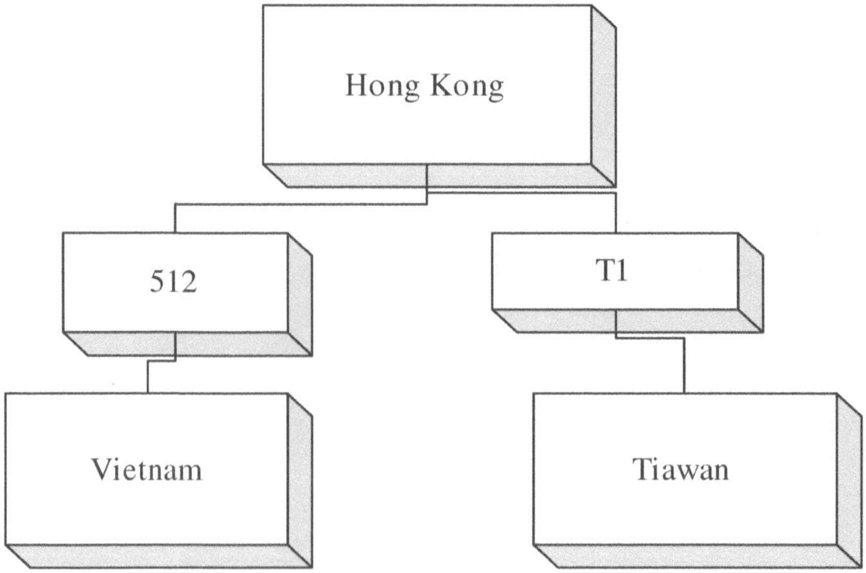

Comments:

For ABC Toys, assuming that the LANs within each location are not further segmented, we will need a minimum of four routers, with two for each connection, or a total of three routers, with the one in Hong Kong being multi-port capable. In any case, a minimum of 5 subnets will be necessary.

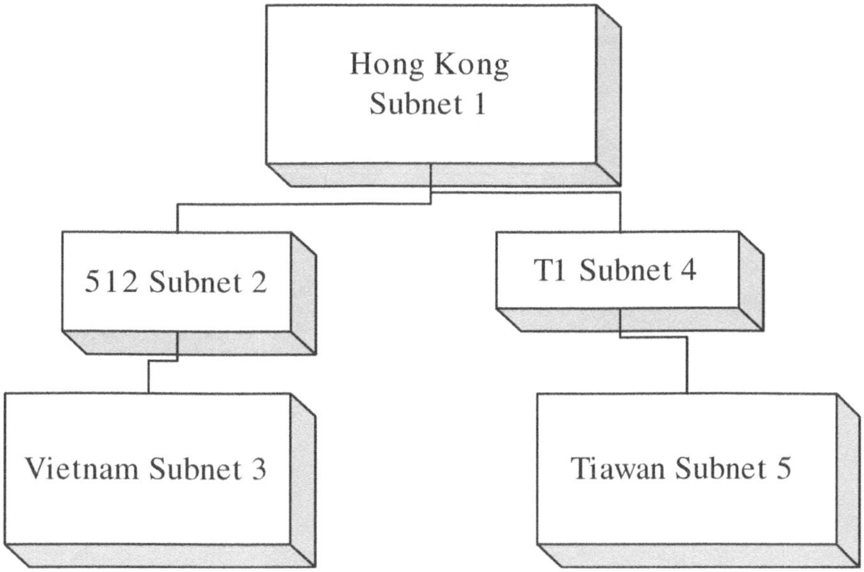

Regarding IP address configuration in a subnetting plan, you will most likely need to determine the following (given a particular network address):

- Network Class
- Subnet Mask
- Number of Subnets
- Nodes/Hosts per Network

The best way to have yourself familiarized is to practice with a Subnet Calculator. There are many FREE subnet calculators on the web, including:

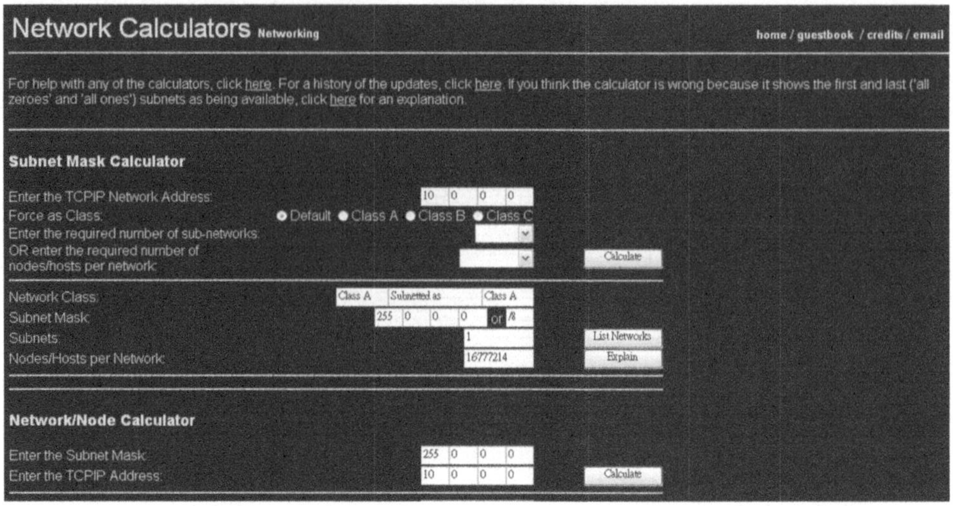

Figure 5.3 Network Calculator

This Network Calculator is available at
http://www.telusplanet.net/public/sparkman/netcalc.htm >

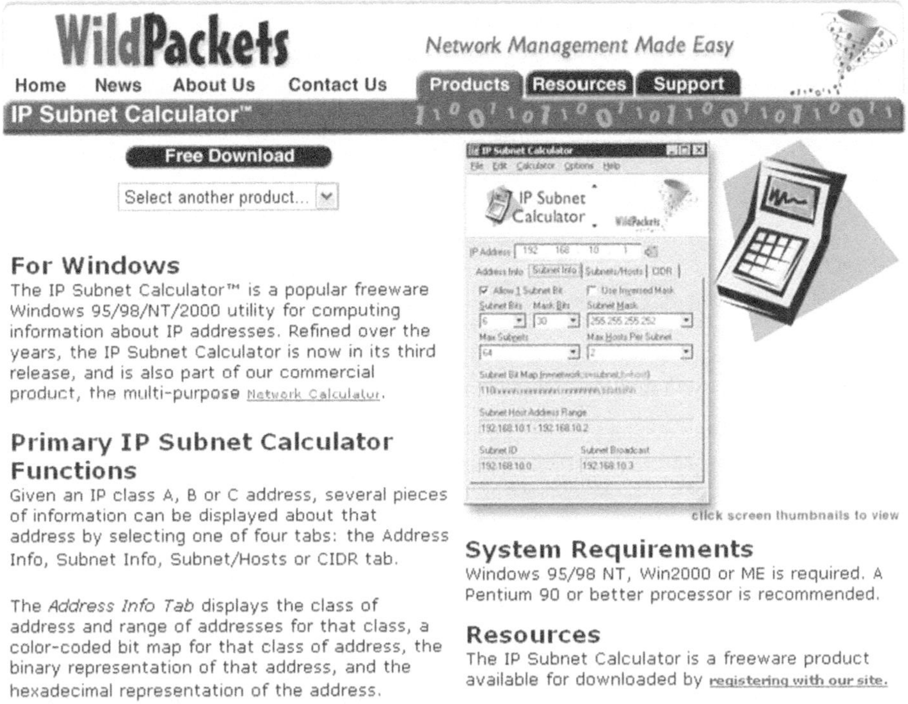

Figure 5.4 Second Network Calculator

This Network Calculator is available at

http://www.wildpackets.com/products/ipsubnetcalculator >

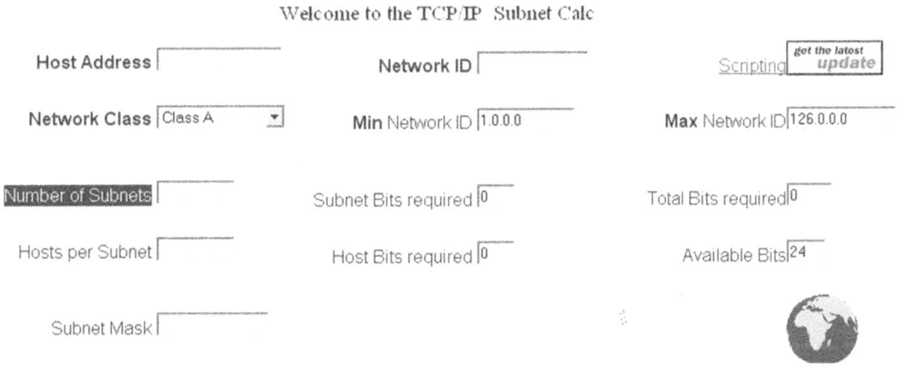

Figure 5.5 Third Subnet Calculator

This Network Calculator is available at http://www.learnquick.com/tcptrainbody.html >

It is worth to note that, as according to RFC 791, subnetting with a subnet address of zero is illegal because of the confusion that can be caused between a network and a subnet that have the same addresses.

Pop Quiz 5.1

Pop Quiz 5.1 *Questions*

1) True or false: Subnetting with a subnet address of zero is illegal.
2) How many octets are available in a 32bit IP address?
3) An IPv6 address is a ______ bit address.

Pop Quiz 5.1

Pop Quiz 5.1 *Answers*

1) True according to RFC 791.

2) Four

3) 128

III Windows 2000 Routing

The term "Software routing", in Microsoft context, means routing with Windows 2000 server. In Windows 2000, routing is performed via the RRAS service. This service allows a Windows 2000 Server computer with multiple NICs to function as a multiprotocol router, a demand-dial router, and a remote access server. Routing And Remote Access snap-in is the tool to use for enabling and configuring RRAS or for disabling the service.

In terms of hardware, Windows 2000 RRAS can run over all major LAN and WAN network adapters, so long as these adaptors are supported by Windows 2000. In terms of protocols, RRAS can route IP, IPX, and AppleTalk simultaneously. In terms of Demand-Dial Routing, RRAS can route IP and IPX over on-demand or persistent WAN links, or over VPN connections running PPTP or L2TP.

Routing can be configured statically via the route command (as in the exhibit below), although a dynamic routing protocol is preferable. RRAS supports RIP 1, RIP 2 and OSPF.

```
C:\Documents and Settings\ycthk>route print
===========================================================================
Interface List
0x1 ........................... MS TCP Loopback interface
0x2 ...00 d0 09 2c cc af ...... DAVICOM 9102-Based PCI Fast Ethernet Adapter - P
acket Scheduler Miniport
===========================================================================
===========================================================================
Active Routes:
Network Destination        Netmask          Gateway       Interface  Metric
          0.0.0.0          0.0.0.0      192.168.0.1    192.168.0.80      30
        127.0.0.0        255.0.0.0        127.0.0.1       127.0.0.1       1
      192.168.0.0    255.255.255.0     192.168.0.80    192.168.0.80      30
     192.168.0.80  255.255.255.255        127.0.0.1       127.0.0.1      30
    192.168.0.255  255.255.255.255     192.168.0.80    192.168.0.80      30
        224.0.0.0        240.0.0.0     192.168.0.80    192.168.0.80      30
  255.255.255.255  255.255.255.255     192.168.0.80    192.168.0.80       1
Default Gateway:       192.168.0.1
===========================================================================
Persistent Routes:
  None
```

Figure 5.6 documents and Settings

The route print command displays the content of the routing table. You may use the route add command to add new entries here.

Example Case – MediAssociate – Part 2

The company is structured in a way that reflects the services it offers. There are mainly 3 departments in the company, one for each main service.

MediAssociate has a very advanced IT infrastructure. It deploys fiber optics in its downtown San Jose office. The network is running 25 NT 4 Servers and 300 clients. To speed up research, they use a T3 line to connect to the Internet. In addition, there are 4 Solaris workstations specially designed for a fault tolerant web site configuration.

What routing strategy would be appropriate?

Comments:

There are 300 clients, so for sure you will need to segment the network. To simplify routing configuration and improve network performance, IP should be used as the primary protocol (and preferably the only protocol) in the network.

There are three departments in the office, so you may consider to create one subnet for each. The case does not mention the head counts for each department, so you must be flexible: for a large department you may want to use more subnets.

Windows 2000 Server is the ideal choice for routing. In fact, a single Windows 2000 server with multiple NICs can do the job satisfactorily (if this system is dedicated for routing and nothing else).

Below is a proposed network layout:

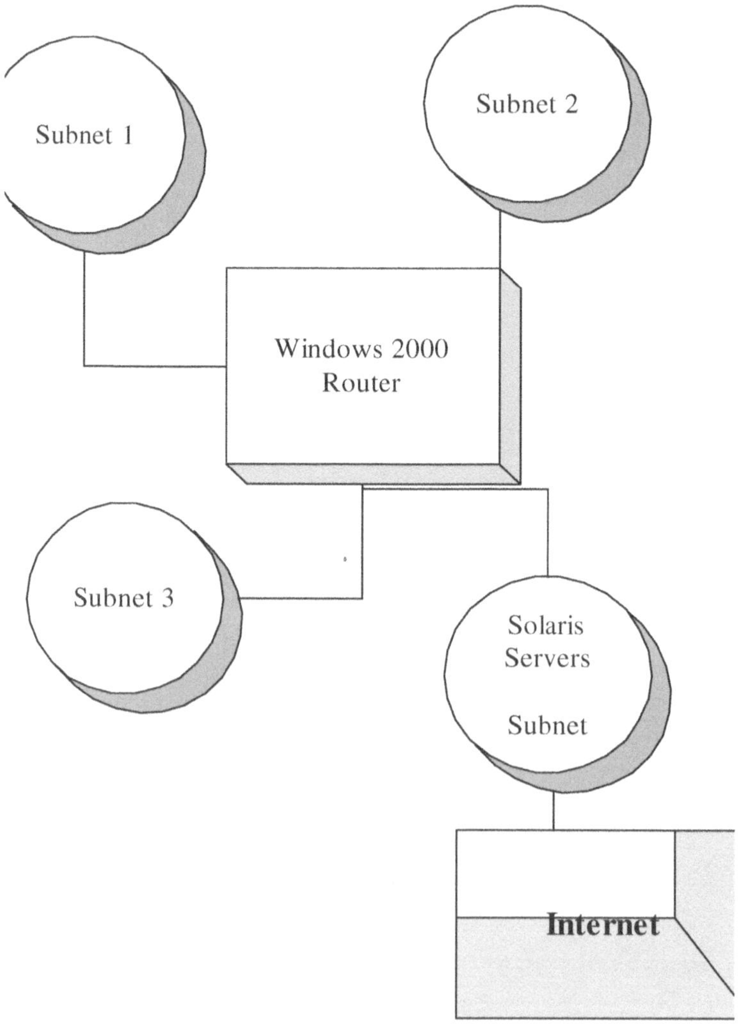

Figure 5.7 Network Layout

Remember, routing updates can consume quite a lot of bandwidth. To minimize bandwidth consumption, follow the guidelines below:

Maintain a static routing topology. Changes in routing topology lead to routing updates.

Use static routes if the network is small and simple. Static routes require no routing updates at all

Choose an efficiency routing protocols. RIP and RIP2 are considered less efficiency than OSPF because they periodically exchange the entire routing table with the other routers on the network.

In fact, RIP and RIP2 can function only within 15 hops, meaning they may not be suitable for large and complex networks at all.

Special Topic: OSPF

Shorts for Open Shortest Path First, OSPF is a routing protocol developed for IP networks by the Internet Engineering Task Force (IETF) to perform routing updates using the Shortest Path First (SPF) algorithm. It has the following characteristics:

It is an open standard that has its specification is in the public domain.

It uses the SPF algorithm (which is also known as the Dijkstra algorithm) to calculate the shortest path to reach each node, which is very processor intensive.

It is classified as a link-state routing protocol.

It sends link-state advertisements (LSAs) to all other routers within the same hierarchical area.

Special Topic: RIP and RIP V2

Shorts for Routing Information Protocol, RIP is one of the most popular routing protocols in use today. The IP version of RIP is defined in RFC 1058 and STD 56. Its second generation (known as RIP2) is described in RFC 1723. The primary enhancement of RIP2 includes:

- Enables RIP messages to carry more information than before
- Allows authentication mechanism to be in place for securing table updates
- Supports subnet masks

RIP and RIP2 send routing-update messages when:

- when the network topology changes
- at regular intervals

RIP routers maintain and use only the best route, which is the route with the lowest metric value to a destination. By using only a single routing metric – the hop count - to measure the distance between source and destination, RIP can sometimes misjudge the actual routing cost.

To prevent routing loops from continuing indefinitely, the maximum number of hops in a path is 15. Any path with a hop count above this value is considered unreachable.

Pop Quiz 5.2

Pop Quiz 5.2 *Questions*

1) What routing protocols are supported by RRAS?
2) Which RRAS supported routing protocol is highly processor intensive?
3) What command do you use in the command prompt to add a static route?
4) What switch do you use in the route add command to make an entry persistent?

Pop Quiz 5.2

Pop Quiz 5.2 *Answers*

1) RIP V1, RIP V2, OSPF
2) OSPF
3) route add
4) -p

IV Windows 2000 DHCP

DHCP Integration with the Local Network

Shorts for Dynamic Host Configuration Protocol, DHCP enables hosts on an IP network to obtain their configurations from a centrally managed server to reduce the administrative work necessary to administer the IP infrastructure. It is described in RFC 2131, and is using UDP as its transport protocol:

Client sends messages to the DHCP server on UDP port 67

DHCP server sends messages to the client on UDP port 68

Even with DHCP, there are three methods for assigning IP addresses:

Automatic allocation – have DHCP assigns a permanent IP address to a client.

Manually configured allocation – have the client's IP address assigned by hand, but uses DHCP to convey the address to the client.

Dynamic allocation – have DHCP assigns an IP address to the client for a limited lease period. This is the most common way of address assignment.

Regarding DHCP in LAN, the four important issues are:

The integration of DNS and DHCP

The integration of WINS and DHCP

DHCP redundancy

DHCP performance

In the past, there was no way for DHCP to interact with DNS, leading to the possibility of incorrect information being maintained by DNS for a DHCP client.

With Windows 2000, DHCP servers and clients can register with DNS, if and only if they support Dynamic DNS updates.

In Windows 2000, the DHCP server can register with a DNS server and update two types of resource records:

- pointer (PTR)
- address (A)

The A record provides the name-to-address mapping, while the PTR record provides the address-to-name mapping. Windows 2000 can perfectly fit into the DDNS and DHCP environment. In fact, every Windows 2000 client will attempt the registration of its A and PTR records automatically.

For non-Windows 2000 computers, the Windows 2000 DHCP server will register the DHCP clients' A and PTR records when requested. Such ability enables DHCP to act as a proxy for DNS registration on behalf of older clients running Windows 95 and Windows NT 4.0.

Keep in mind though, that Windows 2000 DHCP is not compatible with any static DNS service, such as the legacy Unix/Linux DNS flavor. So, as recommended by Microsoft, use only Windows 2000 as your choice for DNS. If this is not possible, follow the guidelines below to avoid DNS lookup failure:

- Enable WINS lookup for legacy Windows DHCP clients (if WINS is available)
- Configure IP address reservations with infinite duration for DNS only DHCP clients.

DHCP Performance and Redundancy

For redundancy purpose, you may configure multiple DHCP servers on the same LAN.

For this to work without producing address duplication errors, you must make sure that overlapping address scopes do not exist among the DHCP servers. Also, Windows 2000 DHCP will not function correctly with the presence of the services below:

- Small Business Server SBS
- Regarding performance Internet Connection Sharing ICS

Always remember the fact that the more address lease requests the more overhead will be brought to your network. You may want to setup longer lease durations in order to reduce the amount of lease renewal requests. To so do, you must ensure that there are enough IP addresses for allocation, or some of your clients will fail to obtain addresses.

Serving DHCP Clients

Do not forget the role of DHCP Relay Agent. If your DHCP clients are located across a router from the subnet where the DHCP server resides, they will be unable to receive an address from the server. To correct this problem, you must configure a DHCP relay agent on the client subnet (to be precise, on the router itself or on a Windows 2000 Server computer with DHCP Relay service running), and configure a scope to match the network address of the client subnet. Do not include this scope on segment where the DHCP server resides.

In some circumstances you may be requested by your clients to migrate their existing NT4 DHCP settings into a new Windows 2000 server. To do so, you should first backup the existing DHCP database, and then perform the steps below:

Export the registry entries to a file

Copy the DHCP database to the new server

Import the registry entries into the new server

Authorize and start the new DHCP service in Active Directory

Last but not least: make sure you have all your DHCP services authorized in Active Directory!

DHCP Integration with RRAS

When there are clients that need to connect to your network via RAS, you may want to assign them with dynamic IP addresses. You can have a RRAS pool configured to use DHCP. RRAS uses DHCP to lease addresses in blocks of 10 and have them stored locally in the registry. These leases are to be released when RRAS is shutting down. To ensure that the remote clients can obtain the correct address configuration settings, enable the DHCP Relay Agent in the Routing and Remote Access Manager.

Example Case – MediAssociate – Part 3

The company is expected to expand its network of affiliated professionals. Currently they have more than 25000 professionals in their network nationwide. These professionals are allowed to connect to the head office via dial up access. Due to the fast growth in business, it is estimated that in three years time the number of professionals that work with the company will be doubled.

Since to a certain extent these professionals are not in-house staffs, the company will want to have a separate community for them. This community should manage their own password and lockout policy on their own.

Comments:

There are currently 25000 remote access users. The number is expected to go double in three years. DHCP is the only way to go for managing such a large amount of clients. Reserve a large enough address pool for these user clients. Acquire enough Windows 2000 servers with enough modem banks to handle the usage volume.

IAS should be used to authenticate and log these users. However, a single IAS server in this case may not be enough. Consider to deploy multiple subnets for these users, each with different sets of servers to handle the workload.

Pop Quiz 5.3

Pop Quiz 5.3 *Questions*

1) True or false: Windows 2000 DHCP will not function correctly with the presence of Small Business Server.
2) True or false: Windows 2000 DHCP functions perfectly with Internet Connection Sharing.
3) In Windows 2000, DHCP servers and clients can register with DNS if:
4) What must be present in a subnet without a DHCP server?

Pop Quiz 5.3

Pop Quiz 5.3 *Answers*

1) True
2) False
3) Dynamic DNS update is supported.
4) DHCP Relay Agent

V Windows 2000 DNS

As mentioned earlier, use WINS only if there are legacy NETBIOS clients! Otherwise, a pure DNS environment is always recommended.

The different types of resource records in DNS include:

SOA, Start Of Authority - identifies the name server that is the best source of information for the data within a domain

NS, Name Server - identifies an authoritative name server for a domain

A, Address - maps a name to an IP address

CNAME, Canonical NAME - maps an alias to the official host name

WKS, Well-Known Service – identifies the services provided by a particular protocol on a particular interface

PTR, PoinTeR - maps an IP address to a name

MX, Mail eXchange - specifies a host for mail processing

The major types of name servers include:

PRIMARY - The primary name server for a zone

SECONDARY - used as backup in case the primary one fails

In Windows 2000 Active Directory, the domain controllers can also act as the DNS servers when Active Directory Integrated Zone is deployed.

To migrate your environment to pure DNS, you must configure your clients by configuring the appropriate DNS settings in the Internet Protocol Properties. You will also need to setup the proper zone(s) on your DNS server.

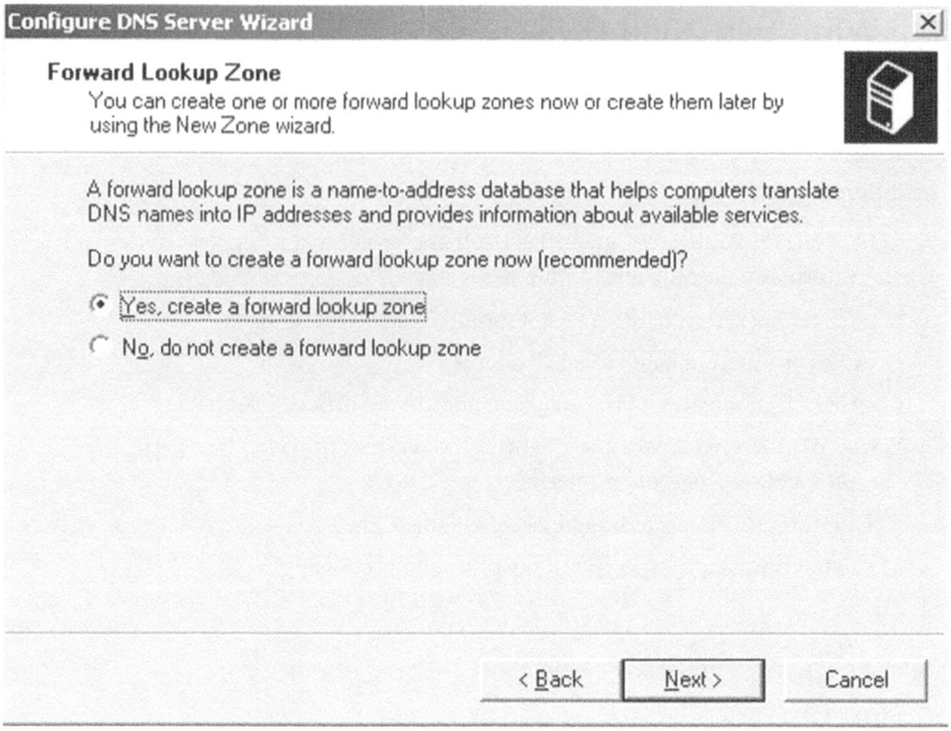

Figure 5.8 Configure DNS Server

The Configure DNS Server Wizard assists you in the creation of different DNS zone files. >

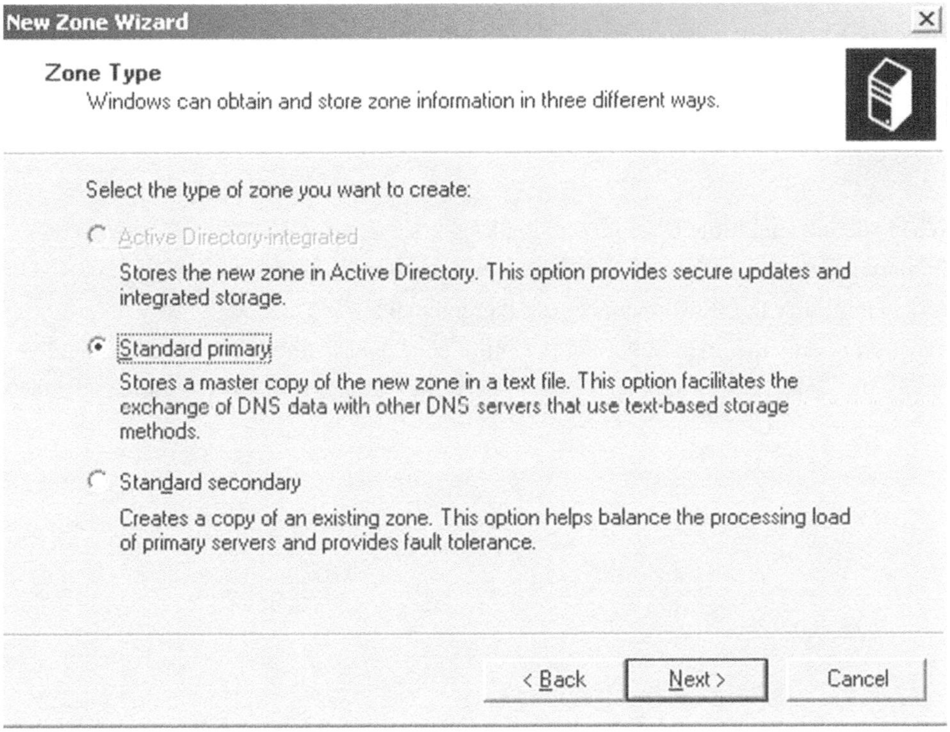

Figure 5.9 New Zone Wizard

Different types of zone can be created with the New Zone Wizard.

If the server itself is a domain controller of Active Directory, you can use the Active Directory Integrated zone type. This is the most reliable and secure zone type available.

If you have couple Windows 2000 DNS Servers and a few legacy DNS servers coexisting in the network, you can have them work together by enabling the Active Directory integrated DNS servers to also act as the primary server, then set up the legacy servers as the secondary servers and allow the zone data to be transferred to them. However, for performance reason, you should use pure Windows 2000 DNS solutions whenever possible.

Once DNS is set up in your network, you can troubleshoot the DNS service by using:

the monitoring and logging options in the DNS Service snap-in

the NSlookup command

When you have multiple DNS servers in place, zone transfer will take place between the Primary and the Secondary servers. These zone transfers produce network overhead. One way to minimize the slowdown is to use Incremental Zone Transfer – a way of transferring only the updates but not the entire zone data. Although you may manually reduce the zone transfer frequency, it will be at the expense of name resolution accuracy.

VI Windows 2000 WINS

In a WINS environment with non-WINS clients, you may use a WINS proxy agent to listen for broadcast name registrations and resolution requests and have them forwarded to the WINS server. To configure a WINS proxy agent, you must have a WINS enabled client available on the same client segment. Edit the registry by setting the value for the EnableProxy entry to 1 and then restart that computer.

As recommended by Microsoft, for performance reason the number of WINS server should always be minimized to an extent that allows a minimum degree of redundancy (that is, two WINS servers). The maximum number of WINS server should never exceed 20. Also, should it be necessary to configure WINS Proxy, one such proxy agent per client subnet is enough. Running multiple WINS proxy agents on the same subnet is entirely meaningless.

Example Case – ExGovern – Part 1

ExGovern is an agency specialized in working with government and non-profit organizations since 1979. Its governmental experience includes working with:

Cities
Counties
State Agencies
Federal Agencies
School Districts
Highway Districts
Port Authorities
Utility Districts

Currently its network is running Windows NT 4 and 3.51. For clients, they have NT 4 Workstations, Win95/98 and a small number of Apple Macintosh. The IT Manager of the company only wants to upgrade the Server and some of the NT Workstation to W2K, and nothing else.

There will be 4 sites in the network due to the physical locations of ExGovern's different offices. These sites will be linked with 256K dedicated lines to the central office.

WINS will be implemented in the network even after the Windows 2000 upgrade.

Comments:

In terms of DNS, after the implementation of Windows 2000 Server, you will want to request DHCP to register the non-Windows 2000 clients with DDNS on their behalf.

Macintosh computers support TCP/IP, and you may give them static configuration. For name resolution, you may use static entries for them in DNS and in WINS.

Since the majority of clients are NETBIOS based, maintaining WINS in addition to DNS is a logical choice (according to Microsoft). Keep in mind though, whenever WINS is involved, pay attention to the following issues:

WINS Proxy Agent (for non-WINS clients)

WINS Replication

Name Resolution Redundancy and Performance

As for DHCP, you may configure redundancy for DNS and WINS. For DNS, the best way is to set up and deploy Active Directory integrated zones on multiple DNS servers. An Active Directory-integrated zone is the master copy of a new zone that makes use of Active Directory to store and replicate the zone data.

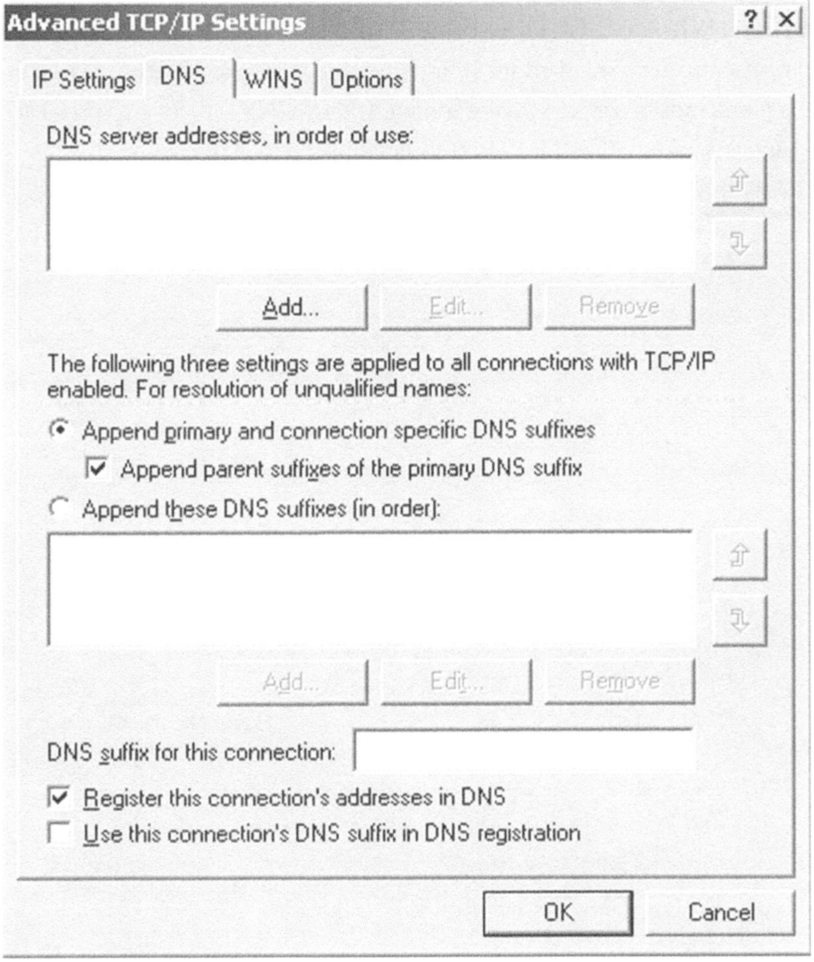

Figure 5.10 DNS Settings

For redundancy, you may configure your clients to use multiple DNS servers.

For WINS, you may configure multiple WINS servers to replicate with each others.

For replication to occur, each WINS server must be configured as either a pull or a push partner with at least one other WINS server. A push partner is one that notifies its pull partners when its database has changed. A pull partner is one that initiates the replication process based on a pre-determined time schedule. The default relationship for replication is a Push / Pull partnership.

Windows 2000 WINS uses broadcast based IGMP (shorts for Internet Group Management Protocol, a standard for IP multicasting as defined in RFC 1112) for automatic partner discovery and configuration. If the WINS servers are spread across different subnets, ensure that IGMP traffics are allowed to go through.

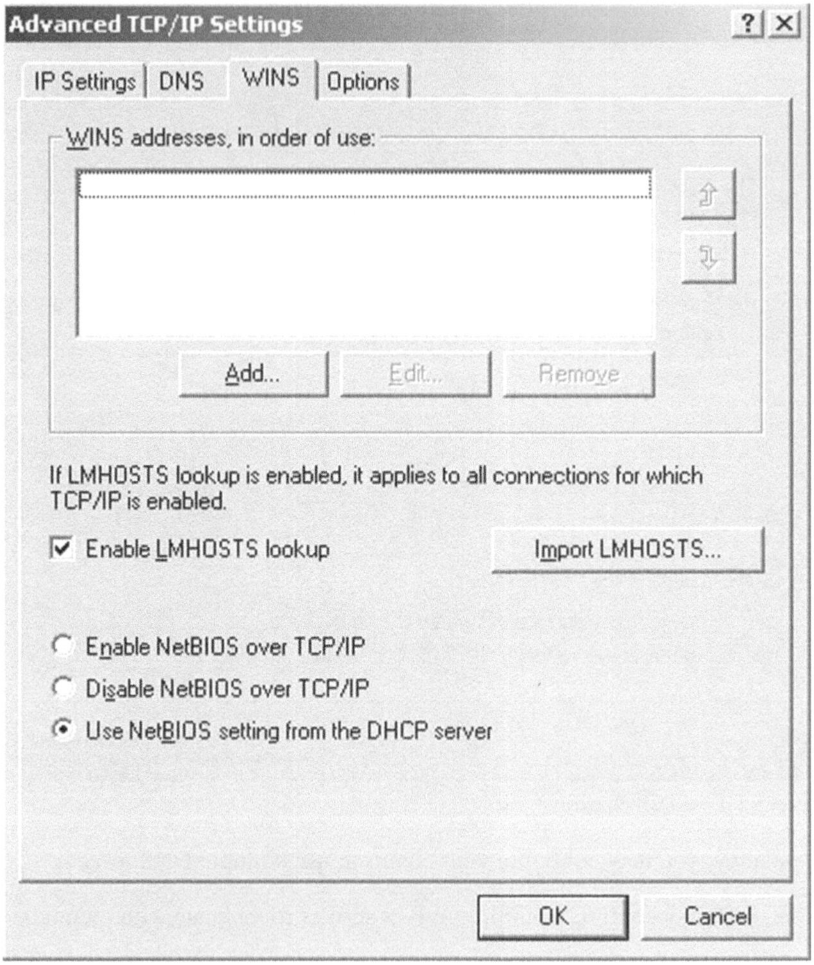

Figure 5.11 WINS Settings

For redundancy, you may configure your clients to use multiple WINS servers.

If name resolution is so critical that down time cannot be tolerated at all, consider to run these services in a Windows 2000 Cluster. A cluster requires two or more Windows 2000 Advanced Servers / Datacenter Servers and special hardware for configuration. It is the most reliable solution, and is the most expensive one too.

Apart from redundancy, the deployment of multiple DNS and WINS servers can in fact share the workload. For load sharing to take place, however, you must ensure that different clients have their servers "in order of use" settings set differently so that client requests can be spread across these servers evenly.

Name resolution for remote offices involves serious performance issues. Things slow down whenever name resolution traffic has to travel across the WAN link. If you are deploying WINS, you should set up a WINS server that is local in the remote location, and have this server replicate regularly with your primary WINS server. For DNS, you should configure the remote office DNS server to point to your DNS server as the forwarder.

VII Windows 2000 Name Resolution Security

One good thing about the use of DNS Active Directory integrated zone is security. You may choose to allow only secure updates if dynamic update is made possible for your DHCP clients. If you are extremely nervous on the issue of security, you may enable IPSec for servers running DNS, WINS or even DHCP. However, before doing so, you must consider whether or not your clients are IPSec-capable. Special attentions must be paid to ensure that the authentication and negotiation settings are 100% compatible.

DNS is a security concern when your LAN is connected to the internet. If external clients can access your internal DNS server, your IP structure can be exploited. One way to circumvent this security hole is to use two DNS servers to maintain two sets of zone data, with one set for public use and another for pure internal use. The DNS server that hosts the "public" set should be placed outside of the firewall, while the "internal" one should be under firewall protection.

Pop Quiz 5.4

Pop Quiz 5.4 *Questions*

1) In a Windows 2000 network, what is needed for the non-WINS clients to enjoy WINS support?
2) In WINS, what partner initiates the replication process based on a pre-determined time schedule?
3) True or false: only DNS but not WINS can be configured for redundancy.
4) IGMP is defined in which RFC?

Pop Quiz 5.4

Pop Quiz 5.4 *Answers*

1) WINS Proxy Agent
2) Pull
3) False. Both DNS and WINS support redundancy configuration.
4) RFC 1112

VIII Global Catalog

Every domain controller in a forest has to store the following directory partitions:

a domain directory partition
a schema directory partition
a configuration directory partition

These partitions are kept as full and writeable copies by a Global Catalog, which itself is built automatically by the Active Directory replication system into a domain controller. In addition to these partitions, the Global Catalog also stores a partial copy of all other domain directory partitions in the forest. These additional directory partitions are read-only and are partial because of the fact that only a limited set of specific attributes are included for each object included.

All of the directory partitions on a Global Catalog are stored only in the directory database Ntds.dit on that server as additional information. The first domain controller in a forest is automatically designated as a Global Catalog, although you may manually designate any domain controller as Global Catalog server through the NTDS Settings Properties dialog box accessible within Active Directory Sites and Services.

In a native-mode domain, a Global Catalog is REQUIRED for logging on to the domain. To ensure smooth and efficient logons, you should always place at least one Global Catalog in every site. Ideally, all logons should be facilitated by Global Catalog locally without going through any WAN links.

Although logon process can proceed with cached logon information when no Global Catalog is available in the same site, Microsoft prefers to see "Global Catalog on each local site" as the correct strategy (and the correct answer too), especially when your network has slow and unreliable links. For fault tolerance, enable at least one Global Catalog on "each side" of the link.

Keep in mind though, any strategy involves tradeoff. To be up-to-date, Global Catalog receives regular updates for objects in all domains through replication. If changes to Active Directory frequently occur, you might take into account the issue of replication traffic. Fortunately, as said by Microsoft, most of your Active Directory network traffic will be query-related rather than update-related.

Domain Controller and Global Catalog

As pointed out by Microsoft, updates to the directory that cause directory replication traffic should not occur frequently in a normal environment. To achieve the best network performance, you should place at least one domain controller in each site so that user queries can be served over the fastest links available. If unfortunately there are sites in your network that are connected by slow links, you may configure domain controllers to receive directory replication updates only during off-peak hours.

It is recommended that you make the domain controller at a site to also act as a Global Catalog so that the server can fulfill queries about objects in the entire forest. As mentioned before, this requires a balanced consideration due to the possible increase in replication traffic.

In domains with more than one domain controller, you should not enable the domain controller holding the infrastructure master role as a Global Catalog. The infrastructure master is responsible for updating references from objects in its domain to objects in other domains. It compares its data with that of a Global Catalog. If it coexists on the same domain controller with the Global Catalog, it will cease functioning. The rationale behind this is that such coexistence will disallow the infrastructure master to find data that is out-of-date, that no replication will ever happen. However, if all of the domain controllers in a domain are hosting the Global Catalog, they will always be current and will not matter which domain controller holds the infrastructure master role.

Pop Quiz 5.5

Pop Quiz 5.5 *Questions*

1) True or false: In a Windows 2000 network, Global Catalog is built automatically by the Active Directory replication system.
2) True or false: The Global Catalog stores a partial copy of all other domain directory partitions in the forest.
3) True or false: In a native-mode domain, a Global Catalog is optional for logging on to the domain.

Pop Quiz 5.5

Pop Quiz 5.4 *Answers*

1) True
2) True
3) False. Global catalog is REQUIRED for domain logon.

IX Windows 2000 Dfs

Shorts for Distributed file system, the Microsoft Dfs consists of two sides:

- software on the network servers to manage and host Dfs components
- software on the clients that links the shared folders located on the different file servers

The beauty of Dfs is that:

- operation is entirely transparent
- a single namespace is used for easy access
- load sharing
- high availability of data

Dfs uses a tree structure, with a root located on a Windows 2000 server. From that root, links to shared folders distributed throughout your organization can be defined without regard to their physical location. Such a consistent naming convention and mapping for distributed resource together with the capability to run regardless of the file client being used make Dfs the choice for large enterprise network running Active Directory.

Below are the official Microsoft reasons for deploying Dfs:

- You have many users that need to access distributed shared resources across a site or sites.
- Most of your users require access to multiple shared resources.
- User accesses to shared resources must be uninterrupted.
- Load balancing for your network is preferred.

Dfs Failover

Dfs functionality is deeply integrated with Active Directory. Since the Dfs topology is published to Active Directory, any changes to a domain-based Dfs topology are automatically synchronized with Active Directory, making it always possible for you to restore a Dfs topology should Dfs root go offline.

In fact, the key advantage of integrating Dfs into Active Directory is that, in the case of a root failure, Dfs can detect its occurrence and allows another server to acquire the root and continues running.

There are significant difference between a domain based Dfs and a non-domain based one. In addition to the fact that Domain-based Dfs stores its configuration information in Active Directory for high availability, the following characteristics highlight its nature and features compare to the local stand-alone Dfs:

It must be hosted on a Windows 2000 domain server such that it can eventually got replicated to every domain controller

It allows root-level shared folders.

It supports root and file replication through the File Replication service (FRS)

Stand-alone Dfs, on the other hand, stores its configuration in the local registry, and cannot use FRS replication nor hosts replicas at the root level. Its existence is primarily for backward compatibility only.

Dfs Root

Dfs provides users with a single access point to shared folders that are distributed throughout a network. As mentioned earlier, it organizes shared folders on different computers into a single, logical and hierarchical file system to facilitate network navigation and administration without sacrificing network permissions.

Only Windows NT 4.0 Server and Windows 2000 servers can host Dfs roots for large hierarchies of Dfs namespaces. All other physical shares can be included only as links but not roots. Also, for security purpose or for working with Windows 2000 FRS, the underlying file system for shared folders to be published in Dfs must be NTFS and nothing else.

Since the Dfs root is the launching point into the namespace, the recommended practice is to keep the root clean: do not place too many files in the root. Instead, organize hierarchy nicely into sub-directories will make things much more organized.

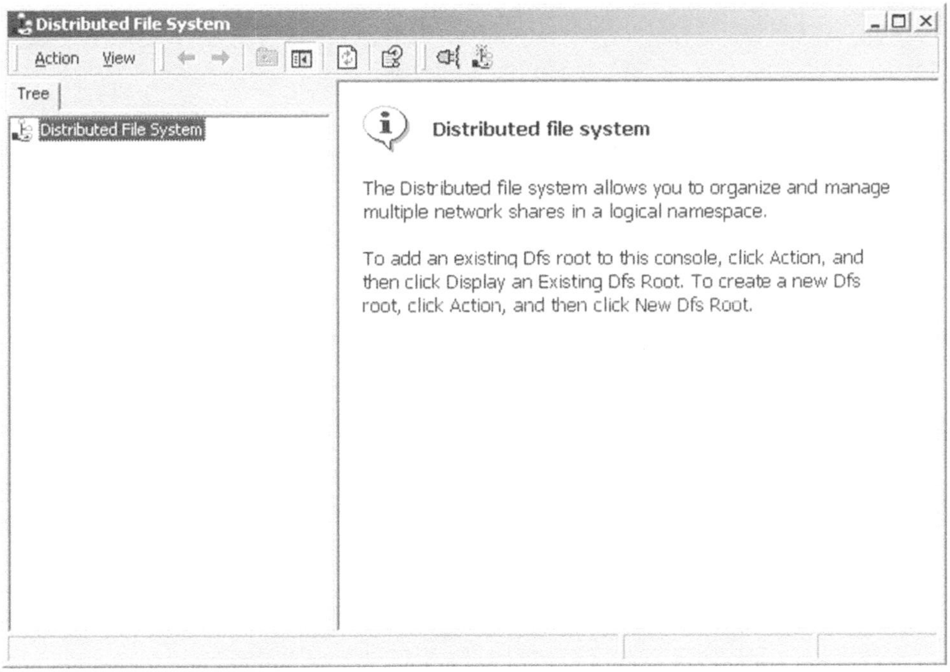

Figure 5.12 Distributed file system

The Dfs Snap-In allows you to configure Dfs on your system. >

In the world of Dfs, we have a single Dfs shared folder (known as the Dfs root) to open access to the actual shared folders in the network (known as the Dfs links). Two types of Dfs roots are available in Windows 2000: standalone and domain based.

Stand-alone Dfs root:

stores the Dfs topology on a single computer

no replication, making fault tolerance impossible

Domain Dfs root:

- stores the Dfs topology in Active Directory
- supports file replication for fault tolerance
- supports DNS
- supports multiple levels of Dfs links

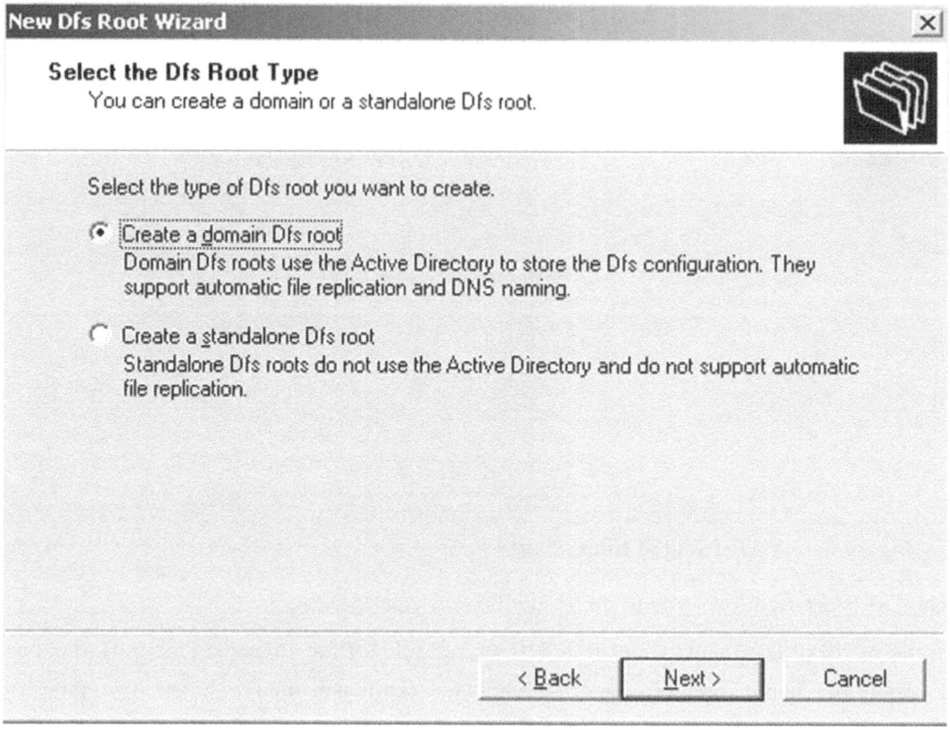

Figure 5.13 Dfs Root

You may create standalone or domain based Dfs root via the Dfs Snap-In.

It is quite obvious that the Domain Dfs root is the preferred choice. Each domain based Dfs root or link can reference a replicated set of shared resources, and the Dfs clients can automatically select the nearest replica without manual intervention.

Dfs Replication

Dfs replication is done via FRS (File Replication Service), although such replication is disabled by default. Remember, Dfs shares on the network other than Windows NT 4.0 and Windows 2000 cannot participate in file replication via FRS.

To enable replication, you must use the Distributed File System snap-in to configure the Replication Policy. By default, FRS is installed and configured to automatically start on all Windows 2000 domain controller. For member severs, however, the service must be started manually. In theory, Active Directory replication and the FRS are mutually independent. In practice, however, they share the common replication topology and methodology. Active Directory even uses FRS to synchronize the directory among all domain controllers.

Under Dfs, changes made on any member will be replicated automatically to every member. The more replication, the higher the bandwidth use. Therefore, you must be very careful when deploying Dfs. If your network cannot afford the high overhead of such replication, you may want to disable them and perform manual Dfs synchronization during off-peak hours.

Another restriction: each Windows 2000 server can only host one Dfs root. If you have multiple Dfs roots, you must use multiple servers to host them.

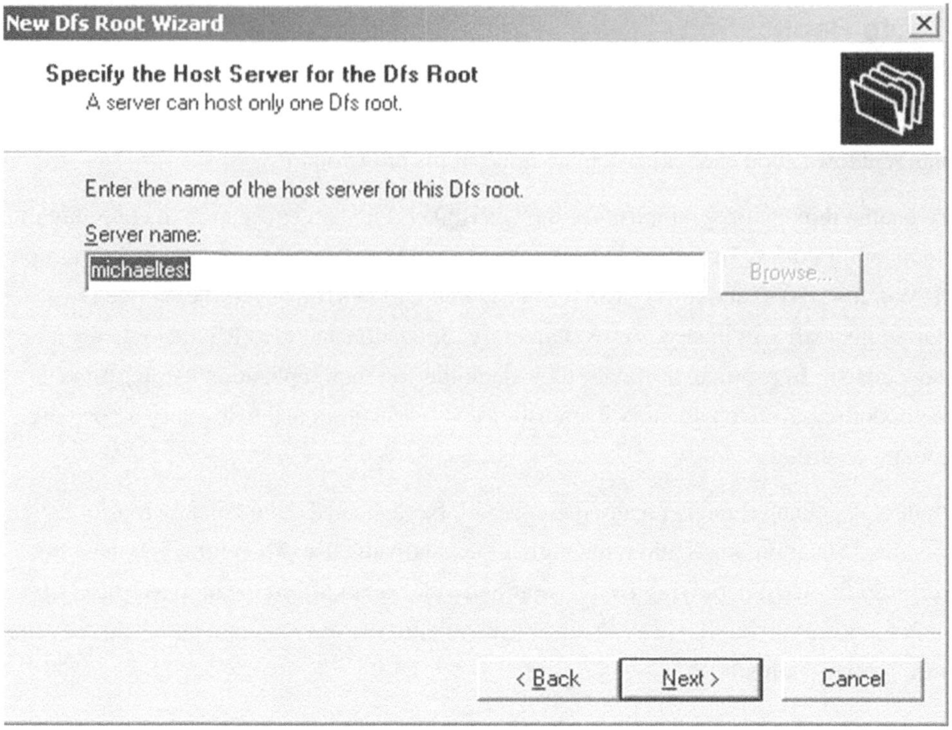

Figure 5.14 Dfs Host Server

You must specify a host server for every Dfs root you create.

Accessing Dfs

Dfs allows users to log on just once for multiple access. A user can access a Dfs volume via a uniform naming convention (UNC) name with the proper client installed.

According to Microsoft, the client statuses are as follow:

Windows 95:

Dfs-aware client is available for download.

Supports only Microsoft SMB volumes.

The net use command cannot be used beyond the share level.

Windows 98:

Dfs-aware client is built-in.

Supports only Microsoft SMB volumes.

The net use command cannot be used beyond the share level.

Windows NT 4.0:

Dfs-aware client is built-in.

Supports SMB and non-SMB volumes.

The net use command can be used beyond the share level.

Windows NT 2000:

Dfs-aware client is built-in.

Can intelligently select replicas based on site location.

Supports SMB and non-SMB volumes.

The net use command can be used beyond the share level.

Includes a shell extension to Windows Explorer for further Dfs exploration.

Pop Quiz 5.6

Pop Quiz 5.6 *Questions*

1) What tool do you use to enable replication in Dfs?
2) What type of Dfs root stores Dfs information on a single computer?
3) Fault tolerance is possible with what types of Dfs root?
4) Dfs replication is done via:

Pop Quiz 5.6

Pop Quiz 5.6 *Answers*

1) Distributed File System snap-in
2) Stand-alone
3) Domain Dfs Root only
4) FRS

X Accessing Active Directory

When Active Directory is in place, the following methods of directory access can be used:

LDAP	The Core protocol supported by Active Directory.
MAPI RPC	Used by MAPI Address Book provider
Replication RPC	Used by Active Directory replication over IP transport.
Replication SMTP	Message-based replication protocol used by Active Directory.

Table 5 Active Directory

Of the above methods, LDAP is the major protocol in use. Shorts for light weight directory access protocol, LDAP can be used for directory searching and information retrieval. In fact, Active Directory itself is an LDAP directory that requires and supports RFC 2247–compliant distinguished name.

In order to accomplish an LDAP search, the following information, in general, are required:

A search base that defines the location in the directory as the point where the LDAP search begins.

A search scope

How many "levels" of search should be conducted.

Whether subtrees should be searched or not

Search filter

Other controls

Below are the types of client that are available with Windows 2000 Server:

Administrative clients - example: the Active Directory Users and Computers MMC snap-in

Windows Address Book - a generic LDAP search client that is designed to work with any LDAP server, and is integrated into:

1. Windows 2000
2. Internet Explorer version 4.0 and later
3. Windows 95 shell
4. Windows 98 shell

XI Chapter 5: Review Questions

Case Question 1

You are a Network Consultant with specialized skills in designing Windows 2000 network. You are recently requested by the Excel Forwarder Corp to design the Windows 2000 network for the entire company.

Background

Excel Forwarder Corp, an international freight forwarder and Customs Broker, has been providing Logistics and Transportation services since 1929. Excel also provides logistics and distribution services as well as purchase order management and ancillary freight services in addition to freight forwarding and Customs Brokerage.

With over 65 years in the business, Excel offers fully computerized documentation and tracking in all areas of its operations. Some of the services offered by Excel are:

- Customs Broker
- Freight Forwarding
- NVOCC
- Logistics Management
- Distribution
- Consulting
- Insurance
- Air Freight
- Purchase Order Expediting
- EDI Services

Divisions

The company divides its operations into two main categories: Air and Ocean. The management structure is as follow:

Air – One director, directly reports to the CEO. Under the director are a group of managers responsible for running the different service departments.

Ocean – One director, directly reports to the CEO. Under the director are a group of managers responsible for running the different service departments.

The CEO admits that there are overlapping of activities and resources among Air and Ocean. However, he does not plan to modify this structure as of the time being.

Locations

There is one headquarters for all of its operations. This headquarters is located in New York. Besides, there are 3 local offices in different regions of the states.

Excel has the following locations:

NY - Headquarter

Miami Ocean & Air

Los Angeles Air & Ocean

Chicago Air & Ocean

Since the headquarters does not have enough space, Excel recently rented a small office place, which is one street block away from the headquarters. The two are connected with ISDN BRI.

IT Structure

The headquarters is running a NT4 network. The PDC of the single account domain is located in the headquarters. There are 5 BDCs for the account domain, and the BDC's are installed in the local offices. In addition, there are resource domains defined. All servers are running with dual 300mhz processors and 256M RAM.

Excel uses State of the Art software to insure that all documentation is prepared quickly and correctly. The software runs on NT Workstation that has TCP/IP configured.

The Excel Trade BBS allows the customers to receive email responses to the leads. This BBS runs on a standalone Linux server.

Excel is also in the process of finalizing the installation of new software that will enable its clients to track their shipments on the Internet.

Future Prospect

Excel has recently become the partner of XSite, a web site that provides a central search engine for local, state and federal government agencies.

This new site is useful in a sense that it eliminates the need to track down all the various agencies to locate available services.

This partnership is expected to draw substantial new businesses to Excel. The CEO of Excel is looking into enhancing its existing IT structure in order to cope with the growing demand for its services.

The latest forecast from Excel is that in 5 years time the number of employees will be doubled.

Questions

1. Which of the following correctly describe the current company model of Excel Forwarder?

A. regional
B. national
C. international
D. merger
E. None of the choices.

---

2. What is the planned organization structure for Excel Forwarder in regards to its major divisions?

A. no change
B. consolidation
C. further segmentation
D. further diversification
E. None of the choices.

---

3. What action should you take regarding the connectivity option of the small office place that is one street block away from the head office?

A. change to RAS dial via modem
B. change to 256K leased line
C. use Frame Relay
D. use ATM
E. no change is needed
F. None of the choices.

4. Which of the following projects seems to receive the highest priority?

A. Server hardware upgrade
B. Organization restructuring
C. The Excel BBS
D. The partnership with XSite
E. None of the choices.

---

5. Which of the following statements signals the importance of infrastructure scalability for Excel Forwarder?

A. In 5 years time the number of employees will be doubled
B. Excel is in the process of finalizing the installation of new software that will enable its clients to track their shipments on the Internet.
C. Excel recently rented a small office place, which is one street block away from the headquarters.
D. The CEO admits that there are overlapping of activities and resources among Air and Ocean. However, he does not plan to modify this structure as of the time being.
E. None of the choices.

---

6. Which of the following protocols can you use to set up a mesh topology between all the Excel's locations to allow for secure communication?

A. PPP
B. SLIP
C. PPTP
D. EAP
E. TLS

7. To configure connectivity among all Excel's locations, at a minimum how many subnets must you configure?

A. One subnet per location and one subnet per WAN link
B. One subnet per WAN link only
C. Two subnet per LAN link only
D. One subnet per location and two subnets per WAN link
E. Two subnets per location and two subnets per WAN link

---

8. When you configure the subnets in different locations, which of the following guidelines must you meet?

A. Subnets must be well connected with stable connections
B. Subnets must have domain controller installed
C. Subnets must have Active Directory installed
D. Subnet communications must be encrypted
E. Subnet communications must be packet switched

---

9. Through subnetting, which of the following can be achieved within each Excel's location?

A. smaller broadcast domains
B. bigger broadcast domains
C. ease of maintenance
D. ease of administration
E. lower TCO

10 What is the minimum number of domain controllers that should be placed at each location, if logon performance is essential?

A. one
B. two
C. three
D. four
E. five

Case Question 2

You are a Network Consultant with specialized skills in designing Windows 2000 network. You are recently requested by Joe's Canoe Company to design the Windows 2000 network for the entire company.

Background

Joe's Canoe Company is a company that produces canoes of different kinds. Most of its customers are in the Vancouver area.

Since 1950 Joe has been designing and manufacturing Cedar Canvas Canoes. Through the years, as materials advanced, Joe began building Fiberglass, Kevlar and high tech Carbon Fiber Canoes. Joe's Master builders have 5 decades of canoe design and building experience, in all types, from the classic Cedar strip to the family cottage canoe & the most advanced Carbon Fiber high performance canoes.

According to the CEO, staffs in the company are on average at the age of 50 and above. Somehow they are a bit resistant to new technologies. Currently they are running on a Win NT network.

Per your interview with the marketing manager, there is an increase in the demand for canoes in California; a local canoe manufacturer has approached The Company from San Jose about a possible merger between the two companies. Your understanding on this is that, in the next one or two years, these two companies will still market their canoes separately under different brand names, however, the management will definitely want to see some sort of synergy in between.

Last month a new representative office was opened in Kansas City, as the company can receive tax deduction from the city government.

Structure

So far there is only one office location for Joe's Canoe. There are 3 different departments: Marketing, Accounting, and Production. Each department has its own management team. The team leaders need to report to the CEO directly.

Currently there are about 500 staffs. Of this amount, 60% of them will need to use computers in their daily operations.

Dealer Locations

The CEO's successor, James, has its roots as an IT consultant. He knows the importance of IT deployment. He likes to have all its dealers placing orders online to save processing costs. He recently built a VPN among the company and all its dealers.

As of today, there are 6 dealers selling canoes for the company:

Algonquin Bound - Madawaska

Frontenac Outfitters - Sydenham

Gordon Bay Marine - Mactier

Muskoka Store - Graven Hurst

Adventure Guide - Kitchener-Waterloo

Boundary Bay Waterspouts - Whiterock, BC

James is a MCP on NT 4.0. He likes to use Microsoft products. He wants you to implement a network design using Windows 2000 and active directory.

There was a NT4 network implemented for the company. It consists of two domains containing accounts and resources. In addition, there are some other resource only domains that trust these two domains.

James is not happy with the fact that trust relationships are so complicated to setup. He also dislikes that fact that scalability is limited with SAM.

Questions

1. RIP is deployed in Joe's Canoe head office's 4 subnets network after the upgrade to Windows 2000. How do you reduce the traffic generated by the routing updates?

A. Use static routes instead
B. Use a relatively dynamic topology
C. Purge the routing entries regularly
D. Use OSPF instead
E. None of the choices

---

2. You are told by the James that he wants to further divide the head office network into 19 subnets. You have concerns regarding the hop counts. Which of the following routing protocol can function even when there are more than 16 hops (Choose all that apply)?

A. RIP
B. RIP V2
C. OSPF
D. Static routes
E. None of the choices.

---

3. By configuring RIP to send updates only to the manually configured neighbors in the head office network, what can be achieved?

A. less routing update traffic
B. less processor load on the routers
C. smaller routing table size
D. more secure routing
E. None of the choices.

4. The hop count from Algonquin Bound to Frontenac Outfitters through link A is 11, while the hop count through link B is 8, and the hop counts through link C and link D are 12 and 13 respectively. If RIP V2 is to be used, which link will be the "first choice" for the IP traffic between them?

F. A
G. B
H. C
I. D
J. None of the choices

---

5. The hop count from Muskoka Store to Adventure Guide through link X is 18, while the hop count through link Y is 21, and the hop counts through link Z and link U are 11 and 3 respectively. If RIP is to be used, which links will be functional (Choose all that apply)?

A. X
B. Y
C. Z
D. U
E. None of the choices.

---

6. To facilitate searching of Active Directory objects in a forest comprising multiple domains and trees, which of the following should be properly placed?

A. Global Catalog
B. Dfs Root
C. Domain Master
D. Infrastructure Master
E. Proxy Server

---

7. To facilitate searching of data files in a domain environment where resources are scattered around, which of the following should be properly deployed?

A. Global Catalog
B. Domain based Dfs Root
C. Registry based Dfs Root
D. Domain Master
E. Infrastructure Master

Case Question 3

You are a Network Consultant with specialized skills in designing Win2000 directory services. You are recently requested by MediAssociate to design the Windows 2000 network for the entire company.

Background

Since 1986, MediAssociate has been conducting research for legal and health care professionals involved in medical malpractice, personal injury, product liability and workers' compensation cases. Target customers are those who are overwhelmed with complicated health care issues and baffling medical jargon. The founders of MediAssociate have been in the medical-legal consultant field for over ten years. They have been providing consulting services for attorneys, physicians and other legal nurse consultants.

Services

MediAssociate searches medical literature for articles, standards and guidelines that will enhance customer's understanding of the case. The search is conducted by RNs experienced in the field, is supplemented with summaries of key articles, and conference sessions to answer the questions.

MediAssociate locates qualified expert physicians and nurses whose accurate opinions will bolster customer's position. Its nationwide network of specialists includes both consulting and testifying experts. MediAssociate can find the ideal expert fast, then help the customer to prepare that expert for deposition or trial.

MediAssociate nurses will accompany the customers during their Independent Medical Examinations. These nurses will be prepared to offer testimony during deposition and trial.

IT Structure

To offer the services listed above, MediAssociate has a very advanced IT infrastructure. Its network in the down town San Jose office is connected with fiber optics. The network is running 25 NT 4 Servers and 300 clients. To speed up research, a T3 line is installed for connecting to the internet. In addition, there are 4 Solaris workstations specially designed for a fault tolerant web site configuration.

Organization Structure

The company is structured in a way that reflects the services it offers. There are mainly 3 departments in the company, one for each main service.

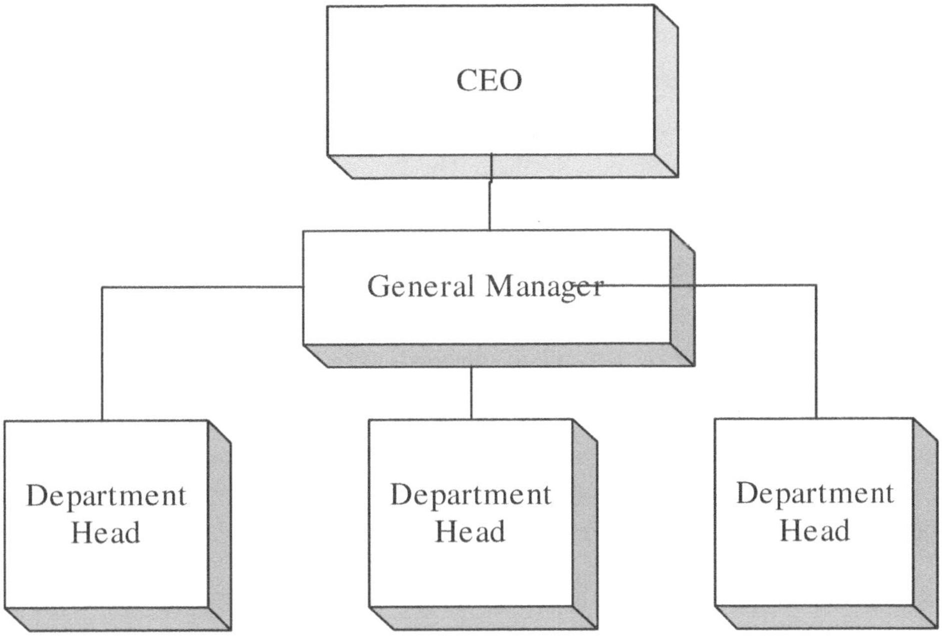

Figure 5.15 Company Departments

Visions

The company is expected to expand its network of affiliated professionals. Currently they have more than 25000 professionals in their network nationwide. These professionals are allowed to connect to the head office via dial up access. Due to the fast growth in business, it is estimated that in three years time the number of professionals that work with the company will be doubled.

Since to a certain extent these professionals are not in house staffs, the company will want to have a separate community for them. This community should manage their own password and lockout policy on their own.

The existing NT4 network was built with scalability in mind. There are 2 account domains together with 5 resource domains.

The CIO wants to upgrade the network to Windows 2000. He is impressed by the stability of the new OS.

One thing the CIO really wants to implement is some sort of Smartcard devices for the in house staffs to log onto the network. He believes in technologies like Smartcard being the trend of the future.

Questions

1. Which of the following is the ideal addressing mechanism for use with the network clients after the network is migrated to Windows 2000?

A. DHCP
B. APIPA
C. Static
D. DDNS
E. WINS

2. Which of the following is the ideal addressing mechanism for use with the network servers after the network is migrated to Windows 2000?

A. DHCP
B. APIPA
C. Static
D. DDNS
E. WINS

3. You are configuring the Windows 2000 DNS service for the San Jose office network. For the Win95 clients to perform dynamic updates to the Windows 2000 DNS, which of the following is required?

A. DHCP Relay Agent
B. DNS Proxy Agent
C. WINS Proxy Agent
D. DHCP Proxy
E. None of the choices.

---

4. You are told to further divide the San Jose office network into more smaller subnets. For cost saving purpose, you plan to deploy router based DHCP Relay Agents. With such arrangement, which of the following are no longer needed in the network (Choose all that apply)?

A. DHCP server in the client subnets
B. Workstation based DHCP Relay Agent in the client subnets
C. DHCP server for the entire network
D. Domain controllers
E. Active Directory store

---

5. You are configuring the Windows 2000 DHCP service for the San Jose office network. By shortening the DHCP address lease duration for the clients, you may:

A. enhance DHCP performance
B. reduce network traffic
C. reduce routing needs
D. increase logon performance
E. accommodate more clients with fewer IP addresses

---

6. You are configuring the Windows 2000 DHCP service for the San Jose office network. By lengthening the DHCP address lease duration for the clients, you may:

A. reduce network traffic
B. reduce routing needs
C. increase file access performance
D. accommodate more clients with fewer IP addresses
E. accommodate less clients with more IP addresses

7. You are requested to set up a Windows 2000 server with IIS 5 to replace all the Solaris Web servers. This single server has to host multiple virtual servers. In terms of IP address configuration, what needs to be done?

A. install multiple NICs onto the Windows 2000 server
B. install multiple NICs onto the Windows 2000 server and assign multiple IPs to each of the NICs
C. setup DHCP for the NICs of the Windows 2000 server
D. assign multiple IPs to a single NIC on the Windows 2000 server
E. None of the choices.

---

8. You are configuring the Windows 2000 DDNS service for the San Jose office network. By using Incremental Zone Transfer, which of the following can you achieve?

A. reduce network traffic
B. reduce routing needs
C. increase file access performance
D. accommodate more clients with fewer IP addresses
E. more accurate name resolution

---

9. You are configuring the Windows 2000 DDNS service for the San Jose office network. For some reasons the Windows 2000 clients fail to register themselves. Which of the following option must you enable?

A. the "Allow dynamic updates?" option on the DDNS server
B. the "Allow dynamic updates?" option on the DHCP scope
C. the "Allow dynamic updates?" option on each client
D. the "Allow dynamic updates?" option on the domain controllers
E. None of the choices

Case Question 4

You are a Network Consultant with specialized skills in designing Windows 2000 network. You are recently requested by Kellok Accounting Service to design the Windows 2000 network for the entire company.

Background

Kellok Accounting Service has been in businesses in the Pacific Northwest for nearly half a century, helping clients to develop effective accounting systems to use as an essential management tool.

Core accounting services

Division AR-1

Financial statements for corporations, proprietorships, and partnerships
Monthly accounting, including computer-generated journals and ledgers
Developing financial accounting and control systems
Analysis and implementation of accounting enhancements
Training in record keeping

Division AR-2

Cash flow management
Compliance with lender requirements
Financing, including banks, SBA, FHA
Consulting and business planning
Budgeting and forecasting

Division AR-3

Computer technology assistance, including network design

Bank reconciliations

Accounts receivable and payable

Inventory control

Depreciation schedules and asset records

Division AR-4

Payroll and other taxes

Executive search for controller/financial staff

Special purpose reports

Locations

Headquarter – Palo Alto

50 staffs

2 NT servers

1 Unix server

AR – 1 Palo Alto

40 staffs

2 NT servers

1 Unix server

AR – 2 Redwood City

40 staffs

1 NT server

1 Unix server

AR – 3 Fremont

70 staffs

3 NT servers

1 Unix server

AR – 4 Oakland

20 staffs

1 NT server

NT Domain Model

All locations are interconnected with 128K ISDN lines.

All locations share the same password and lockout policies.

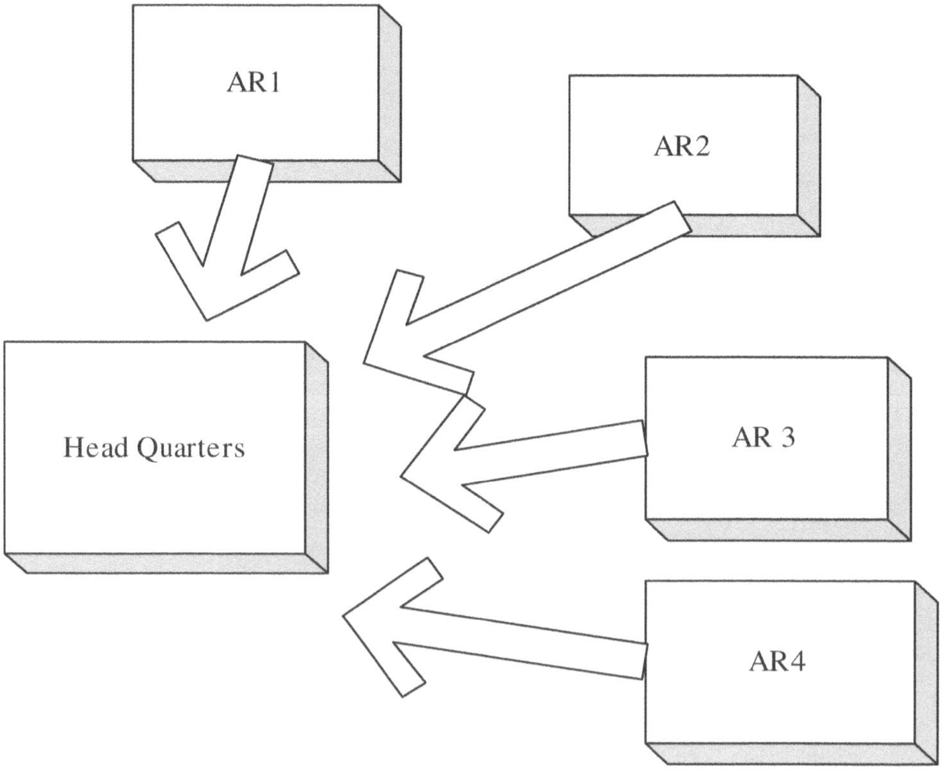

Figure 5.16 NT Domain Model

Questions

1. You are setting up the Windows 2000 infrastructure for Kellok. Kellok needs web presence. What is the benefit of having two identical zones configured on each side of the Kellok's firewall?

A. Security
B. Performance
C. Redundancy
D. Load sharing
E. None of the choices.

---

2. You are setting up the Windows 2000 infrastructure for Kellok. You plan to use multiple Windows 2000 servers to provide DNS services. Which type of DNS zones will you use for maximum reliability and security?

A. Incremental transfer zone
B. Primary zone
C. Secondary zone
D. Active Directory integrated zone
E. None of the choices.

---

3. To ensure that all the remote offices of Kellok are provided with sufficient name resolution performance even with slow WAN links, you should always:

A. Set up a DNS server local to each remote office, and have it point to the head office DNS server as the forwarder
B. Set up a Proxy server local to each remote office, and have it point to the head office DNS server
C. Set up a DNS server local to each remote office, and have it point to the other remote DNS servers
D. Enlarge the DNS server cache
E. None of the choices

4. You are setting up the Windows 2000 infrastructure for Kellok. You want to configure an Active Directory integrated zone on a Windows 2000 DNS server and fail. You can successfully create the other zone types though. What is the likely reason?

A. The DDNS service has not been authorized explicitly
B. The Windows 2000 server is a domain controller upgraded from NT4.
C. DDNS has not been enabled on the server
D. WINS has not been enabled on the server
E. The Windows 2000 server is not a domain controller.

---

5. You are setting up the Windows 2000 DNS service for Kellok. What is the best way to secure DNS zone transfer without sacrificing performance?

A. Use Active Directory integrated zone
B. Use Primary zone with one slave zone only
C. Use Secondary zone with no Primary zone
D. Use incremental zone transfer with encryption
E. Enable IPSec on the DNS server

---

6. You are setting up the Windows 2000 DNS service for Kellok. How do you provide 24x7 non-stop DNS service for the network?

A. Run DNS on a Windows 2000 server with RAID 1
B. Run DNS on a Windows 2000 server with RAID 1 or 5 and UPS
C. Configure DNS to replicate with WINS
D. Configure DNS to replicate with DHCP
E. Run DNS on a Windows 2000 cluster

Case Question 5

You are a Network Consultant with specialized skills in designing Win2000 directory services. You are recently requested by ProX Auditing Group to design the Windows 2000 network for the entire company.

Background

ProX Auditing Group uses a logical sequence of steps to perform audits in the most efficient, effective, and timely manner possible. Its audits comply with the highest professional standards and lend credibility to client company's financial statements. Its experts can assist the clients in improving internal controls and operating efficiency, as well as recommend enhancements to make client companies more profitable.

Services

ProX offers the following audit services:

ProX Austin

General financial audits

Review of agreed-upon procedures

Analysis of internal and operating controls

Review of computer systems for proper operation and control procedures

ProX Kansas

Due diligence audits for mergers and acquisitions

Federal single audit compliance

Compliance with GAO "Yellow Book" requirements

Compliance with grant requirements

Compliance with loan covenants/regulatory requirements

Client sectors:

- Agriculture
- Auto Dealers and Auto Repair
- Beverages
- Construction and Logging
- Financial Institutions and Trusts
- Governmental
- Health Care Professionals
- Lodging and Food Service
- Insurance Services
- Manufacturing
- Non-Profit Organizations
- Professional Service Firms
- Real Estate
- Retail and Wholesale Businesses
- Timber
- Trucks and Transportation

1. You plan to deploy Dfs in ProX. Which of the following client types require that an additional component be downloaded and applied in order to access the SMB volumes only (Choose all that apply)?

A. Windows 95
B. Windows 98
C. Windows ME
D. Windows NT 4.0
E. Windows 2000

---

2. You plan to deploy Dfs in ProX. Which of the following client types allow the use of the net use command beyond the share level (Choose all that apply)?

A. Windows 95
B. Windows 98
C. Windows 3.11
D. Windows NT 4.0
E. Windows 2000

---

3. You plan to deploy Dfs in ProX. Which of the following client types allow your users to access non-SMB volumes (Choose all that apply)?

A. Windows 95
B. Windows 98
C. Windows 3.11
D. Windows NT 4.0
E. Windows 2000

Chapter 5: Review Answers

Case 1 Answers:

1, a

2, a

3, e

4, d

5, a

6, c

7, a

8, a

9, a

10, a

Case 2 Answers:

1, a

2, c d

3, a

4, b

5, c d

6, a

7, b

Case 3 Answers:

1, a

2, c

3, d

4, a b

5, e

6, a

7, d

8, a

9, a

Case 4 Answers:

1, a

2, d

3, a

4, e

5, a

6, e

Case 5 Answers:

1, a

2, d e

3, d e

Total Recall

Chapter 6: Designing a Windows 2000 Network Infrastructure – The WAN Perspective

The objective of this chapter is to provide the reader with an understanding of the following:

1. PKI
2. Windows 2000 Certificate Services
3. Certificate Hierarchy
4. Windows 2000 IAS
5. Windows 2000 NAT
6. ICS
7. APIPA
8. Smart Card
9. Windows 2000 VPN

Getting Ready (Questions)

1) In a typical PKI setup, what keys are involved in a secure transaction?
2) Certificate Services can be used to establish a Windows 2000 Server as a:
3) ICS can run on what Windows platforms?
4) APIPA is most useful when your DHCP server is:
5) VPN works on what type of connection?
6) ICS is best to be deployed on what type of business environment?
7) APIPA is natively supported on which legacy Windows versions?

Getting Ready - Answers

1) Private key and public key.
2) Certificate Authority.
3) Windows 2000 Server, Windows 2000 Professional, Windows ME and Windows 98 SE.
4) APIPA works when the DHCP Server is not available.
5) VPN runs on top of an internet connection.
6) SOHO.
7) All legacy Windows require external APIPA server support.

I Introduction

This chapter continues to talk about "Designing a Windows 2000 Network Infrastructure". However, our focus will now shift to a wide area network perspective.

To be precise, the following topics will be covered:

- PKI
- Windows 2000 Certificate Services
- Windows 2000 IAS
- Windows 2000 VPN
- Windows 2000 ICS and NAT

This chapter is another one of the heaviest chapters in this book, and is the foundation of the Microsoft Exam Objective "Designing for Internet Connectivity" and "Designing a Wide Area Network Infrastructure". The focus is on the security aspect of WAN connectivity. First we will have an overview of the Windows 2000 security features:

- Kerberos V5 protocol for Authentication.
- Public key infrastructure support via the Certificate Services and the smart card facility.
- Virtual Private Networking via L2TP and PPTP.
- Remote Access security via IAS.

With Kerberos, the following are made possible:

- Single logon process.
- Mutual authentication that requires both the client and the server to provide authentication.
- Delegated authentication, allowing user's credential to be tracked end to end.

It is always nice to have such new features. However, will they fit into your existing network environment? The Microsoft answer is "YES", that you should be able to introduce Windows 2000–based servers into your existing network security structure. However, as said by Microsoft, your security strategy will

sooner or later be influenced by the security-specific features of Windows 2000 that you plan to deploy when you upgrade the infrastructure to full-blown Windows 2000. Put it this way, if your network is not yet pure-Windows 2000, some features may not be fully utilized.

On Windows 2000, there isn't much for you to configure regarding Kerberos. There are, however, different issues related to the Certificate Services. We will go through them one by one.

II Windows 2000 PKI

In Windows 2000, you can use the Certificate Services and the certificate management tools to setup your own public key infrastructure. Such an infrastructure allows for the following network security features:

- Smart card logon.
- Client authentication through Secure Sockets Layer (SSL). SSL uses a public key to encrypt data that's transferred over the SSL connection. By convention, URLs that require an SSL connection start with https:.
- Client authentication through Transport Layer Security (TLS). TLS is used for encapsulation of various higher level protocols. For example, the TLS Handshake Protocol can be used to allow your server and clients to authenticate each other and negotiate an encryption algorithm and cryptographic keys before actual data transmission.
- Secure e-mail.
- Digital signatures, the digital codes attached to the electronic messages to uniquely identify the sender.
- Secure connectivity via Internet Protocol Security.
- Set up and manage certification authorities for issuing (and revoking) X.509 V3 certificates. X.509 is the most widely deployed industry-standard certificate type. You can find more information on X.509 at http://www.rsa.com/rsalabs/faq/html/5-3-2.html.
- Integrate commercial third party client authentication into your own internal public key infrastructure if necessary.

PKI is not intended as a replacement to the Windows 2000 domain based logon mechanism. Windows 2000 PKI does not replace the existing way of authorization in your Windows 2000 domain. Instead, it works as a complement.

In certain cases, you may want to deploy third-party PKI. This is especially common when you are setting up a commerce site open to the public, that the outside customers tend to trust the third party CA (such as Revising) rather than your own CA mechanism. When choosing a third party PKI vendor, make sure that it can work with your Windows 2000 infrastructure flawlessly.

If you are to setup your own PKI (mostly for internal use), one recommended way (based on Microsoft's suggestion) is to have it implemented in stages:

1. Install root certification authorities in the parent domains for each Windows 2000 domain tree.
2. Install intermediate certification authorities in the domains of each business unit.
3. Install and configure issuing certificate authorities and services in the domains for each user group at each site.

Windows 2000 Certificate Services

You rely on the Certificate Services to issue and manage certificates. Certificate Services allows your Windows 2000 server computer to act as a CA that receives certificate requests from clients and servers. These requests for new certificates are sent mostly over HTTP and e-mail. The information included in the requests is to be verified by you before the corresponding X.509 certificates should be issued.

Shorts for certification authority, a CA is a facility that is entrusted to accept a certificate request, verifies the requester's information, and issue the certificate accordingly.

Certificate Services turns your Windows 2000 server into a CA and supports issuing certificates for the following standards / technologies:

Secure/Multipurpose Internet Mail Extensions
Digital signatures for use in SSL
Digital signatures for use in TLS

Generally, you will be performing the following activities when deploying Windows 2000 Certificate Services:

4. Install and configure one or more certification authorities.
5. Modify the default security permissions for certificate templates IF NECESSARY.
6. Install and configure the support systems and the applications.
7. Configure the Public Key Group Policy.
8. You may OPTIONALLY configure Web Enrollment Support on another computer.
9. You may OPTIONALLY develop custom certificate enrollment applications for submitting requests to the Certificate Services.

Pop Quiz 6.1

Pop Quiz 6.1 *Questions*

1) Windows 2000 CA can issue certificates for what certificate standards?
2) What TLS Protocol can be used to allow your server and clients to authenticate each other and negotiate an encryption algorithm and cryptographic keys before actual data transmission?
3) True or false: Windows 2000 PKI replaces the existing way of authorization in a Windows 2000 domain.

Pop Quiz 6.1

Pop Quiz 6.1 *Answers*

1) Secure/Multipurpose Internet Mail Extensions, Digital signatures for use in SSL, Digital signatures for use in TLS
2) TLS Handshake Protocol
3) False. Windows 2000 PKI does not replace the existing way of authorization in your Windows 2000 domain. Instead, it works as a complement.

Certificate Services Policy Modules

Windows 2000 uses the policy module to determine whether a certificate request must be approved, denied, or queued for later decision. A default policy module is included in Windows 2000 to incorporate the CA policy for both the enterprise CA and the standalone CAs. Most of the time you can use the pre-defined module with small changes to suit your need, although you may go extra miles by building custom policy modules to suit your specific needs.

Different CA Policies

Enterprise CA Policy:

This kind of policy uses Active Directory to determine the identity of the requester and automatically determines whether the requester has security permissions to receive such certificate. Response is almost immediate, and is generated without the need for human intervention.

Stand-alone CA Policy:

This policy sends certificate requests to a pending queue and wait for the administrator to take his/her time making approval. You may choose to set this policy to automatically approve all certificate requests. However, such attempt is considered as unsafe, as the stand-alone CA cannot verify the identity of the requesters even with the presence of Active Directory.

Custom Policy:

This can be accomplished by using the customizable policy module DLL. To create a custom policy requires that you use the Microsoft Platform SDK. More information on this topic can be found at: http://windows.microsoft.com/windows2000/reskit/webresources. Keep in mind though, that custom policy should not be used with the Enterprise CAs, or the integration with Active Directory may be interrupted.

By default, Windows 2000 enterprise CAs are installed. To modify the default configuration as well as to specify the types of certificates to be issued, use the Certification Authority console MMC snap-in.

Before you can determine what PKI certificate service policies are necessary, always identify the applications you want to deploy first. Identify these applications together with:

- all uses for certificates
- users that will require certificates
- computers that will require certificates
- services that will require certificates
- types of certificates intended for being issued

You may then make your decisions accordingly. Regarding the type of certificate services to deploy, you must consider the following factors:

- the types of certificates to be issued
- the number of entities that need certificates
- the locations of the groups

You may use different types of CAs to serve different users. Depending on the number of users to serve, multiple CAs may have to be deployed to meet the demand.

Example Case – SBP Associates

SBP Associates has been in the consulting business in the San Francisco Bay Area for 10 years. Its business is characterized by long-standing partner relationships with clients. It takes an entrepreneurial approach to servicing clients. Its service units work closely together, share resources, experiences and strategies.

Organization Structure

The CEO of the company reports directly to the board of directors. Under the CEO there are two divisions. The internal division handles all the internal affairs, while the Service Division provides service to the customers.

Under the Service Division, there are 4 departments:

Department of Executive Management

100 people, head office, SF

EM.Service.SBP.com

Department of Administrative Services

100 people, Oakland office

AS.Service.SBP.com

Department of Information Services

36 people, San Jose office

IS.Service.SBP.com

Department of Accounting

550 people, Milpitas office

AT.Service.SBP.com

Comments:

If SBP is running Windows 2000 Active Directory, the best type of CA to be deployed is the enterprise CA. All requests should be made online to minimize human intervention.

Different departments may use their own CAs, as each CA can have its own distinct set of proof-of-identity requirements for its certificate requesters.

Watch out for the number of people in each department. For larger department (like the Accounting department in this case), consider to deploy more CAs for supporting the corresponding larger group of users.

Different Certificate Types

Below are the basic security requirements for the certificates you deploy:

- Length of the private key.
- Cryptographic algorithms used with certificates.
- Lifetime of certificates.
- Certificate renewal cycle.
- Private key storage and management requirements.

Typically speaking, user certificates should deploy 1,024-bit keys, while root CAs should deploy the stronger 4,096-bit keys. Certificate lifetimes are determined by many different factors, and it is your duty to make the appropriate judgment.

To deploy the appropriate certificates in your network, it is always a good idea to consider using the "standard" Certificate Templates. A list of the available certificates is available at the URL below:

http://www.microsoft.com/windows2000/techinfo/reskit/en-us/default.asp?url=/WINDOWS2000/techinfo/reskit/en-us/deploy/dgch_pki_uttv.asp

Keep in mind that the standalone CAs do not use certificate templates. Certificate requests made to these CAs must have all of the information necessary for defining the type of certificate manually specified.

Online VS Offline Requests

Online certificate templates are for issuing certificates to requestors who:

have Windows 2000 accounts

are capable of obtaining certificates directly from an enterprise CA

If the requestors do not fulfill any of the above criteria, offline certificate templates will have to be used instead. The primary difference between the two is that with online certificate requests, identification information about the requestor is extracted from the requestor's Windows 2000 account and included in the issued certificates. On the other hand, offline requests require that the requestor's identification information be manually entered at the time the requests are made.

Example Case – B2Bexpert

You are a Network Consultant with specialized skills in designing Win2000 infrastructure. You are recently requested by B2BExpert to design the Windows 2000 network for the entire company.

Background

B2Bexpert is an open, business-to-business electronic marketplace for building materials that enhances the customer-supplier relationship. The B2BExpert marketplace enables buyers and sellers of building materials to benefit from timely and relevant market information, broader customer reach, highly efficient transactional capabilities, and more automated logistical and back-office processes allowing greater control over the relationship side of business.

The B2BExpert marketplace will initially focus on structural lumber, but quickly move into other building materials, starting with structural panels. Ultimately, B2BExpert's marketplace will support the buying and selling of all building materials used in residential home and light commercial construction, such as engineered wood products, millwork, siding, roofing, gypsum wallboard, insulation, and other major building materials.

B2BExpert's customers are buyers and sellers of truckload and railcar quantities of building materials including producers, wholesalers, and retailers.

B2BExpert Services

B2BExpert has partnered with a number of partners, allowing members to choose from a variety of value-added services to fulfill transactions in the B2BExpert Marketplace. B2BExpert works with individual members to design specific service packages. Members will always control the extent to which the services are used.

Comments:

B2Bexpert operates an open business-to-business electronic marketplace. This marketplace will likely involve transactions on the Internet. When doing business over the net, it is always recommended that a trusted third party CA such as Revising be used.

Watch out for the namespace strategy of B2Bexpert. It may use the same namespace both internally and externally. If there is a need to authenticate the internal users, an in-house enterprise CA should be setup for this purpose. Do not use third party CA for internal use.

Special Topic: Establishing a Certification Hierarchy

As said by Microsoft, anyone can create a CA. So, to make sure that your CA hierarchy is valid and entrusted, you must carefully plan for the policies and procedures that your CA has in place. At the end of the day, "trust is the key to the whole thing".

A root CA, which is also known as a root authority, is supposed to be the most trusted type of CA in your organization. The physical security and the certificate issuance policy of this CA must be rigorous enough to prevent possible tampering and to maintain the integrity of your PKI.

Technically it is perfectly all right for you to use your root CA to issue certificates to end-users. In fact, in a small organization a root CA may be the only CA that is available. However, for a large organization where multiple CAs are needed, the primary duty of the root CA would be to issue certificates to its subordinate CAs.

A subordinate CA is a CA that has been certified by another CA in your organization to issue certificates. Think of it this way: the root CA delegates some of the jobs to the subordinate CAs. Subordinate CAs can further certify other CAs, thus forming a complete CA hierarchy.

Always remember, the very first step of establishing a certification hierarchy is to install a root CA. This root CA will create a self-signed certificate to identify itself. After trust in a root authority has been established, you can install the subordinate CAs and request for certification from the root CA.

It is technically possible to use the following non-Windows 2000 CAs as the root CA in your infrastructure:

An outside CA

An inside CA running on non-Microsoft platform

If your organization is using a third-party certification authority from outside your organization as the root authority (which is a common practice for E-Commerce oriented companies), you must obtain the root certificate and distribute it to your internal clients and servers that needs to establish trust in the third-party root authority. To distribute such a root certificate, you may use the certificate trust list (CTL) of the Group Policy. Similar actions are required if you are using a non-Microsoft certification authority inside your organization as root.

Example Case - MyTeapots

Since 1970 MyTeapots has been offering products of slate, natural rock, and exquisite crystal water fountains. As a mail order house located in Texas, MyTeapots has its warehouse located in San Jose to serve the customers in the Bay Area. Another office will be opened in New York shortly.

There are 5 departments in the company. The TEA department handles the sales of Tea leaf. The TEAPOT department handles the sales of teapots. The ACCESSORIES department handles the sales of Tea accessories. The WAREHOUSE department handles the inventory. The ADMIN department handles the in house administration.

The management of the company has decided to upgrade to W2K and deploys a single domain model. There will be 2 sites: one in Texas and one in San Jose. The 2 sites will be connected with a 64KBPS links.

You are asked to implement certificate based authentication for the entire organization internally.

Comments:

In the company there are primarily two locations. The ideal setup would be to have:

a root CA in the head office

a subordinate CA in the head office

a subordinate CA in San Jose

This is technically all right if you simply have one CA in the entire company. However, the root CA is supposed to be highly secured, and is not supposed to have its hands on the daily routine works.

Pop Quiz 6.2

Pop Quiz 6.2 *Questions*

1) What CA Policy uses Active Directory to determine the identity of the requester and automatically determines whether the requester has security permissions to receive such certificate?
2) What CA policy sends certificate requests to a pending queue and wait for the administrator to take his/her time making approval?
3) What CA policy requires the use of customizable policy module DLL?
4) For security purpose, root CAs should deploy keys of how many bits?

Pop Quiz 6.2

Pop Quiz 6.2 *Answers*

1) Enterprise CA Policy
2) Stand-alone CA Policy
3) Custom policy.
4) 4096

III Windows 2000 Remote / Internet Connectivity

RRAS

RRAS is an integrated service. It provides the following major functions:

Remote access: It supports PPP and the new Extensible Authentication Protocol (EAP) to enable special vendor-provided authentication methods for remote clients (such as retina scan, smart card…etc).

Routing: It supports both local (LAN-to-LAN) routing and remote (demand-dial) routing, as well as direct connections between offices. It supports the OSPF and RIP2 routing control protocols for IP, and RIP and SAP for IPX.

IAS

Shorts for Internet Authentication Service, IAS allows you to manage authentication, authorization, accounting and auditing of dial-up or VPN users centrally. In fact, IAS turns your Windows 2000 server into a RADIUS server that can authenticate users in databases on Windows NT 4.0 or Windows 2000 domain controller.

Since the IAS server handles the private data communications, hackers love to hack it. Microsoft suggests the following strategies when using IAS:

Install IAS on a computer dedicated solely for RADIUS and nothing else.

Have the IAS computer physically secured.

Protect your IAS server with a firewall.

Use longer shared secrets.

Make use of the account lockout feature.

Enable only authentication protocols that your users will be using. PAP and LAN Manager protocols are considered as the very weak forms of authentication, and should be avoided unless you need to support legacy clients.

Enable logging of both authentication and accounting records, and back up all log files on a regular basis.

Since IAS uses the global catalog to authenticate users, you should install IAS on a server near your global catalog server to minimize latency.

If you want to use remote access policies to restrict access for all but certain groups of users, create a Universal Group for all the users to whom you want to allow access, and create a remote access policy that grants access for that universal group. However, do not put the users directly in the Universal Group, but create groups within the Universal Group instead.

Use a user principal name to refer to users for scalability in a very organization.

Improve throughput (if necessary) by increasing the number of concurrent authentication calls in progress allowed at a time between the IAS server and the domain controller. Note: Doing this requires that you edit the registry.

A RADIUS client can be either a NAS or a RADIUS proxy. All NASs that are compliant with RADIUS RFC 2138 are supported. You may specify clients either with IP addresses or with domain names. Microsoft suggests that you specify RADIUS clients by IP address so that IAS won't need to resolve host names at startup (thus minimizing delays). On the other hand, specifying a RADIUS client by DNS name gives you more administrative flexibility and allows you to map multiple IP addresses of the RADIUS clients to a single name.

In the world of RADIUS, realm names are used to provide the identification necessary to forward authentication requests to the server that holds the user's logon credentials. Note that Windows 2000 IAS does not use realm names for routing purposes.

NAT

NAT and ICS are always the choice for a Small Office/Home Office (SOHO) network. A SOHO network is small, and is usually peer-to-peer based with only a single subnet. There is no need for dedicated routers, DHCP servers, nor WINS servers. What they really need is low cost internet connectivity.

Since there is usually no resource for hiring an administrator to manage the network, the goal for a SOHO infrastructure is "simplicity". Windows 2000 offers the SOHO the ability to auto-assign private IP addresses to internal computers through Automatic Private IP Addressing (APIPA). Addresses

obtained via APIPA are good for internal use only. To be able to access the internet, either NAT or ICS must be deployed.

NAT enables your internal private IP addresses to be translated into valid public IP addresses. This keeps the internal network secure while allowing all the internal hosts to access the outside world without the need to maintain a public address range.

Microsoft recommends that you do not use NAT on a network that has the following services or computers running:

Windows 2000 domain controllers

DNS servers

Gateways

DHCP servers

Systems configured for static IP

Keep in mind though, that NAT is just a translation function that translate (or map) IP addresses. You cannot rely on NAT to allow 2 computers to access the internet with one valid address concurrently. If you can afford to buy only one IP address, you should use ICS. In fact, using ICS is more economical, as NAT requires a Windows 2000 Server to run, whereas ICS can run on cheaper Windows 2000 Professional or Windows 98 Second Edition computers.

ICS

Internet Connection Sharing (ICS) is a simple package that can run on Windows 98, ME and 2000. It consists of the simplified versions of DHCP, NAT, and DNS functions, and allows all of your computers on the network to access the internet by sharing a single internet connection.

You can configure ICS on any remote access or LAN connections, as long as you have a computer with a network connection to a local ISP and a network interface card for connection to the in-house peer-to-peer network. ICS gets its IP address from the ISP and automatically configure your internal network interface with the static IP address of 192.168.0.1 (which is part of the IP

address range of 192.168.0.0 to 192.168.254.254). To allow your in-house PCs to work with ICS, configure them to receive addressing configuration dynamically. Disable any running DNS and DHCP service in the network and allows ICS to take things over.

There is not much you can configure on ICS. While NAT allows manual configuration of IP addresses, subnet masks and many other features, ICS uses a fixed IP address range and allows almost nothing to be customized.

Automatic Private IP Addressing on Legacy Clients

We mentioned APIPA in the previous section. Windows 2000, ME and 98 can self-assign an IP address from the 169.254.0.0/16 address range when there is no DHCP server available. To support this functionality on Windows 3.11 and Windows NT, you must manually setup an APIPA server on a Windows 2000 Server computer:

1. Run the Routing and Remote Access Manager.
2. Configure NAT.
3. Add the interface that distributes the IP addresses.
4. Configure the IP address range in the NAT properties.

Example Case – LaserPoint

LaserPoint has been importing laser pointers by the thousands since 1994. Its business model is quite unique: it operates from the garages of the partners to reduce overhead to almost zero, which allows them to provide low prices for the customers. There are 5 garages in this business. All of these garages have cable modems connectivity.

Products
Products sold by LaserPoint include:

Sales Team 1

Green Laser Pointers

Keychain Pointers

Pattern Pointers

Full Size Pointers

Ballpoint Pen Pointers

Sales Team 2

Laser Yoyo

Laser Glove

Laser Aimer Gunsight

Diode Modules

Spectacle Binoculars

Organization

Each sales team has about 3 members. They are all working in the downtown garage location.

Comments:

Each sales team has about 3 members. There are only two sales teams. And they are all working in the downtown garage location. You should treat this as a SOHO scenario because:

- There are too few users.
- The users are mainly sales professionals who are unlikely to have time and skills to manage the network.

ICS is the simplest solution for this garage location if internet connectivity is desired. It is simple because it does not need nor allow you to modify the following default configuration items:

- the DHCP allocator
- the range of private IP addresses to be distributed
- the DNS proxy
- inbound mappings

If ICS is to be used on top of a modem that requires dialing, consider the "Enable on-demand dialing" option. Also, make sure that the computers used by the sales team members are all configured to obtain IP addresses automatically.

As there is a need for all the garages to connect to each others via the internet, you will need to configure VPN connectivity as well. Fortunately, ICS and VPN can co-exist smoothly. All you need to do is to create a VPN connection to tunnel from the computer on the Internet connection sharing network to the tunnel server on the other side of the Internet. The VPN connection will then be authenticated and completely secured.

Smart Card

We mentioned in the previous sections the support for EAP. EAP is needed if you want to deploy smart card as the logon authentication device.

Shorts for Extensible Authentication Protocol, EAP is an extension to PPP that provides a standard mechanism for support of additional authentication methods, such as:

token cards
smart cards
one-time passwords
certificates

EAP is especially good for use in VPN connections that are subject to the following attacks:

dictionary attacks
password guessing

Windows 2000 provides both the EAP-MD5 CHAP and EAP-TLS authentication methods. The latter is a mutual authentication method that requires both the client and the server prove their identities. If your connection is configured to use EAP-TLS as its only authentication method, ensure that both sides are capable of providing proof of identity, or all connection attempts will fail.

Smart cards are a key component of the public key infrastructure that Microsoft is integrating into the Windows 2000 infrastructure. As a solution that combines both hardware and software, smart cards provide a point of convergence for the public key certificates and the associated keys with its tamper-resistant storage capability and its security-critical computation mechanisms.

To deploy smart card, you must check with your vendor regarding their products' OS compatibility. Windows 2000 is smart card enabled, while older Windows may require special tweaks (on the drivers) before smart card can be fully supported (it all depends on the model and device driver of the smart card device you use).

Pop Quiz 6.3

Pop Quiz 6.3 *Questions*

1) APIPA uses what address range?
2) ICS consists of the simplified versions of:
3) In the world of RADIUS, what are used to provide the identification necessary to forward authentication requests to the server that holds the user's logon credentials?
4) True or false: A RADIUS client can be a NAS but not a RADIUS proxy.

Pop Quiz 6.3

Pop Quiz 6.3 *Answers*

1) 169.254.0.0/16
2) DHCP, NAT, and DNS
3) realm names
4) False. A RADIUS client can be either a NAS or a RADIUS proxy.

IV Windows 2000 VPN

Virtual Private Networking

VPN is the technology that you can use to enable your users to easily and securely connect to your corporate network from remote locations. The VPN connection is made through an ISP, NOT through RAS dial in. Advantages of using VPN include:

Low cost – the medium is the Internet.

Enhanced security -- the connection is encrypted and secure.

Network protocol support – the most common network protocols (in addition to IP) are all supported.

With Windows 2000, you can use the following secure protocols for creating Virtual Private Networks:

Layer 2 Tunneling Protocol (L2TP)

Point-to-point Tunneling Protocol (PPTP)

Internet Protocol Security (IPSec)

When there is a choice that has to be made between L2TP and PPTP, go for L2TP if:

your environment is purely Windows 2000

you want better security than PPTP

On the other hand, IPSec is the standard-based protocol that provides the highest levels of VPN security through encryption. According to Microsoft, it is so secure that almost everything above the networking layer is encrypted.

In Windows 2000, there is no such thing as VPN Manager. You manage your VPN via the Routing and Remote Access Service (RRAS), which oversees both RASA dial and VPN operations in addition to routing.

L2TP and IPSec

Shorts for Layer Two Tunneling Protocol, L2TP is an industry-standard Internet tunneling protocol that is designed to run over IP networks. You can use L2TP to set up tunnels across intervening networks, and allows the communication to be encrypted via IPSec. Note that the Windows 2000 implementation of L2TP does not support native tunneling over X.25, Frame Relay, nor ATM networks.

IPSec is a suite of cryptography-based protection services and security protocols that provides computer-level authentication in addition to data encryption.

Regarding authentication, the following standard PPP-based authentication protocols are supported:

EAP
MS-CHAP
CHAP
SPAP
PAP

For authentication to work, you must ensure that both sides of the connection are using the same authentication protocol. PAP is clear text based and is always discouraged. EAP is always required if smart card authentication is to be deployed.

Regarding Encryption, IPSec Security Association (SA) makes use of the Security Parameters Index (SPI), which is a combination of:

a destination address
a security protocol
a unique identification value

The available encryptions in IPSec include Data Encryption Standard (DES) and Triple DES (3DES). The latter is a strong form of encryption that is subject to export control. Check with your legal advisor before deploying it in your overseas branches.

Always remember, do not deploy NAT and IPSec together, as they do not coexist well. In fact, NAT will modify the packet headers, causing IPSec to reject the returning packets.

PPTP

Point-to-Point Tunneling Protocol (PPTP) as an extension of the Point-to-Point Protocol is the choice to go with if Windows NT is involved in your VPN. PPTP enables the secure transfer of multi-protocol data from a remote computer to a private server. The connection can be on either permanent or on-demand basis. Always remember, if your environment is pure Windows 2000, PPTP is less preferable than L2TP.

Pop Quiz 6.4

Pop Quiz 6.4 *Questions*

1) What VPN protocol should be used when backward compatibility is important?
2) What VPN protocol should be used when the network is purely Windows 2000 based?
3) True or false: Windows 2000 implementation of L2TP supports native tunneling over X.25, Frame Relay, and ATM networks.
4) True or false: IPSec is the standard-based protocol that provides the highest levels of VPN security through encryption.

Pop Quiz 6.4

Pop Quiz 6.4 *Answers*

1) PPTP
2) L2TP
3) False. Windows 2000 implementation of L2TP does not support native tunneling over X.25, Frame Relay, nor ATM networks.
4) True

Example Case – ProTax

You are a Network Consultant with specialized skills in designing Win2000 infrastructure. You are recently requested by The ProTax Group to design the Windows 2000 network for the entire company.

Since 1980, ProTax has established a formal tax service to serve the clients needs. Headed by CPAs with many years of experience in a wide array of industries, ProTax staff works year-round to stay abreast of developments in the ever-changing state and federal tax laws.

IT Structure:

Currently the offices are running a mixture of NT4, Netware and IBM Mainframe Servers. For clients, they have 95, 98 and NT.

Expected IT Structure:

ProTax (Redwood City)

Domain 1

100 Staffs

ProTax (San Mateo)

Domain 2

120 Staffs

ProTax (San Bruno)

Domain 3

65 Staffs

You are asked to upgrade the entire network infrastructure.

Comments:

In the ProTax case, since there are 3 locations, the most economical way of connecting them together is VPN. If every server is upgraded to Windows 2000 to run with Active Directory, you may consider to deploy a L2TP based VPN. However, there are still many existing NT servers, and you are not yet sure if these servers are to be upgraded. Most importantly, if any of the NT Servers is to directly involve in a VPN connection, PPTP will be your safest bet.

VPN connection is also possible between clients and servers. The end clients can be running Windows 2000 Pro or Windows NT/98/ME. The general guideline to follow is identical: as long as both sides are Windows 2000, use L2TP. Otherwise, use PPTP.

V Chapter 6: Review Questions

Case Question

You are a Network Consultant with specialized skills in designing Win2000 network. You are recently requested by LoveSherpa Inc to design the network infrastructure for the entire company.

Background

LoveSherpa is a company producing and selling the LoveSherpa series of bag - soft-sided pet carrier approved for in-cabin use by major airlines. The LoveSherpa bags are recognized as the premiere soft-sided pet carrier that can provide a safe comfortable trip for the pets by plane, train or automobile.

Locations

Established in New York, it has two branches in East Asia and one branch in London. Due to the expanding demand for this kind of products, instead of manufacturing everything on its own, it is outsourcing many of the production works.

Products

The following products are produced by their contractor in China:

LoveSherpa Lite
The Classic LoveSherpa Traveler
The Kartu Bag
LoveSherpa French Sac
The Ultimate LoveSherpa

The following products are produced by their contractor in Korea:

LoveSherpa Back Pac the All-in-One Bag

Delta Airlines Deluxe Pet Carrier By LoveSherpa

The LoveSherpa-on-Wheels

The LoveSherpa Roll-Up

Original LoveSherpa Bag

Network Structure

Due to the close relationship with the contractors, the company actually shares all its network resources with them. Instead of running its own network, it aims at building a "mega network" that integrates the domains of the contractors into its envisioned directory structure. The domain name for external use will be lovesherpa.com, while the internal one will be LS.com. Also note that there will be one W2K server and one NT4 server available in the head office. The network will run only TCP/IP and nothing else.

Questions

1. You want to centralize the administration and authentication of all RAS accesses for LoveSherpa. Which of the following should you deploy (Choose all that apply)?

A. IAS
B. NAT
C. ICS
D. CA
E. VPN

---

2. LoveSherpa has remote clients that consists of Win98, Windows 2000 and NT4. These clients need to access LoveSherpa's server via dial-up connections. Which of the following protocols should be used?

A. PPTP
B. L2TP
C. DHCP
D. WTLS
E. PPP

---

3. You plan to implement IPSec for LoveSherpa's head office and its London branch. Before you configure IPSec, what should you acquire for the servers on both sides?

A. A root CA
B. A subordinate CA
C. Certificates
D. An IKE scheme
E. A digital digest

4. You plan to implement IPSec for LoveSherpa's head office and its London branch. You need to install and configure certificates. How many CA as a minimum should you setup internally if outside CA is not preferable?

A. One
B. One on each side
C. At least two
D. You can issue certificates without CA
E. None of the choices

---

5. You plan to implement VPN for LoveSherpa. There are Windows 2000 and Windows 95 clients in the London office. PPTP is chosen over L2TP. What is the primary rationale behind this decision?

A. Compatibility
B. Security
C. Performance
D. Collaboration
E. Integrity

---

6. You plan to implement VPN for LoveSherpa between the head office and the East Asia offices, excluding the London office. There are only Windows 2000 clients in the East Asia offices. L2TP is chosen over PPTP. What is the primary rationale behind this decision?

A. Compatibility
B. Security
C. Cost
D. Collaboration
E. Export control

7. On one of the East Asia office, you want to cut cost by reducing the available internet connection to one. However, all of the staffs over there still want to access the internet for fun during lunch hours. Which of the following should be enabled in that office?

A. IAS
B. RADIUS
C. ICS
D. EFS
E. NAT

---

8. You are setting up the PKI for LoveSherpa. You want the CA to function with minimal human intervention. You want requests to be processed entirely automatically. Which of the following CA policy will you use?

A. Enterprise CA
B. Stand-alone CA
C. Web-enabled CA
D. Outside CA
E. Integrated CA

---

9. Which of the following are the valid reasons for LoveSherpa to deploy multiple subordinate CAs in its PKI (Choose 2)?

A. Cost
B. Performance
C. Access control
D. Security
E. Integrity

10. You want to enforce the use of smart cards for remote clients' logon attempts. Which of the following protocols must be in place?

A. EAP
B. TLC
C. PPTP
D. PAP
E. PABP

---

11. You plan to implement IAS for LoveSherpa. You want to optimize the performance. Which of the following guidelines should you follow when configuring IAS?

A. Place it close to a Global Catalog.
B. Enable Multilink.
C. Enable the fastdetect switch at Windows 2000 startup.
D. Use only static IP addresses to reference the clients.
E. Disable the use of any NetBIOS related interface.

---

12. You plan to create a VPN that uses L2TP and IPSec among all the LoveSherpa locations. Which of the following PPP-based authentication protocols are supported (Choose all that apply)?

F. EAP
G. MS-CHAP
H. CHAP
I. SPAP
J. PAP

---

13. You plan to create a VPN that uses L2TP and IPSec among all the LoveSherpa locations. For this to work, which of the following must be disabled entirely in LoveSherpa's network?

A. NAT
B. DHCP
C. DNS
D. RRAS
E. IAS

Chapter 6: Review Answers

1, a

2, e

3, c

4, a

5, a

6, b

7, c

8, a

9, b d

10, a

11, a

12, a b c d e

13, a

Total Recall

Total Recall

Chapter 7: Putting It Altogether

The objective of this chapter is to provide the reader with an understanding of the following:

1. The application of the skills learned in the previous chapters
2. The exam scenarios

Getting Ready (Questions)

1) Round-Robin DNS is mainly used for what network service?
2) High Availability database service can be achieved through which of the following technologies?
3) What technology has its focus on improving client web browsing performance?
4) NAT cannot co-exist with what security technology?
5) What is the primary reason to use PPTP as the VPN protocol instead of L2TP?

Getting Ready (Answers)

1) Web service.
2) Windows 2000 Cluster.
3) Proxy Server.
4) IPSec
5) Platform compatibility.

I Introduction

This chapter attempts to help you consolidate and apply what you have learned in the previous chapters. A case is developed to illustrate the kind of scenario and questions you will see in the exam.

II The case of SuperBanc

SuperBanc

Profile:

A multinational investment banking services organization

Corporate Head Office in San Jose, California

Comprised of 3 separate operating companies with primary headquarters (each with about 400 staffs) located in North America, Europe and Asia.

Each operating company is an autonomous business unit

Over 32 smaller regional offices (each with, on average, 8 staffs) under their respective regional HQs to provide a complete range of investment banking services

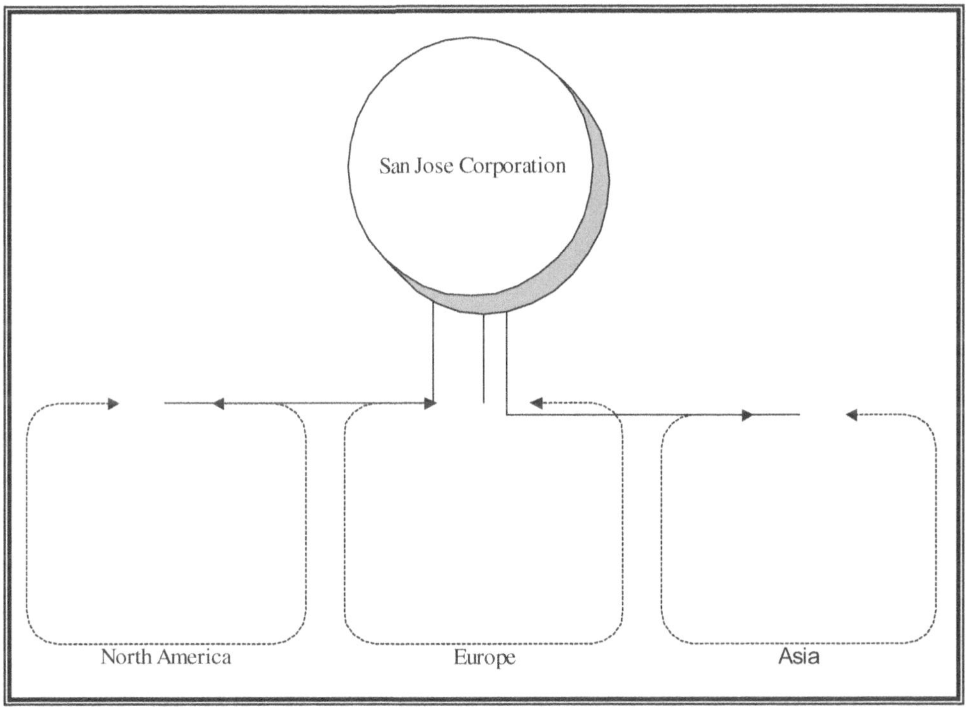

Figure 7.1 SuperBanc

Existing IT Environment:

No central IT group for all operating companies

Each operating company has its own IT standards

Local offices maintain their own file and print servers

Regional offices maintain their domain controllers

Most applications run on the UNIX operating system

DHCP and DNS are managed under UNIX

Server Platforms breakdown:

Windows NT Server 4.0 – 80%

Novell NetWare – 10%

Unix – 10%

Desktop Platforms breakdown:

Windows NT Workstation 4.0 – 50%

Windows 95 – 40%

Windows NT Workstation 3.51 – 10%

Expected IT Infrastructure:

Develop a company-wide Active Directory structure

Retire NetWare

Use Windows 2000 as the mainstream OS

Retain UNIX for the critical application

III DNS for SuperBanc

What DNS namespace structure will you use for SuperBanc?

Question Exhibit:

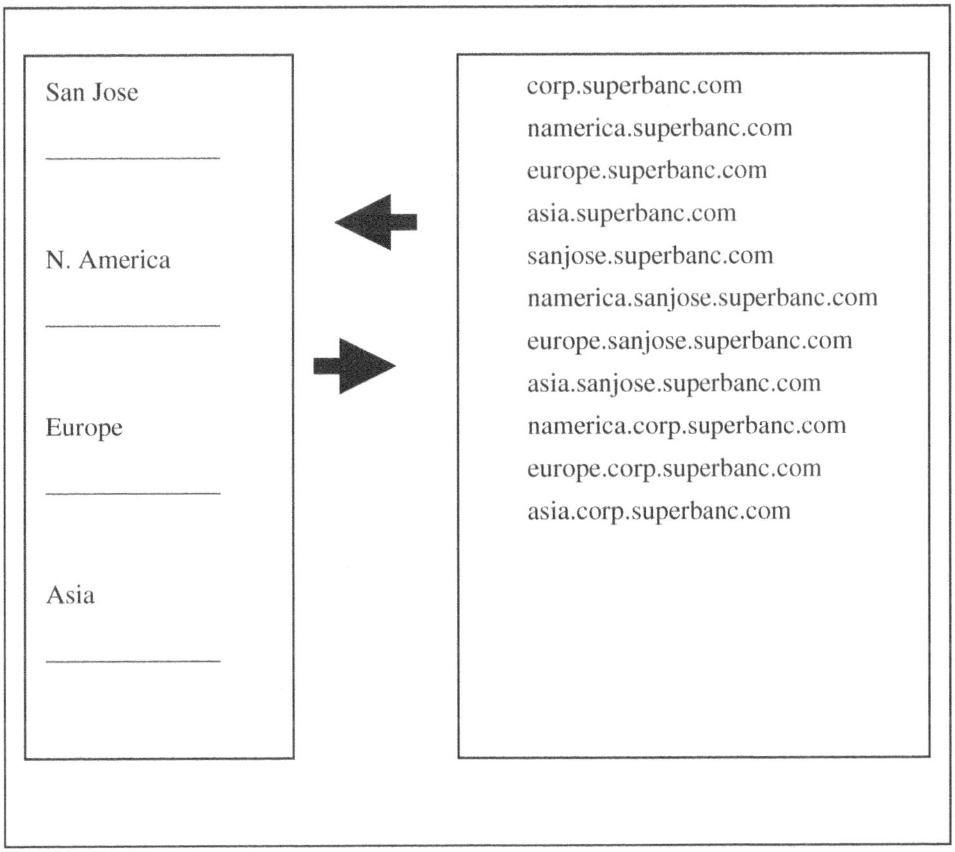

A typical namespace structure of a multinational company usually involves a single domain tree and a series of sub-domains that represent each regional operation. So, in the above question, the suggested DNS namespace would be:

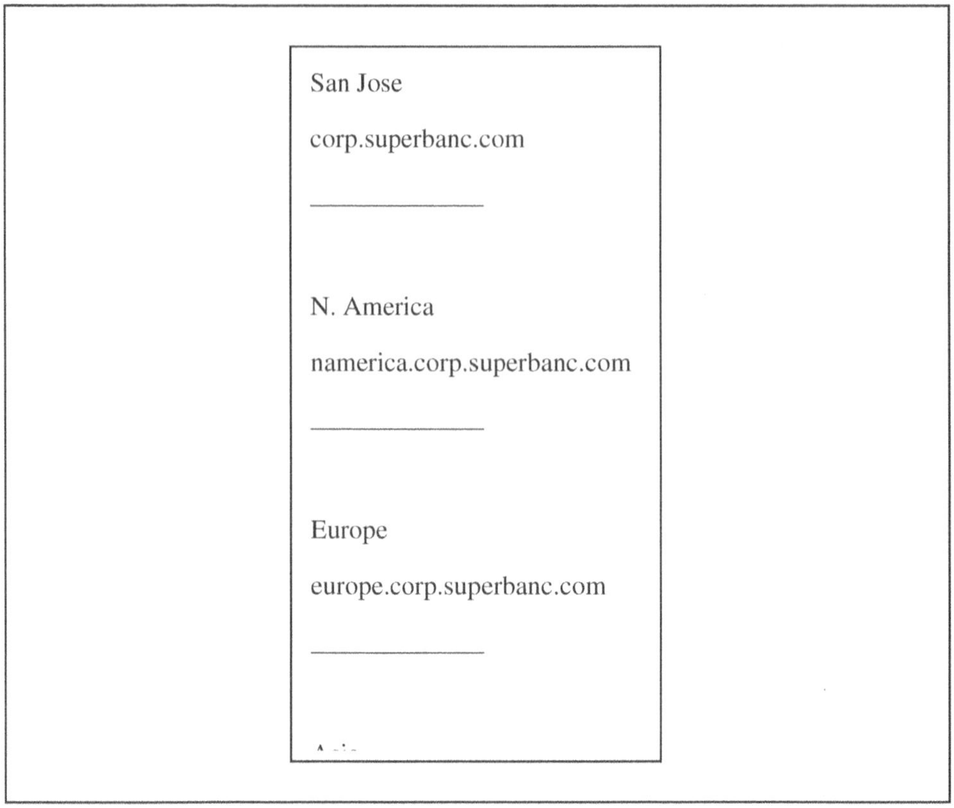

Figure 7.2 SuperBanc announced

San Jose is the location of the head office. It does not represent any specific operation. Now, consider the scenario below:

SuperBanc announced that it just finished acquiring a bank called AFAB in Africa. SuperBanc will become the largest shareholder of AFAB, and will retain AFAB's separate identity, although collaboration between the two is likely to happen. AFAB's existing management will continue to run the company.

With the introduction of AFAB, what will be the new DNS namespace structure?

Question Exhibit:

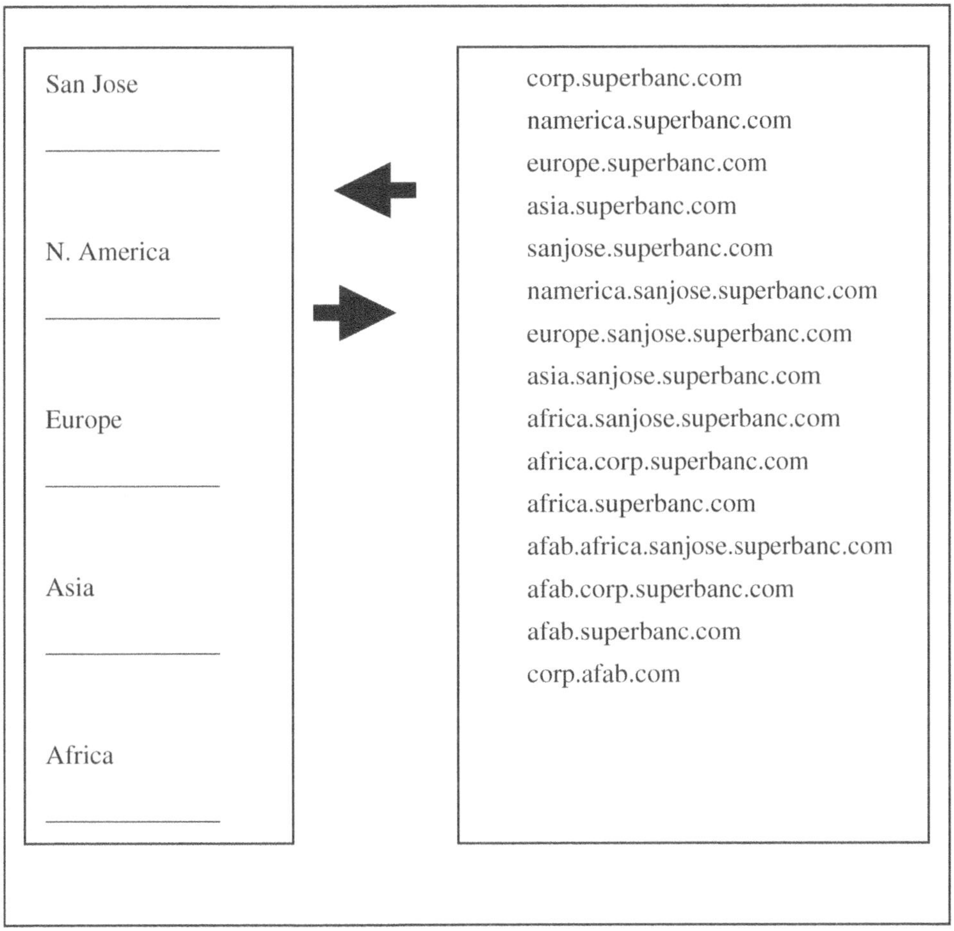

Figure 5.17 DNS Namespace Structure

Since AFAB's identity as well as its management are to be retained, AFAB should not be treated as a sub-domain of superbanc.com. Instead, it should start its own tree in the same forest or even in a separate forest:

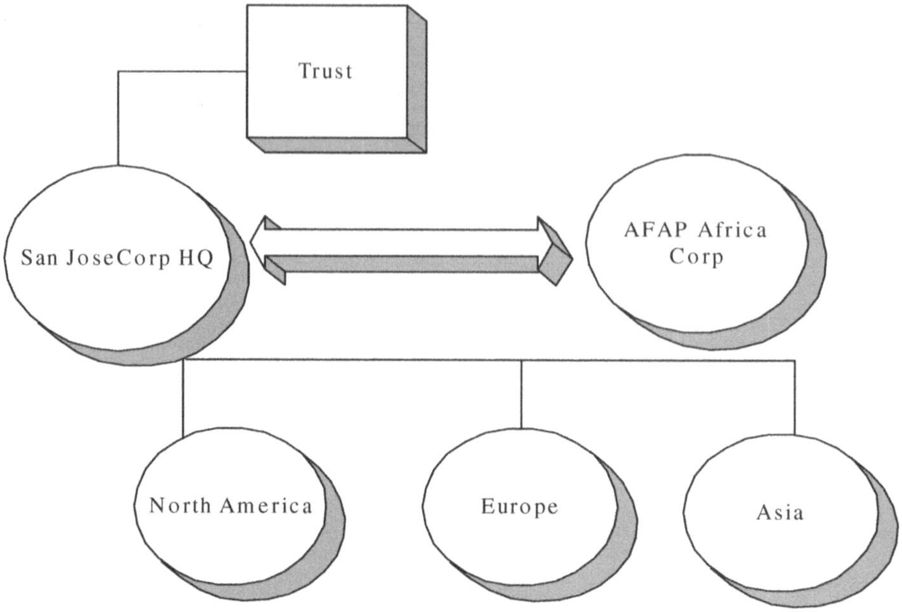

Figure 7.3 AFAB Identity

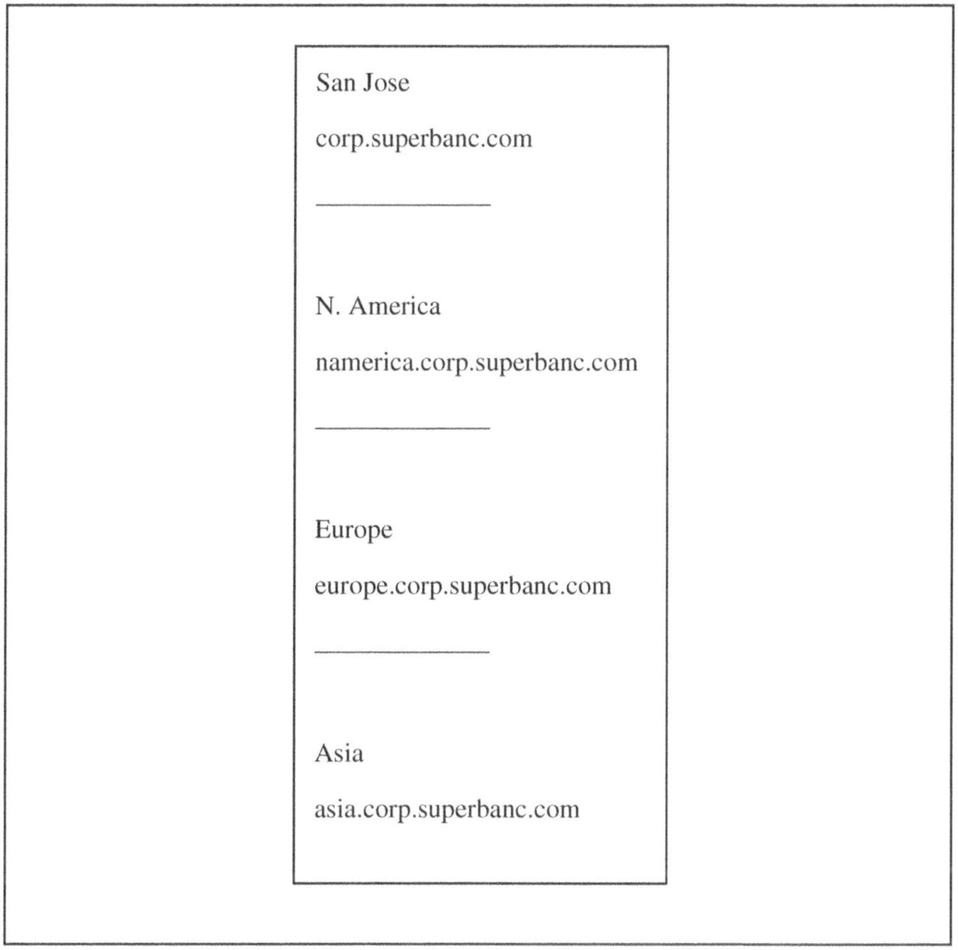
San Jose
corp.superbanc.com
N. America
namerica.corp.superbanc.com
Europe
europe.corp.superbanc.com
Asia
asia.corp.superbanc.com

If it turns out that AFAB's operation is entirely merged into SuperBanc's framework, that AFAB's branches in Africa are to be treated as SuperBanc's African branches, then it may make sense to redefine the corporate structure of SuperBanc as well as its DNS structure as below follow:

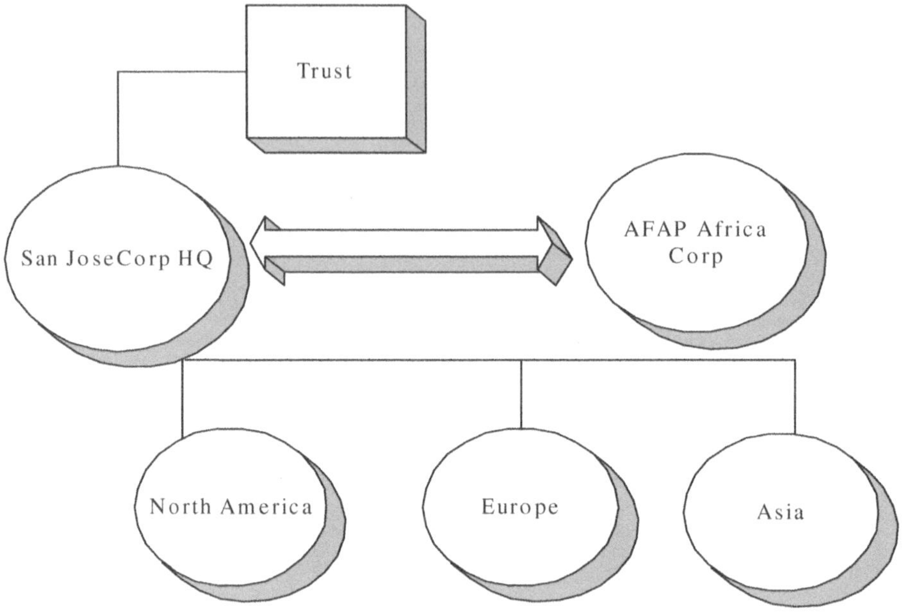

Figure 7.4 AFAB's Operation

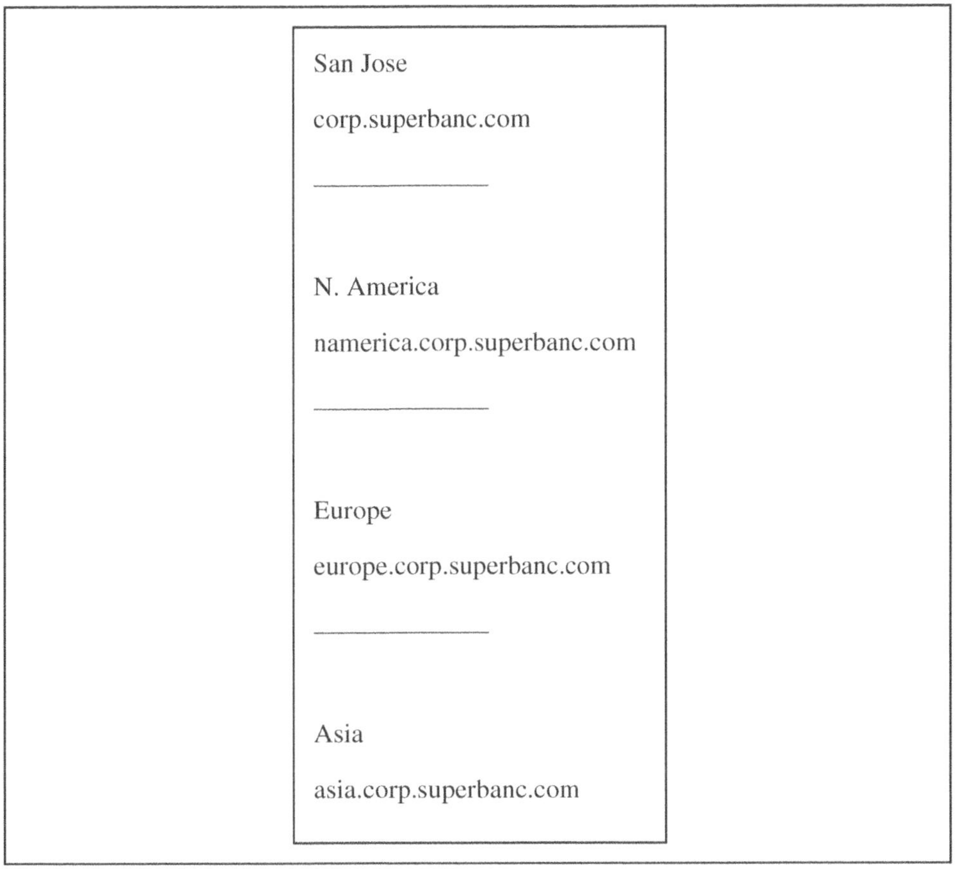

Figure 7.5

What is the appropriate DNS server placement strategy for SuperBanc?

Question Exhibit:

San Jose

N. America

Branches in North America

Europe

Branches in Europe

Asia

Create a standard primary zone for corp.superbanc.com

Create a standard primary zone for namerica.corp.superbanc.com

Create a standard primary zone for europe.corp.superbanc.com

Create a standard primary zone for asia.corp.superbanc.com

Create a standard secondary zone for corp.superbanc.com

Create a standard secondary zone for namerica.corp.superbanc.com

Create a standard secondary zone for europe.corp.superbanc.com

Create a standard secondary zone for asia.corp.superbanc.com

Create a DNS server as a forwarder to corp.superbanc.com

Create a DNS server as a forwarder to namerica.corp.superbanc.com

Create a DNS server as a forwarder to europe.corp.superbanc.com

Create a DNS server as a forwarder to asia.corp.superbanc.com

First of all, let's clarify the exact structure of SuperBanc's network:

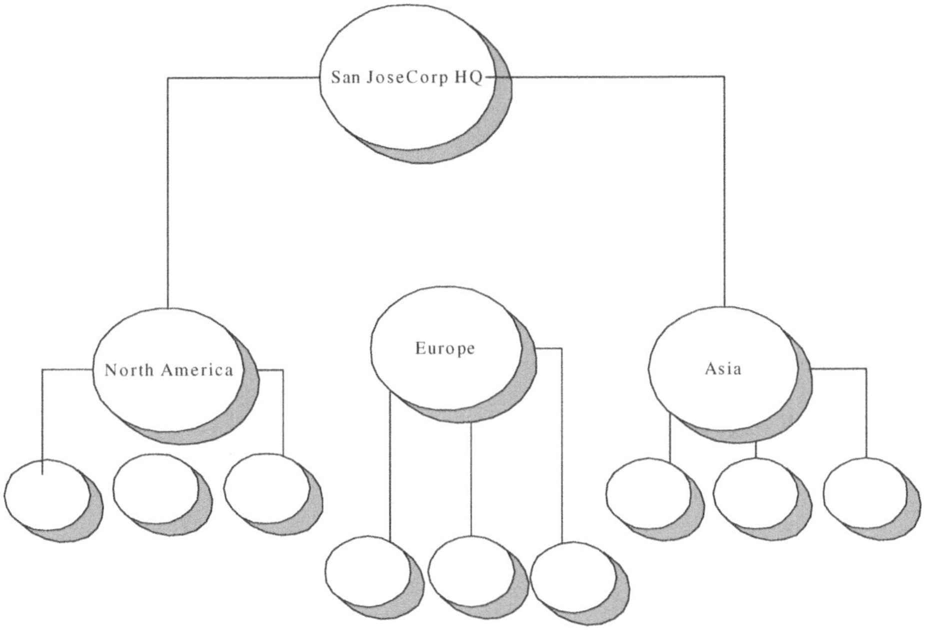

Figure 7.6 SuperBanc's Network

Now, let's answer this question: do we need to have a DNS server on EACH office location? This really depends on the volume of use in the different locations. In the above case, this is probably not desirable, as there are too many locations, that the need for administering a DNS server in each location may not be justified at all.

How about the arrangement of the DNS zones? Let's visualize the appropriate arrangement as below:

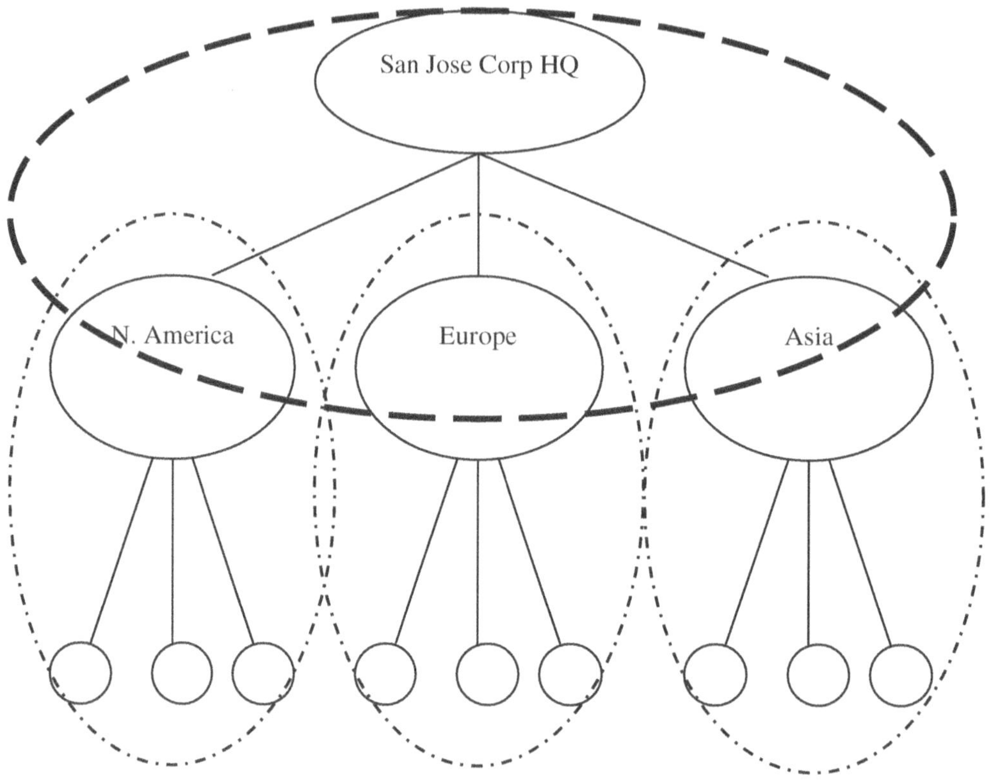

The above illustration actually echoes what we have discussed before regarding the namespace structure of SuperBanc. We should define 4 zones:

corp.superbanc.com

namerica.corp.superbanc.com

europe.corp.superbanc.com

asia.corp.superbanc.com

Take Europe as an example. What should be done is illustrated as below:

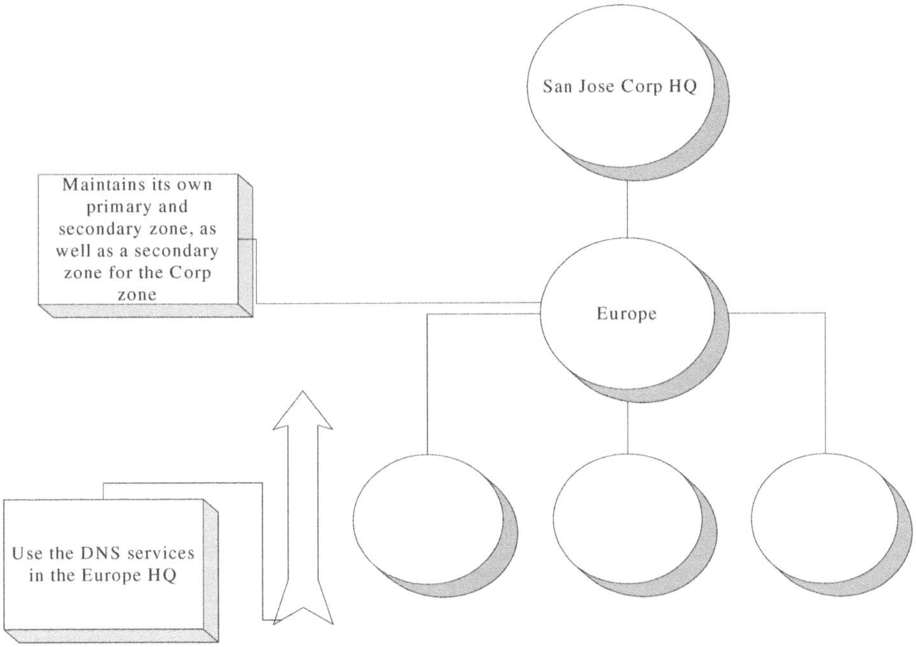

Figure 7.7 The above illustration will translate into the answer below:

San Jose

- Create a standard primary zone for corp.superbanc.com
- Create a standard secondary zone for corp.superbanc.com

N. America

- Create a standard secondary zone for corp.superbanc.com
- Create a standard primary zone for namerica.corp.superbanc.com
- Create a standard secondary zone for namerica.corp.superbanc.com

Europe

- Create a standard secondary zone for corp.superbanc.com
- Create a standard primary zone for europe.corp.superbanc.com
- Create a standard secondary zone for europe.corp.superbanc.com

Asia

- Create a standard secondary zone for corp.superbanc.com
- Create a standard primary zone for asia.corp.superbanc.com
- Create a standard secondary zone for asia.corp.superbanc.com

Now, consider this scenario:

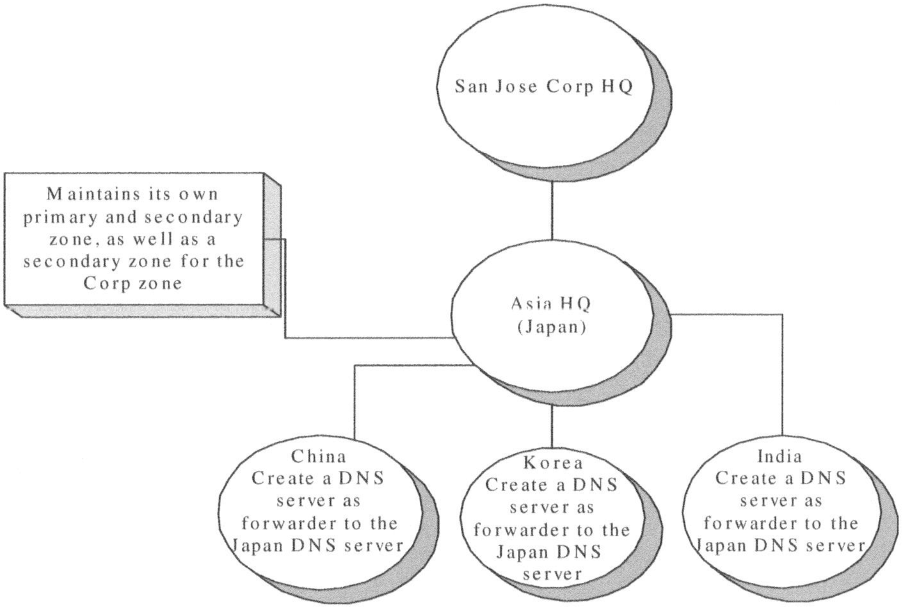

Figure 7.8 San Jose Corp HQ

SuperBanc has designed to consolidate its operations in Asia. Only 4 locations will be maintained in Asia, with the HQ in Japan and the 3 branches in China, Korea and India respectively. Each branch will accommodate about 180 users.

This changes the arrangement for the Asia region entirely. Because of the large number of users in the consolidated offices, it is logical to place DNS servers in these locations to serve the clients locally.

San Jose

Create a standard primary zone for corp.superbanc.com

Create a standard secondary zone for corp.superbanc.com

Asia

Create a standard secondary zone for corp.superbanc.com

Create a standard primary zone for asia.corp.superbanc.com

Create a standard secondary zone for asia.corp.superbanc.com

Korea

Create a DNS server as a forwarder to asia.corp.superbanc.com

China

Create a DNS server as a forwarder to asia.corp.superbanc.com

India

IV IP Infrastructure for SuperBanc

What is the appropriate subnetting strategy for the consolidated Asia operations?

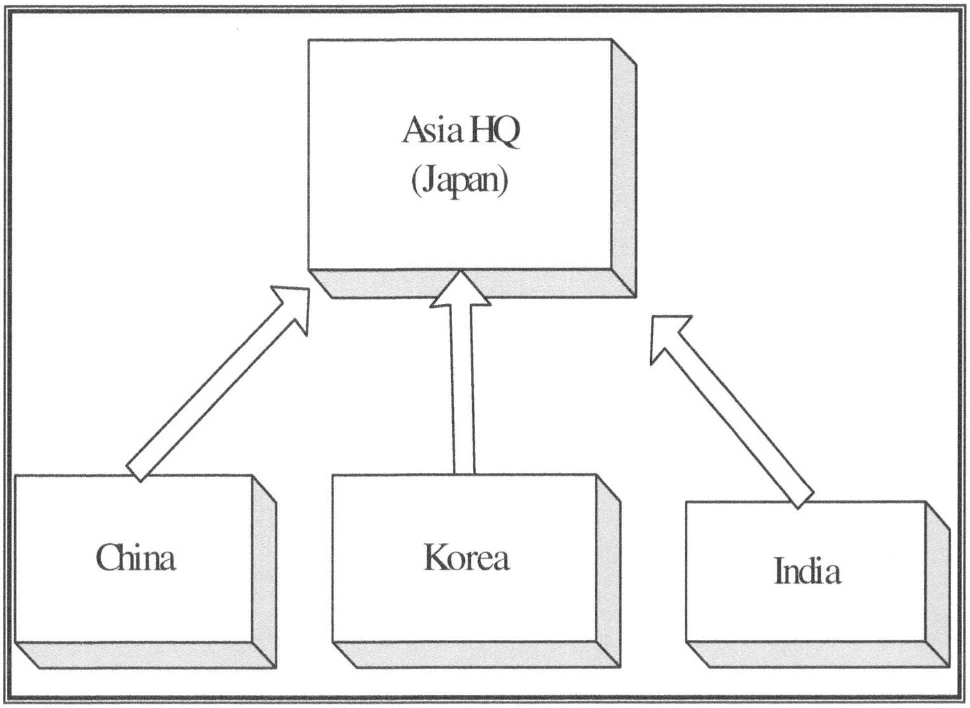

Figure 7.9 Asia HQ Subnetting Strategy

Let's refer back to the now consolidated Asia corporate structure:

The first question to ask is, how many subnets, as a minimum, should be configured? When we say "minimum", that means we do not care about the performance issue (we all know that the more subnets we have the better the segmentation will be).

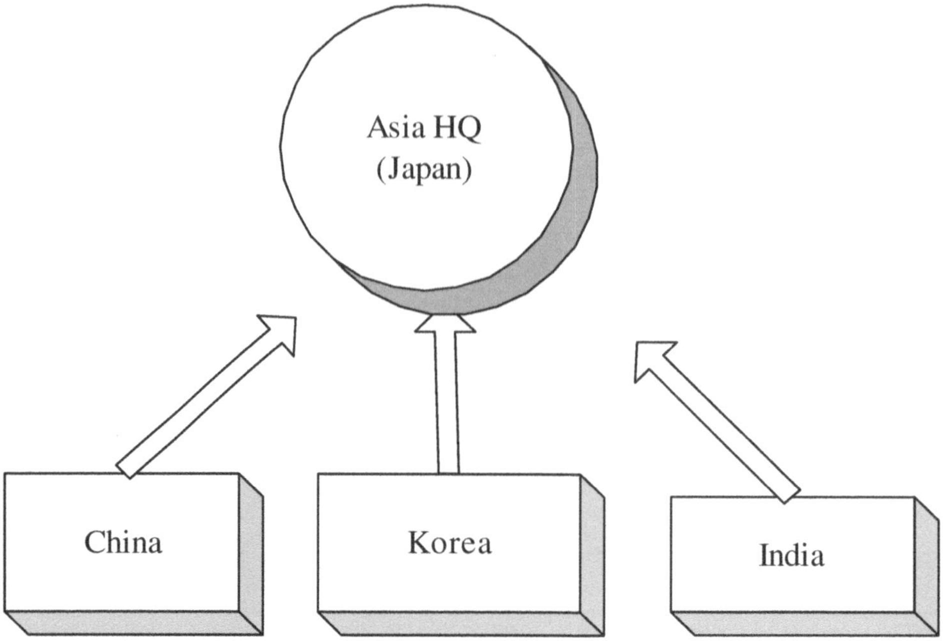

Figure 7.10 Asia HQ Subnetting Strategy

Does the above figure indicate that only four subnets are needed? Not really. Remember what we have learned in Chapter Five?

The type of setting below is required when the connection is made between two remote locations:

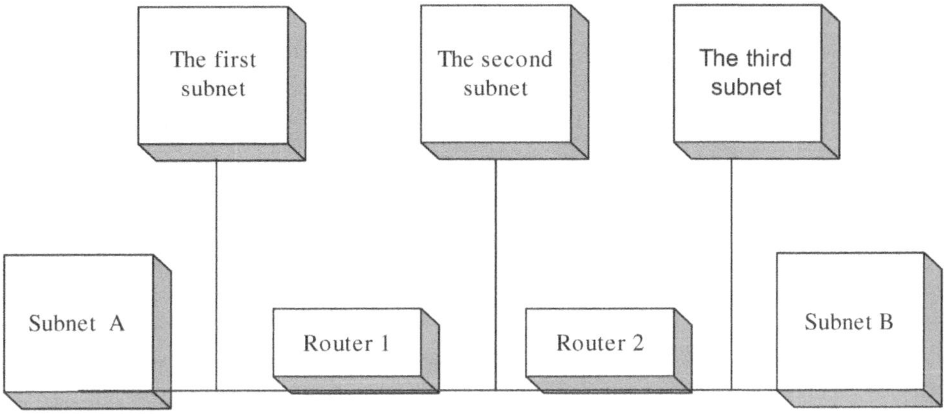

Figure 7.11 SuperBanc IP Infrastructure

That means, you need at least an extra subnet for each link! Now, lets talk about the proper subnet mask to use. As mentioned before,

Japan HQ – 400 users

China – 180 users

India – 180 users

Korea – 180 users

If we are to deploy the minimum number of subnets, the subnet mask for the branches must be able to accommodate at least 180 users, plus room for some flexibility. The HQ, on the other hand, requires a mask that can accommodate at least 400 users per subnet. To determine the correct mask to use, let's check with the table below:

IP Address Table (Class B)

Number of Subnet bits	Subnet Mask	Number of Subnets	Number of Hosts	The first Subnet Address Range	The second Subnet Address Range
2	255.255.192.0	2	16382	64.1-127.254	128.1-191.254
3	255.255.224.0	6	8190	32.1-63.254	64.1-95.254
4	255.255.240.0	14	4094	16.1-31.254	32.1-47.254
5	255.255.248.0	30	2046	8.1-15.254	16.1-23.254
6	255.255.252.0	62	1022	4.1-7.254	8.1-11.254
7	**255.255.254.0**	**126**	**510**	**2.1-3.254**	**4.1-5.254**
8	**255.255.255.0**	**254**	**254**	**1.1-254**	**2.1-2.254**
9	255.255.255.128	510	126	0.129-0.254	1.1-1.126
10	255.255.255.192	1022	62	0.65-0.126	0.129-0.190
11	255.255.255.224	2046	30	0.33-0.62	0.65-0.94
12	255.255.255.240	4094	14	0.17-0.30	0.33-0.46
13	255.255.255.248	8190	6	0.9-0.14	0.17-0.22
14	255.255.255.252	16382	2	0.5-0.6	0.9-0.10

Table 6 IP Address Table (Class B)

Seems like we have plenty of choices if we are given a class B network address. What about if we use a class C network address?

IP Address Table (Class C)

Number of Subnet bits	Subnet Mask	Number of Subnets	Number of Hosts	The first Subnet Address Range	The second Subnet Address Range
2	255.255.255.192	2	62	65-126	129-190
3	255.255.255.224	6	30	33-62	65-94
4	255.255.255.240	14	14	17-30	33-46
5	255.255.255.248	30	6	9-14	17-22
6	255.255.255.252	62	2	5-6	9-10

Table 7 IP Address Table (Class C)

Seems like a Class C address range won't make it, unless we want to further segment the networks into more "smaller" pieces.

Always pay attention to any "growth" clause in the case. If, let's say, the Japan office is going to grow two-fold in the coming year, your choice of subnet mask will have to be ready for such growth:

Number of Subnet bits	Subnet Mask	Number of Subnets	Number of Hosts	The first Subnet Address Range	The second Subnet Address Range
2	255.255.192.0	2	16382	64.1-127.254	128.1-191.254
3	255.255.224.0	6	8190	32.1-63.254	64.1-95.254
4	255.255.240.0	14	4094	16.1-31.254	32.1-47.254
5	255.255.248.0	30	2046	8.1-15.254	16.1-23.254
6	**255.255.252.0**	**62**	**1022**	**4.1-7.254**	**8.1-11.254**
7	255.255.254.0	126	510	2.1-3.254	4.1-5.254
8	255.255.255.0	254	254	1.1-254	2.1-2.254
9	255.255.255.128	510	126	0.129-0.254	1.1-1.126
10	255.255.255.192	1022	62	0.65-0.126	0.129-0.190
11	255.255.255.224	2046	30	0.33-0.62	0.65-0.94
12	255.255.255.240	4094	14	0.17-0.30	0.33-0.46
13	255.255.255.248	8190	6	0.9-0.14	0.17-0.22
14	255.255.255.252	16382	2	0.5-0.6	0.9-0.10

Table 8 IP Address Table

V Administrative Arrangement for SuperBanc

You need to organize an IT team for the consolidated operations in Asia. What will be your strategy?

In a big enterprise that spans multiple regions, there are always at least three levels of administration teams:

Enterprise Team
Regional Team
Site Team

The Enterprise Team should be involved in the top level works, such as the configuration of password policies and the management of the Active Directory schema. The Regional Team should be responsible for second tier tasks such as DNS / WINS server settings, managing WINS replication and monitoring event logs. The Site Team should act as the local point of assistance in the branch offices, providing simple functions such as DHCP server authorization, end user configuration and miscellaneous day-to-day backups.

In the case of SuperBanc, you may want to assign the Site Team members to work for the locations in China, India and Korea, while keeping the Regional Team members in the Japan HQ. If the Asia operation is going to deploy policies and rules significantly different from the rest of the organization, consider to setup an Enterprise Team in Japan as well.

VI Equipment Arrangement for SuperBanc

The SuperBanc HQ in San Jose is a campus area with multiple buildings:

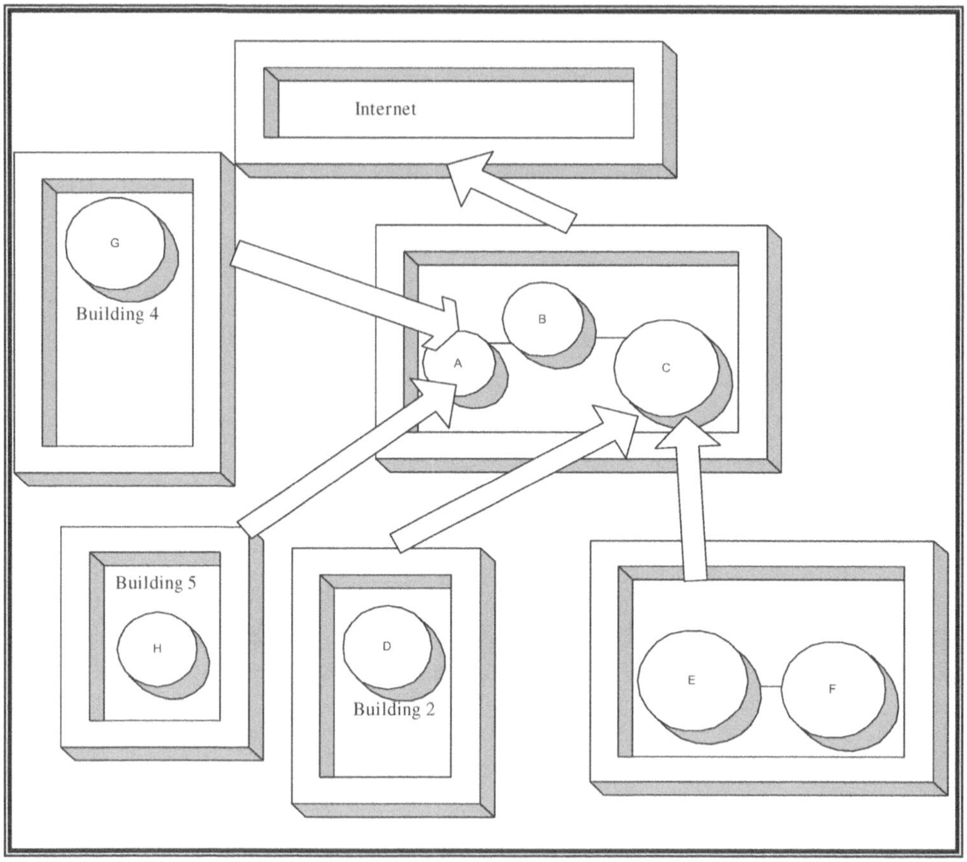

Figure 7.12 SuperBanc's HQ in San Jose

Now, you need to properly arrange the equipments needed:

Question Exhibit:

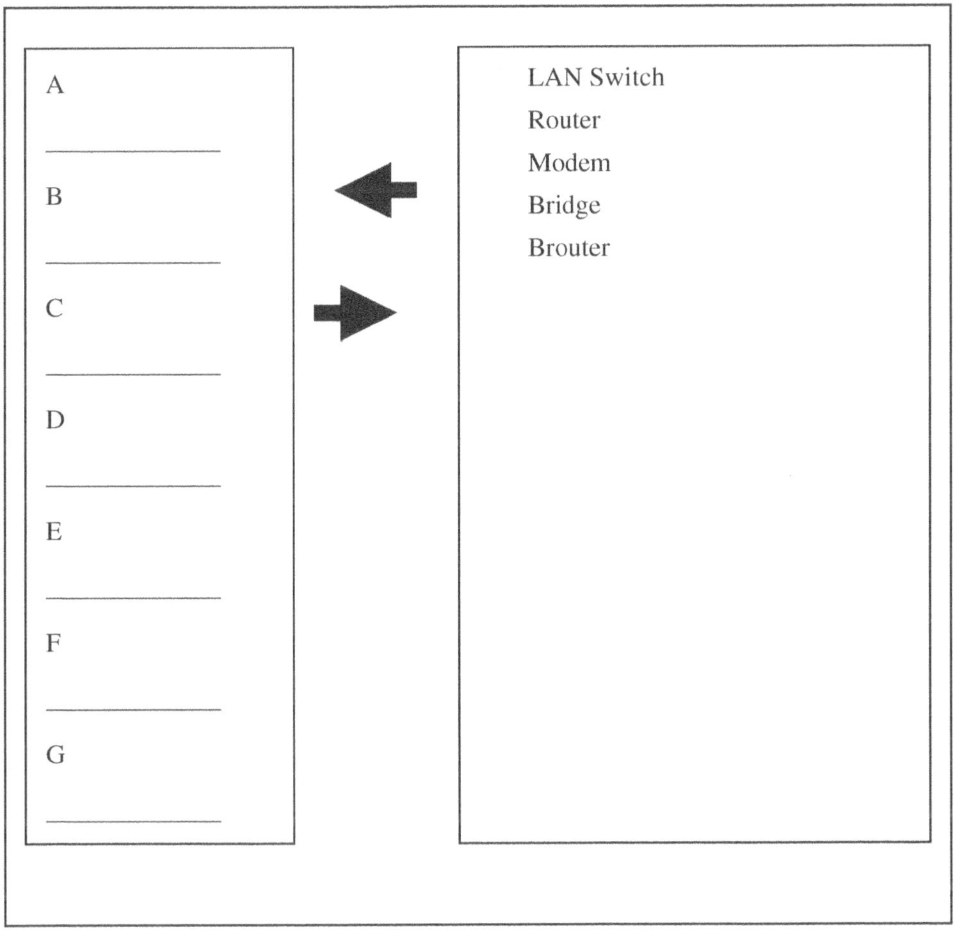

What must be equipped at each segment?

Basically, in a modern network you do not need old time devices like brouters nor bridges. Also, since the buildings are all in the same campus, it makes no sense to have them connected via modems. So, the only choices we have left are LAN Switches and Routers. It is not difficult to come to a conclusion that LAN connections use LAN switches while “remote” building-to-building connections use routers.

VII Remote Access for SuperBanc

All critical servers are located in Building ONE. There are servers that act as:

Domain Controllers

Remote Access servers

Firewall stations (based on Windows 2000)

Application servers

Web servers

Proxy servers

The members of the Enterprise Team specify that sometimes they need to perform remote administration on the domain controllers. They prefer to do this even if they are on field trips to different places in the world.

50 of the managers need to remotely accessing the resources on the network. They want to do this through the Internet connections at home. They use Windows 2000 laptops, and some of them prefer to use Netscape browsers instead of IEs.

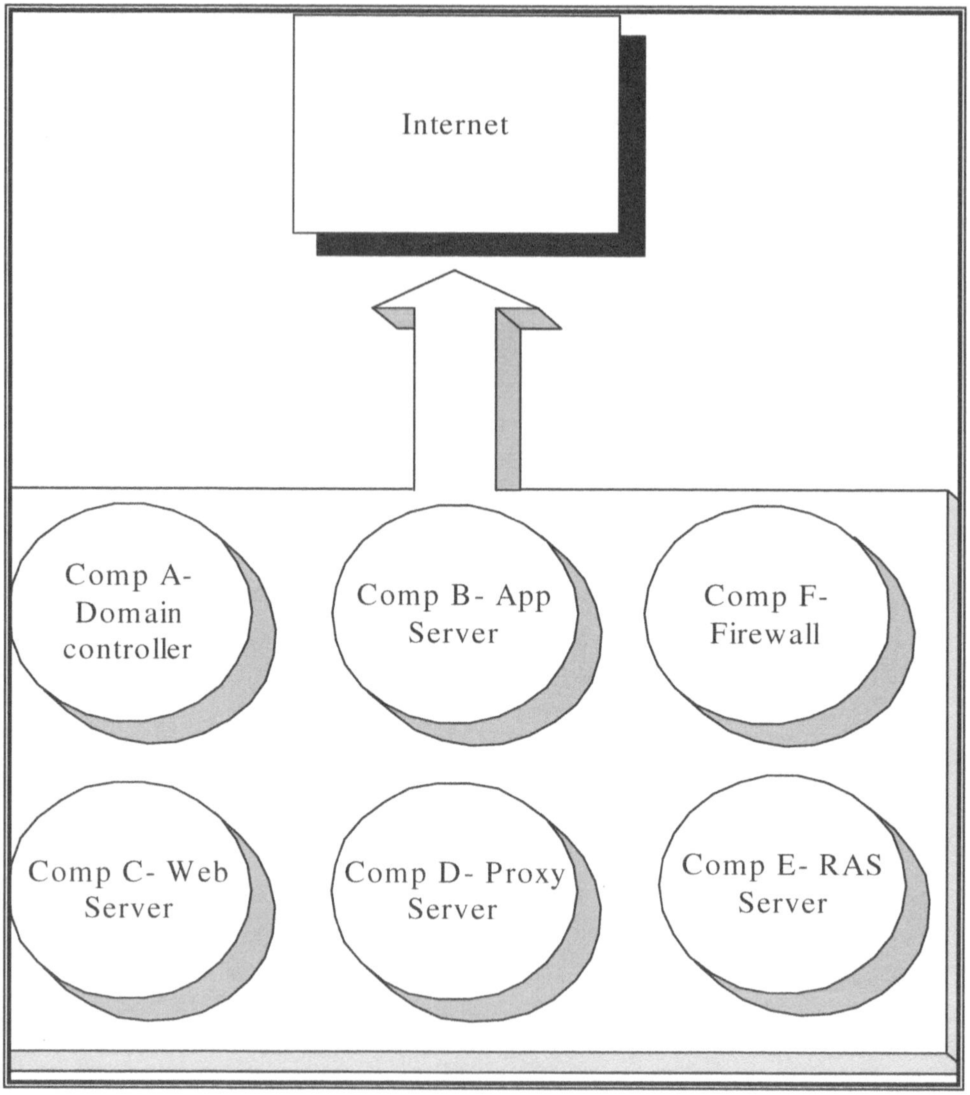

Figure 7.13 Remote Access for SuperBanc

What will be your remote access arrangement for the servers in Building ONE?

Question Exhibit:

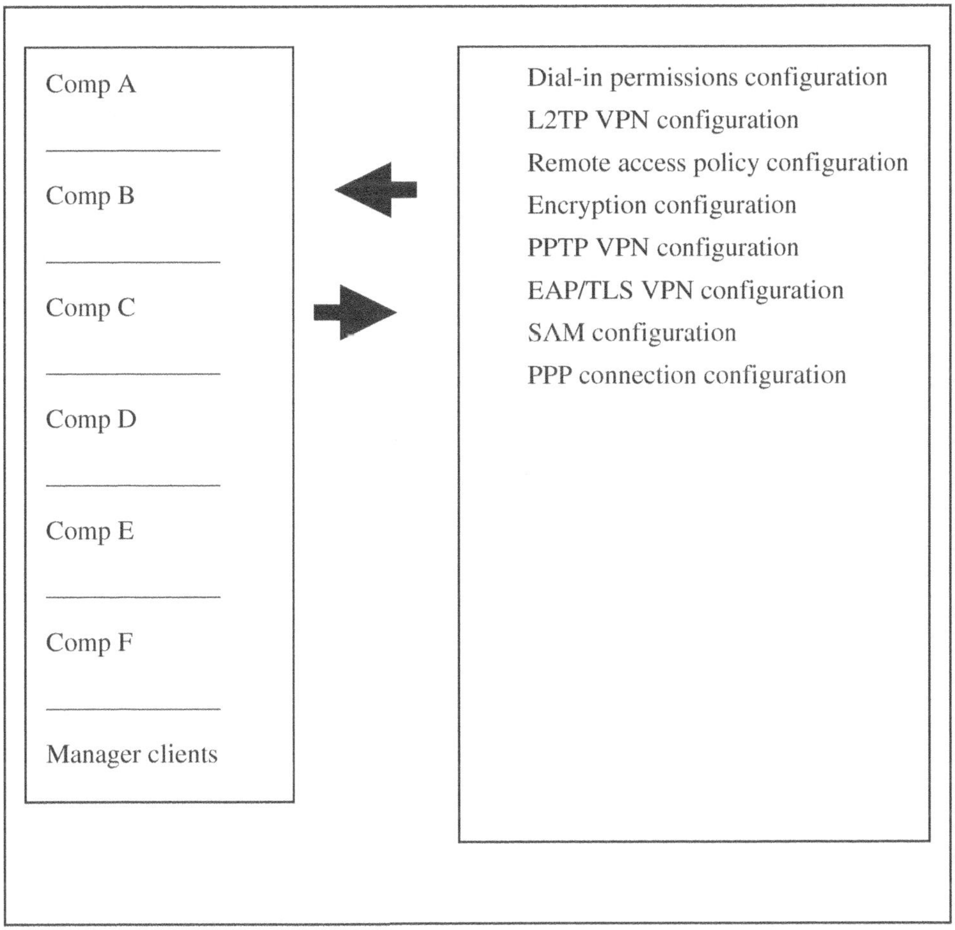

First of all, let's go through the list of options available:

Dial-in permissions configuration – yes, we need this one for the Enterprise IT team.

L2TP VPN configuration – yes, we need this one to support the Manager clients.

Remote access policy configuration – yes, we need this to support the Manager clients.

Encryption configuration – yes, we need this to secure the remote connections.

PPTP VPN configuration – well, since everything is supposed to be Windows 2000, L2TP is preferred over PPTP.

EAP/TLS VPN configuration – we have not been asked to use smart card authentication. No need for this one.

SAM configuration – SAM is the Security Account Manager in NT4.0. No need for this one.

PPP connection configuration – yes, we need this for the dial in clients.

Now, let's take a look at what computers should be involved:

Comp A – this is the domain controller that needs to be remotely administered.

Comp B – it seems like we have nothing to deal with this application server.

Comp C – it seems like we have nothing to deal with this web server.

Comp D – it seems like we have nothing to deal with this proxy server.

Comp E – this RAS server is required for supporting the manager clients.

Comp F – in the world of Windows 2000, VPN does not go through the firewall. Instead, VPN is handled via RRAS.

Based on the above rationales, we can conclude the appropriate configuration:

Comp A

- Dial-in permissions configuration
- Encryption configuration

Comp E

- L2TP VPN configuration
- Remote access policy configuration
- Encryption configuration

Manager clients

- L2TP VPN configuration

Enterprise IT clients

- PPP connection configuration

VIII DHCP for SuperBanc

You need to implement a DHCP strategy for the Europe HQ. Based on the layout below, what is the appropriate placement of the available servers/computers, if only one set of Clustered DHCP Setup is available in Subnet C?

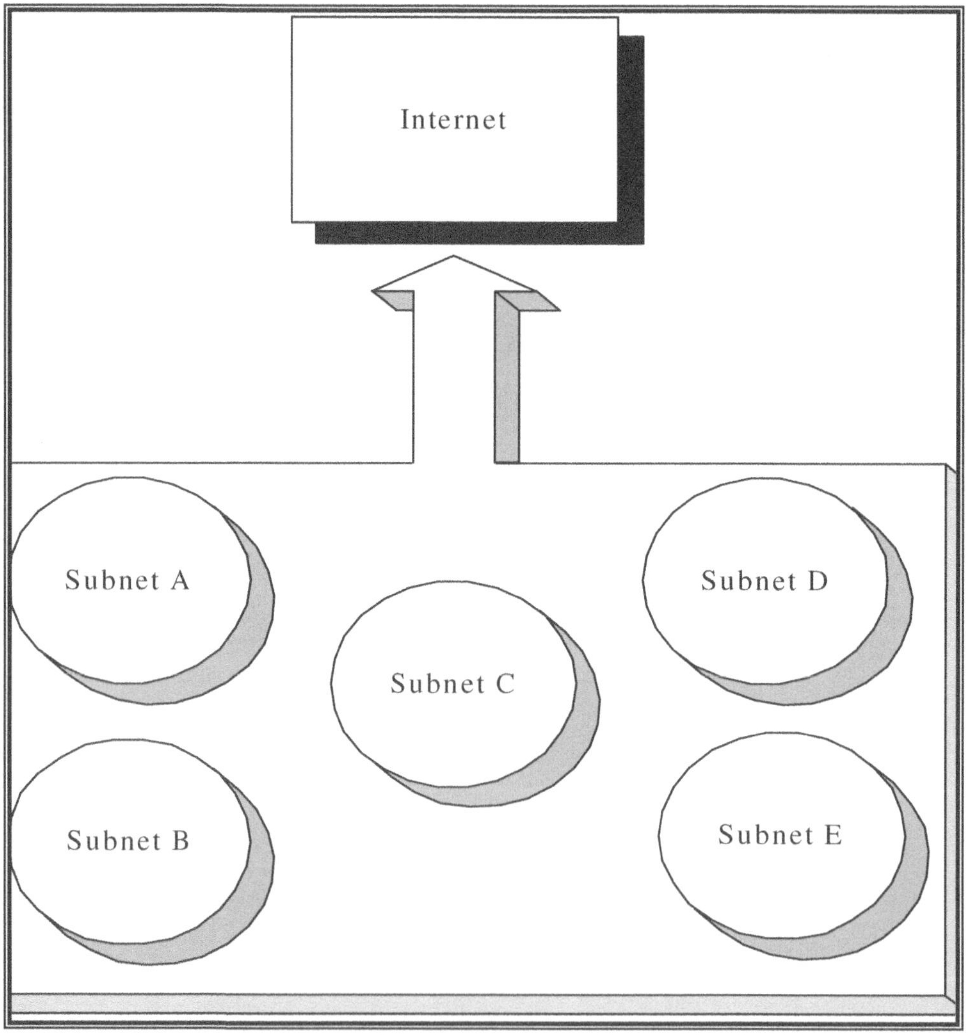

Figure 7.14 DHCP for SuperBanc

Question Exhibit:

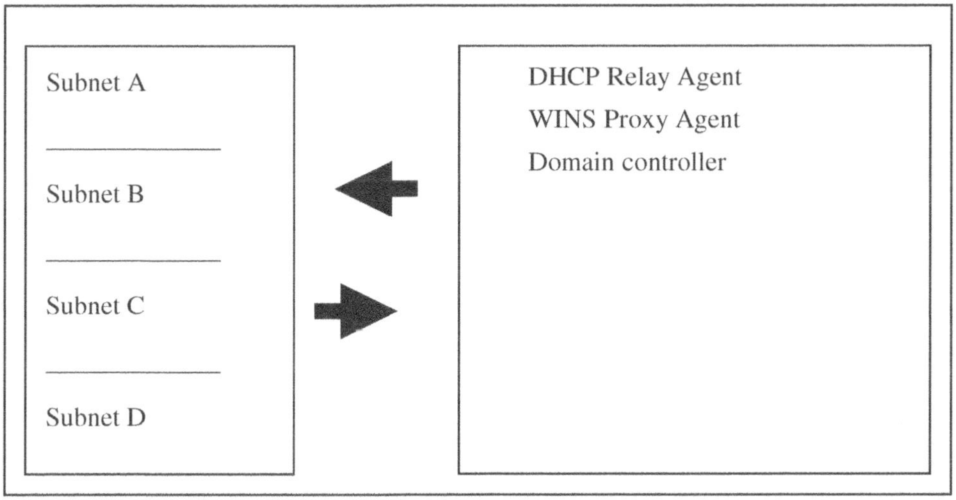

Since Subnet C already has the DHCP Service running, basically nothing else have to be configured for it. Your focus will be on the subnets without local DHCP services, and your only option will always be "DHCP Relay Agent". The other options exist to confuse you only.

Subnet A

DHCP Relay Agent

Subnet B

DHCP Relay Agent

Subnet D

■ DHCP Relay Agent

Subnet E

IX Internet Connectivity for SuperBanc

You need to implement an Internet access strategy for the Japan HQ. Currently the Japan HQ has one T1 connection to the Internet. 90% of the bandwidth usage is for web browsing. Users complain that web access is slow. How do you enhance the overall performance and provide fault tolerance in case the T1 link fails? How do you achieve this in the most cost effective way? How do you enable outgoing web access control?

Question Exhibit:

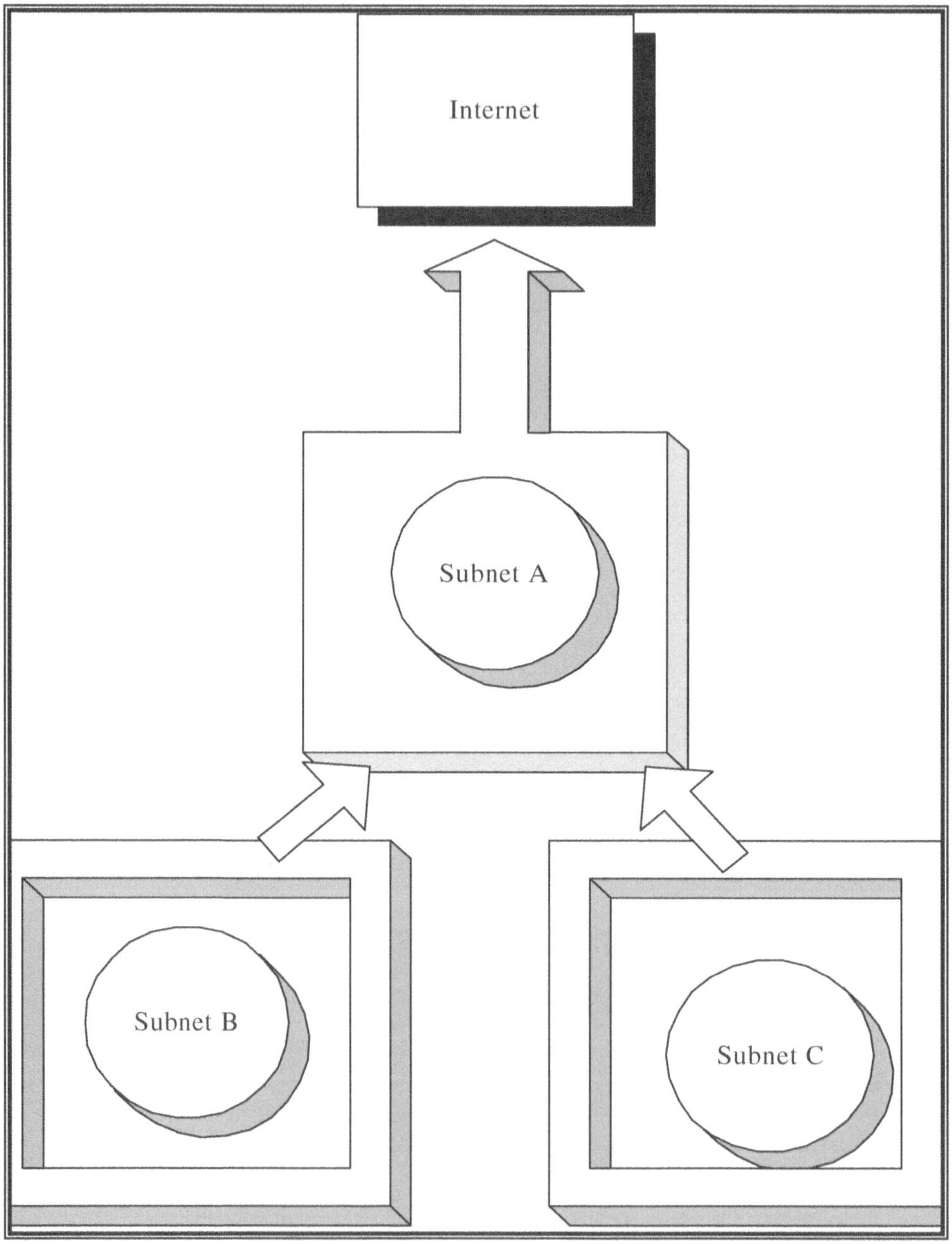

Figure 7.15 Question Exhibit

Depending on the number of users in each building, you may configure multiple Proxy Servers in different building.

Possible Setting

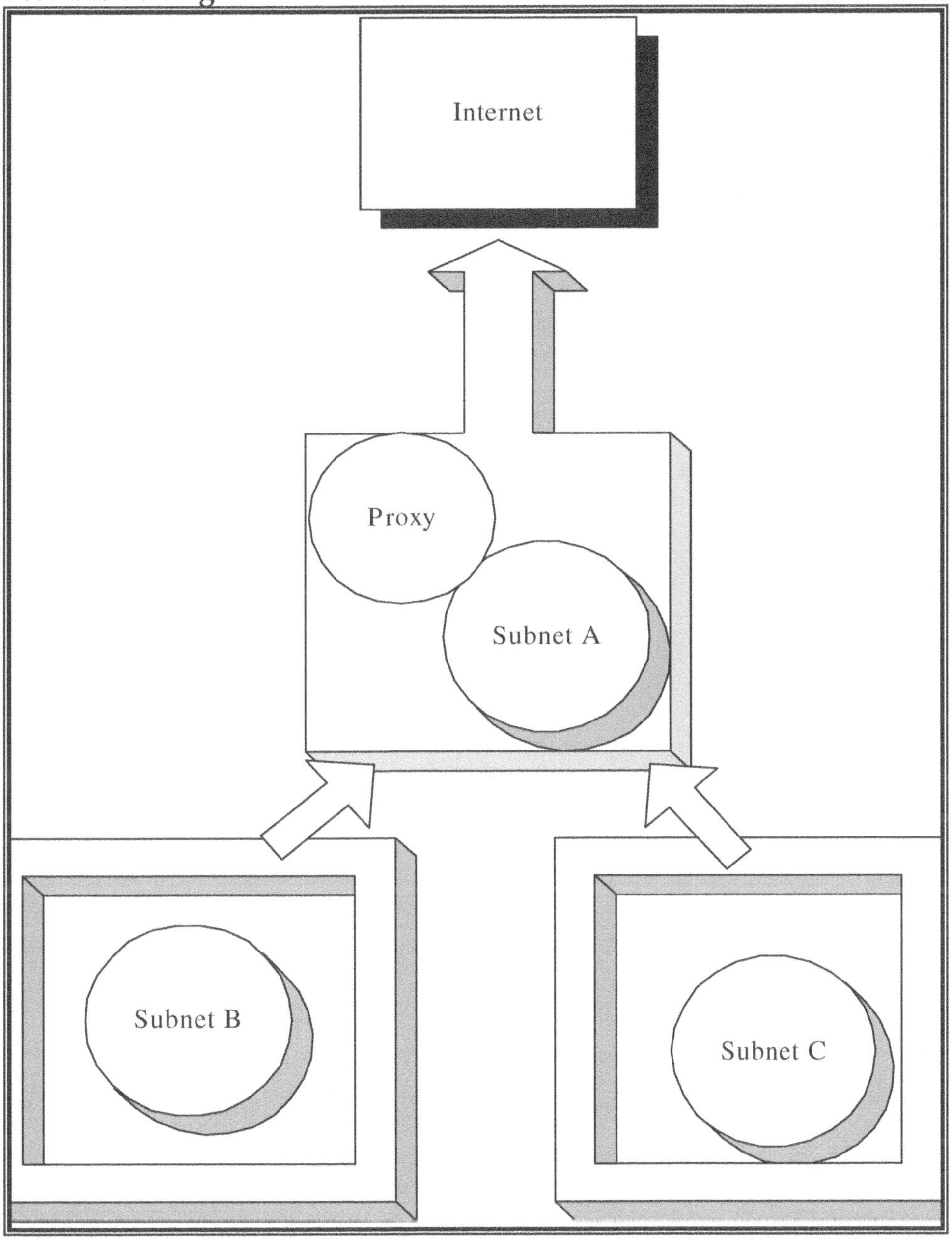

Figure 7.16 Setting One

In Setting One, you place all your Proxy Servers in Building One. This allows centralization of server management. To further maximize performance, the Proxy servers can be configured as an array.

This setting has a drawback. That is, if the number of users in Building Two and Three grow, the links between the buildings will become heavily congested.

Possible Setting Two:

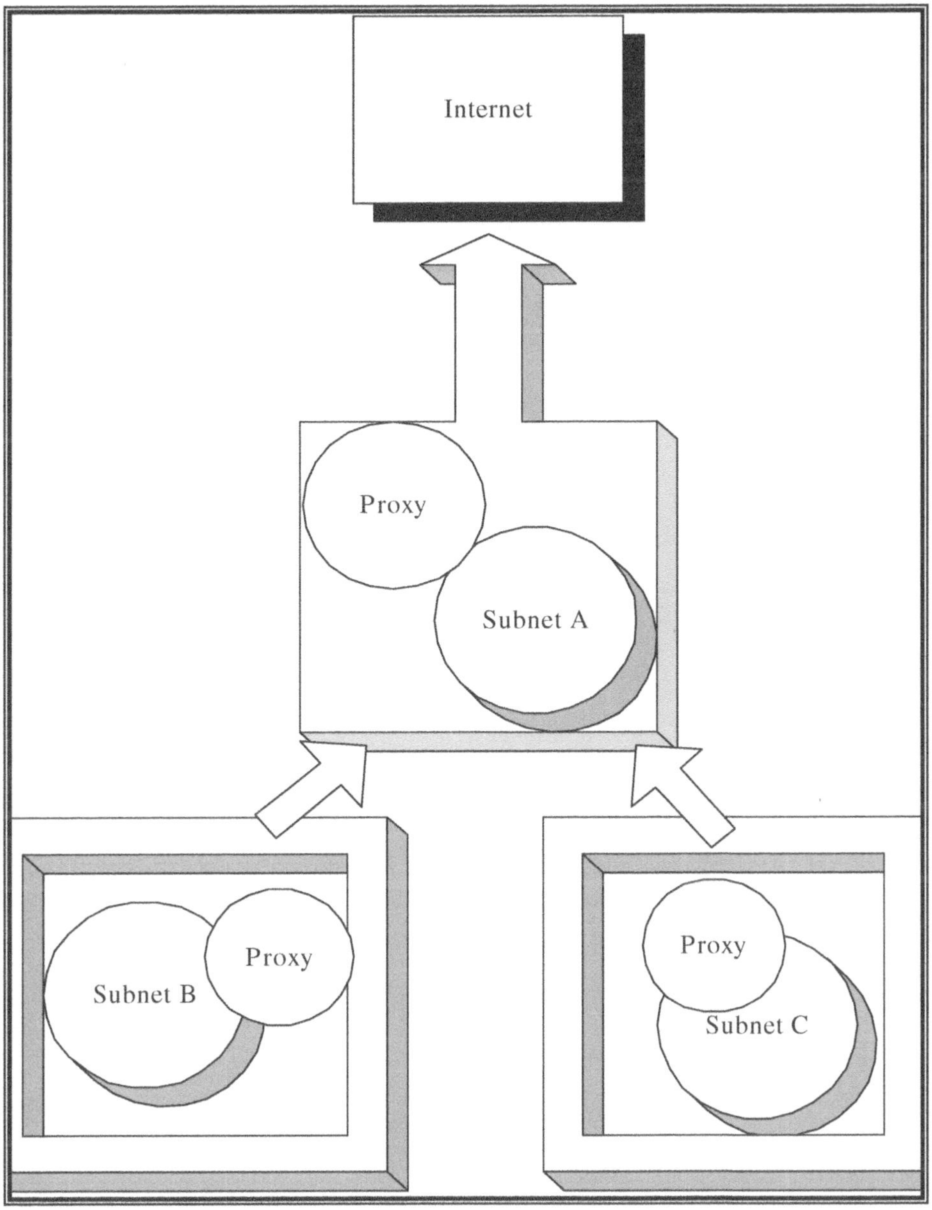

Figure 7.17 Setting Two

In Setting Two, you place the Proxy Servers in every building. This way, caching can be performed at different levels, and can minimize bandwidth consumptions among the intra-building links.

Note that Proxy Server has been discontinued. In the future you may see questions related to the ISA Server instead. The ISA Server Enterprise Edition allows you to manage multiple servers with its central server array management function. Server configurations, access policies, rules, and users and groups can be stored and managed at a single location centrally as a single virtual ISA Server.

If you still want to run Proxy Server 2.0 on a machine which has been upgraded to Windows 2000, you must download the proper Proxy Server updates and have the Proxy Server software reinstalled entirely.

Proxy Server supports two major types of caching methods. With passive caching, contents that have been accessed by the Proxy Server are stored in the local cache. With active caching, Proxy Server can automatically go into the internet and retrieve web contents based on the schedule you defined.

To ensure high availability in case the primary link fails, you should set up an ISDN connection and configure dial-on-demand accordingly.

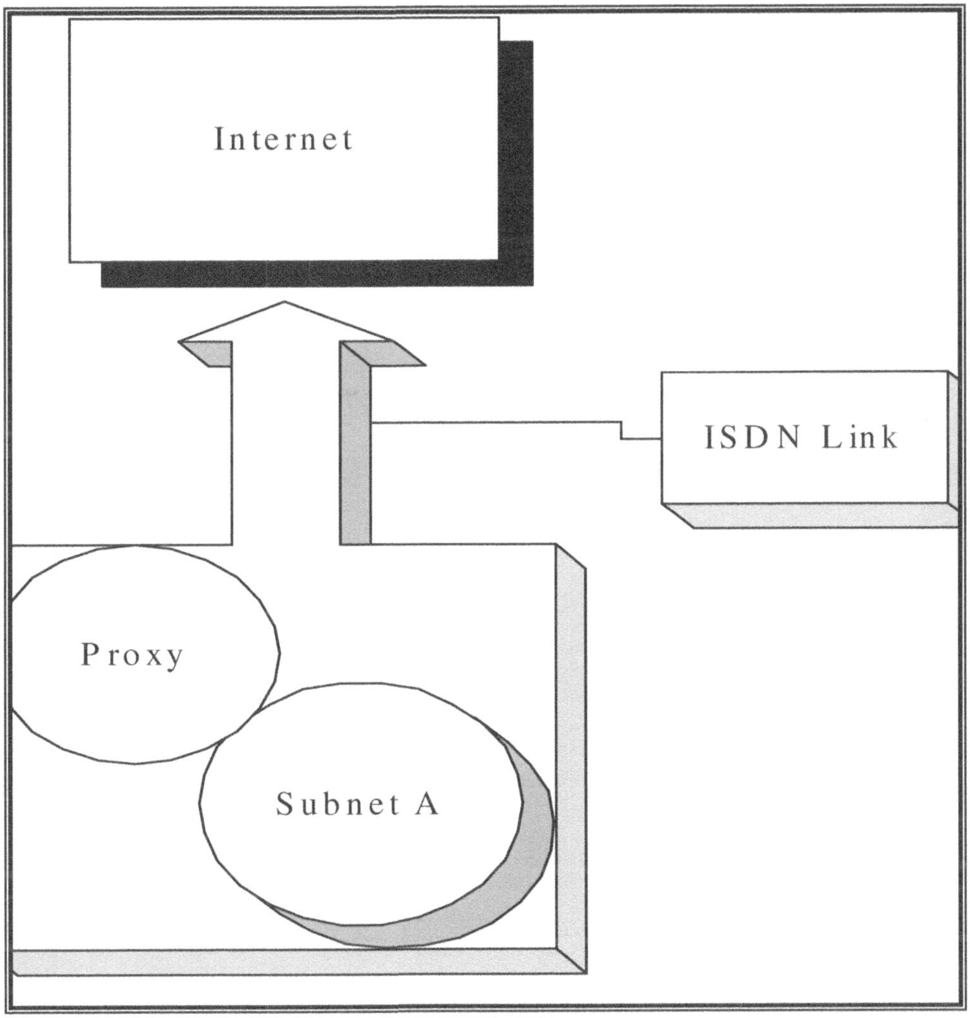

Figure 7.18 Setting Three

X Application Infrastructure for SuperBanc

You need to implement an infrastructure for the new web application that is supposed to run in the North America HQ network. This web application shall consist of the following components:

- ASP modules
- Web Server
- SQL Server Database

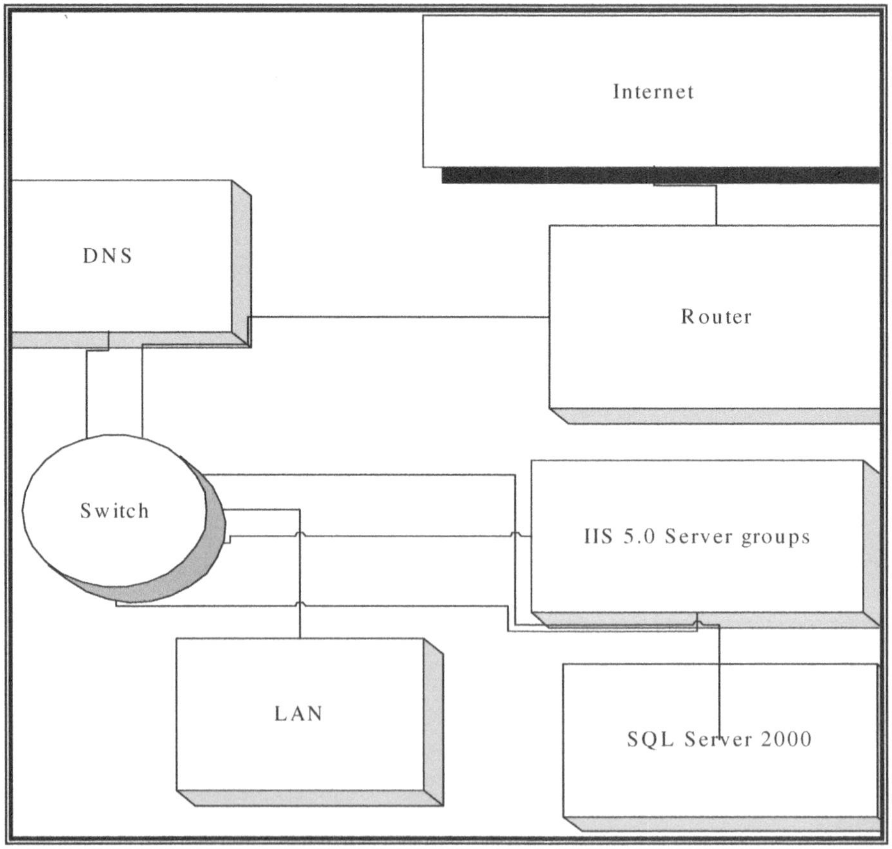

Figure 7.19 Application Infrastructure

You need to fulfill the following objectives:

- Provide load sharing on the web service
- Provide fault tolerance on the SQL database

What strategy should you deploy?

Question Exhibit:

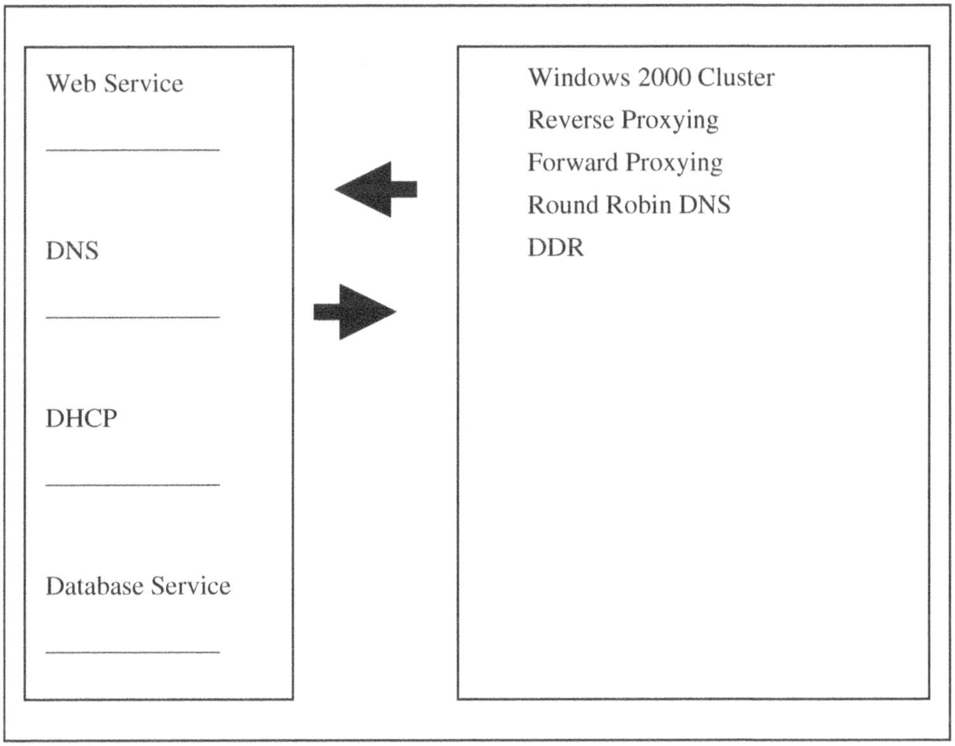

In this configuration, there is nothing special that needs to be done with the DHCP service and the router. To provide load sharing for the web site, one easy way is to use Round Robin DNS. Round Robin DNS is a facility that directs user requests to the different web servers on a round robin fashion. With such functionality, load balancing and high availability can be achieved without investing into the expensive cluster equipments.

With regards to the database operation, it is not possible to “round robin” the database requests due to the difficulty involved in keeping the data in-sync. To ensure high availability, the safest way is to run the database on a Cluster.

DNS

Round Robin DNS

____

Database Service

Windows 2000
Cluster

____

XI Chapter 7: Review Questions

Case 1:

You are a Network Consultant with specialized skills in designing Win2000 directory services. You are recently requested by MyTeapots to design the Windows 2000 network for the entire company.

Background

Since 1970 MyTeapots has been offering products of slate, natural rock, and exquisite crystal water fountains. As a mail order house located in Texas, MyTeapots has its warehouse located in San Jose to serve the customers in the Bay Area. Another office will be opened in New York shortly.

Products

The major product lines available:

Yixing Teapots
Chinese Jade Teapots
Taiwanese Teapots
Japanese Tetsubin
Tea Accessories

In addition, MyTeapots offers fresh hand-picked, full leaf teas. The line of unblended and blended full-leaf varieties include:

China Green Teas
Japan Green Teas
Indian Green Teas
Vietnamese Green Teas
White Teas
Jasmine Teas
Oolong Teas
Black Teas

Departmental Structure

There are 5 departments in the company. The TEA department handles the sales of Tea leaf. The TEAPOT department handles the sales of teapots. The ACCESSORIES department handles the sales of Tea accessories. The WAREHOUSE department handles the inventory. The ADMIN department handles the in house administration.

The management of the company has decided to upgrade to W2K and deploys a single domain model for the Active Directory based network.

There will be 2 sites in the infrastructure, with one in Texas and the other one in San Jose. The 2 sites will be connected with a 64KBPS links.

The management has a strong desire to deploy Proxy Server in the network. There has been one NT4 Proxy Server running on the network. Windows 2000 version is expected.

Questions

1. What is the appropriate domain namespace for the network in Texas?

A. corp.MyTeapots.com
B. www.MyTeapots.com
C. MyTeapots.texas.com
D. corp.texas.MyTeapots.com
E. None of the choices.

---

2. What must be done to provide the maximum possible fault tolerance for the DHCP service running in the Texas network?

A. Configure multiple DHCP servers into a DHCP array
B. Configure RAID 1 for the DHCP Server
C. Configure RAID 5 for the DHCP Server
D. Configure DHCP on a Cluster
E. None of the choices.

---

3. How do you enhance the web client browsing performance in the MyTeapots network in Texas?

A. Configure the proxy servers to form an array
B. Enforce the use of IE 5.x and above
C. Configure the DNS server to support dynamic updates of the web clients
D. Configure the DNS server to support dynamic updates on the Proxy Servers
E. None of the choices.

4. How do you provide firewall capability on the Texas network with the existing server facilities?

A. Enable Packet filtering on the Proxy Server
B. Deploy a tightened policy on the domain controllers
C. Deploy a secured GPO at the domain level
D. Deploy a secured GPO at the site level
E. Install the SNA server on one of the Windows 2000 servers

---

5. What is the minimum number of DNS Server that should be deployed in the Texas network if redundancy is needed?

A. one
B. two
C. one per local subnet
D. two per local subnet
E. one per local subnet plus one per WAN link

---

6. What is the minimum number of DHCP Server that should be deployed in the Texas network?

A. one
B. one per local subnet
C. two per local subnet
D. one per local subnet plus one per WAN link
E. two per local subnet plus one per WAN link

7. What are the benefits brought to the MyTeapots web site by using Round Robin DNS (Choose 2)?

A. Reverse Proxying
B. Load Sharing
C. Fault Tolerance
D. Random routing
E. Enhanced security

Case 2:

You are a Network Consultant with specialized skills in designing Win2000 directory services. You are recently requested by LoveSherpa Inc to design the network infrastructure for the entire company.

Background

LoveSherpa is a company producing and selling the LoveSherpa series of bag - soft-sided pet carrier approved for in-cabin use by major airlines. The LoveSherpa bags are recognized as the premiere soft-sided pet carrier that can provide a safe comfortable trip for the pets by plane, train or automobile.

Locations

Established in New York, it has two branches in East Asia and one branch in London. Due to the expanding demand for this kind of products, instead of manufacturing everything on its own, it is outsourcing many of the production works.

Products

The following products are produced by their contractor in China:

LoveSherpa Lite
The Classic LoveSherpa Traveler
The Kartu Bag
LoveSherpa French Sac
The Ultimate LoveSherpa

The following products are produced by their contractor in Korea:

LoveSherpa Back Pac the All-in-One Bag
Delta Airlines Deluxe Pet Carrier By LoveSherpa
The LoveSherpa-on-Wheels
The LoveSherpa Roll-Up
Original LoveSherpa Bag

Network Structure

Due to the close relationship with the contractors, the company actually shares all its network resources with them. Instead of running its own network, it aims at building a "mega network" that integrates the domains of the contractors into its envisioned directory structure. The domain name for external use will be lovesherpa.com, while the internal one will be LS.com. Also note that there will be one W2K server and one NT4 server available in the head office. The network will run only TCP/IP and nothing else.

Questions

1. You need to configure remote access for LoveSherpa. LoveSherpa's clients consists of:

   Windows 95

   Windows 98

   Windows NT

   Windows 2000

To allow these clients to access the company's network via the internet, which of the following protocols should you use?

A. PPTP
B. L2TP
C. EAP
D. TLS
E. PPP

---

2. You plan to implement IPSec for LoveSherpa's head office and its London branch. You need to secure the communication between these two locations. What action should you take (Choose all that apply)?

A. Configure VPN in the Head Office
B. Configure VPN in the London Office
C. Configure a certificate in the Head Office
D. Configure a certificate in the London Office
E. None of the choices.

3. During the configuration of the WAN link between LoveSherpa's locations, your peer disagree with your decision to use IPSec. Which of the following is an obvious restriction imposed by the use of IPSec?

A. NAT cannot be used
B. DDNS cannot be used
C. L2TP cannot be used
D. PPTP cannot be used
E. RRAS cannot be run

---

4. You need to enhance the web browsing performance for LoveSherpa's clients. What caching mechanism allows caching to take place based on a pre-defined time schedule?

A. Proxy Server passive caching
B. Proxy Server active caching
C. Proxy Server array
D. Proxy Server cluster
E. None of the choices.

---

5. What are the benefits brought to the LoveSherpa's database service by using Windows 2000 Cluster (Choose 2)?

A. Reverse Proxying
B. Load Sharing
C. Fault Tolerance
D. Random routing
E. Enhanced security

6. You are requested to implement an additional subnet on LoveSherpa's LAN in the head office. This subnet will contain 6 clients, all of which are to rely on dynamic addressing. What is the most cost effective way to provide dynamic addressing on this subnet?

A. Install a separate DHCP server in this subnet.
B. Install a DHCP Relay Agent in this subnet.
C. Install a separate bootp router on the other end of this subnet.
D. Install a WINS Proxy Agent in this subnet.
E. None of the choices.

Chapter 7: Review Answers

Case 1:

1, a

2, d

3, a

4, a

5, b

6, a

7, b c

Case 2:

1, a

2, a b c d

3, a

4, b

5, c

6, b

Total Recall

top eBook

ExamInsight For MCP/MCSE Certification: Managing and Maintaining a Microsoft Windows Server 2003 Environment: Examination 70-290

TotalRecall Gives You *Four* Levels of Computer Certification Practice Exams, Books, and eBooks

- Study formats and prices vary so you can choose one that best fits your level of knowledge and skills.
- Each format offers you either free or discounted access to our popular BeachFront Quizzer test engine. See description below.
- ALL come with our exclusive Money-Back Guarantee—pass the exam your first time or get money back!

1. InsideScoop Certification Success Series

Paperback books in the InsideScoop series offer a package of comprehensive study manual and CD-ROM of the BeachFront Quizzer test engine with answers/ explanations linked to relevant chapters in an integrated eBook. The study manual includes detailed information about each core exam topic with pre/post assessment quizzes; an abundance of figures, diagrams and photos; chapter summaries; helpful tips and time management techniques for test taking; lists of useful websites, articles and other learning resources; and an extensive glossary of 600 computer, IT, and telecommunications terms.

Books are $89.99

2. InsidersChoice Certification Success Series

Paperback books in the InsidersChoice series offer a package of comprehensive study manual and FREE download of the BeachFront Quizzer test engine with answers/ explanations linked to relevant chapters in an integrated eBook. The study manual includes detailed information about each core exam topic with pre/post assessment quizzes; an abundance of figures, diagrams and photos; chapter summaries; helpful tips and time management techniques for test taking; lists of useful websites, articles and other learning resources; and an extensive glossary of 600 computer, IT, and telecommunications terms.

Paperbacks are $59.99 and eBooks are $44.99

3. ExamInsight IT Certification System Series

Paperback books and eBooks in the ExamInsight series offer a package of compact study guide and 50% discount to purchase a download of the BeachFront Quizzer test engine with answers/ explanations linked to relevant chapters in an integrated eBook. The study guide includes compact information about each core exam topic with pre/post assessment quizzes; an abundance of figures, diagrams and photos; chapter summaries; helpful tips and time management techniques for test taking; and lists of useful websites, articles and other learning resources

Paperbacks are $39.99 and eBooks are $29.99

4. ExamWise IT Question Book Series

Paperback books and eBooks in the ExamWise series offer a package of Q&A workbook and 30-Day FREE access to a BeachFront Quizzer online practice exam. Each ExamWise Q&A workbook offers you approximately 300 practice questions organized by core exam topic. Questions are arranged in a unique format of two questions per right and page, with answers and brief explanations on the reverse page.

Paperbacks are $39.99 and eBooks are $29.99

The BeachFront Quizzer Test Engine Makes Passing Certification Exams as Easy as a Day at the Beach...

The BeachFront Quizzer test engine was pioneered in 1995 by Bruce Moran, an ex-NASA IT professional turned vocational computer instructor and certification trainer before launching his own book publishing operation in 2002. This popular test engine introduced interactive and adaptive features that other publishers have since tried to imitate, but never duplicate. It offers you four helpful study formats:

1) Adaptive technology generates 15-25 questions in 30-minute sessions to help you identify your strengths and weaknesses for each exam topic.

2) Study sessions help strengthen your weakest exam topics by generating up to 250 questions per topic until you can answer each correctly. Explanations for each question are linked to relevant chapters in an eBook study manual and often to web sites to help you develop a complete understanding of why an answer is correct. By focusing on your rough spots, we'll get you certified fast—guaranteed or get money back!

3) Simulated exams generate randomized questions about core exam topics in 60-90 minute sessions and then provide a score summary by topic. Taking multiple practice exams will build your confidence and ability to concentrate during the real deal!

4) Flash card drills present questions to answer mentally and then allow you to click F4 to display the correct answer.

Visit our web sites for more information:

www.TotalRecallPress.com / www.bfq.com

TotalRecall Certification Publications Microsoft

InsideScoop: TotalRecall's Complete Certification System Series:

InsideScoop to MCP / MCSE Certification: Exam 70-210
Managing Microsoft Windows 2000 Professional

InsideScoop to MCP / MCSE Certification: Exam 70-216
Implementing and Administering a Microsoft Windows 2000 Network Infrastructure

InsideScoop to MCP / MCSE Certification: Exam 70-217
Managing a Microsoft Directory Services Infrastructure

InsideScoop to MCP / MCSE Certification: Exam 70-219
Designing a Windows 2000 Directory Services Infrastructure

InsideScoop to MCP / MCSE Certification: Exam 70-220
Designing Security for a Microsoft Windows 2000 Network

InsideScoop to MCP / MCSE Certification: Exam 70-221
Designing a Microsoft Windows 2000 Network Infrastructure

InsideScoop to MCP / MCSE Certification: Exam 70-227
Installing, Configuring, and Administering Microsoft Internet Security
and Acceleration (ISA) Server 2000, Enterprise Edition

InsideScoop to MCP / MCSE Certification: Exam 70-270
Installing, Configuring, and Administering Microsoft Windows XP Professional

InsideScoop to MCP / MCSE Certification: Exam 70-290
Managing and Maintaining a Microsoft Windows Server 2003 Environment

InsideScoop to MCP / MCSE Certification: Exam 70-291
Managing, and Maintaining a Microsoft Windows Server 2003 Network Infrastructure

InsideScoop to MCP / MCSE Certification: Exam 70-292
Managing and Maintaining a Microsoft Windows Server 2003
Environment for an MCSA Certified on Windows 2000

InsideScoop to MCP / MCSE Certification: Exam 70-293
Planning and Maintaining a Microsoft Windows Server 2003 Network Infrastructure

InsideScoop to MCP / MCSE Certification: Exam 70-294
Plan and Maintain a Microsoft Windows Server 2003 Active Directory Infrastructure

InsideScoop to MCP / MCSE Certification: Exam 70-296
Planning, Implementing, and Maintaining a Microsoft Windows Server 2003
Environment for an MCSE Certified on Windows

InsideScoop to MCP / MCSE Certification: Exam 70-297
Designing Microsoft Windows Server 2003 Active Directory and Network Infrastructure

InsideScoop to MCP / MCSE Certification: Exam 70-298
Designing Security for a Microsoft Server 2003 Network

InsideScoop to MCP / MCSE Certification: Exam 70-299
Implementing and Administering Security in a Microsoft Windows Server 2003 Network

ExamInsight: TotalRecall IT Insight Certification Book Series:

ExamInsight For MCP / MCSE Certification: **Exam 70-210**
Managing Microsoft Windows 2000 Professional

ExamInsight For MCP / MCSE Certification: **Exam 70-216**
Implementing and Administering a Microsoft Windows 2000 Network Infrastructure

ExamInsight For MCP / MCSE Certification: **Exam 70-217**
Managing a Microsoft Directory Services Infrastructure

ExamInsight For MCP / MCSE Certification: **Exam 70-219**
Designing a Windows 2000 Directory Services Infrastructure

ExamInsight For MCP / MCSE Certification: **Exam 70-220**
Designing Security for a Microsoft Windows 2000 Network

ExamInsight For MCP / MCSE Certification: **Exam 70-221**
Designing a Microsoft Windows 2000 Network Infrastructure

ExamInsight For MCP / MCSE Certification: **Exam 70-227**
Installing, Configuring, and Administering Microsoft Internet Security and Acceleration (ISA) Server 2000, Enterprise Edition

ExamInsight For MCP / MCSE Certification: **Exam 70-270**
Installing, Configuring, and Administering Microsoft Windows XP Professional

ExamInsight For MCP / MCSE Certification: **Exam 70-290**
Managing and Maintaining a Microsoft Windows Server 2003 Environment

ExamInsight For MCP / MCSE Certification: **Exam 70-291**
Managing, and Maintaining a Microsoft Windows Server 2003 Network Infrastructure

ExamInsight For MCP / MCSE Certification: **Exam 70-292**
Managing and Maintaining a Microsoft Windows Server 2003 Environment for an MCSA Certified on Windows 2000

ExamInsight For MCP / MCSE Certification: **Exam 70-293**
Planning and Maintaining a Microsoft Windows Server 2003 Network Infrastructure

ExamInsight For MCP / MCSE Certification: **Exam 70-294**
Plan and Maintain a Microsoft Windows Server 2003 Active Directory Infrastructure

InsidersChoice to MCP / MCSE Certification: **Exam 70-296**
Planning, Implementing, and Maintaining a Microsoft Windows Server 2003 Environment for an MCSE Certified on Windows

ExamInsight For MCP / MCSE Certification: **Exam 70-297**
Designing Microsoft Windows Server 2003 Active Directory and Network Infrastructure

ExamInsight For MCP / MCSE Certification: **Exam 70-298**
Designing Security for a Microsoft Server 2003 Network:

InsidersChoice to MCP / MCSE Certification: **Exam 70-299**
Implementing and Administering Security in a Microsoft Windows Server 2003 Network

InsidersChoice: TotalRecall's Insiders Certification System Series:

InsidersChoice to MCP / MCSE Certification: Exam 70-270
Installing, Configuring, and Administering Microsoft Windows XP Professional

InsidersChoice to MCP / MCSE Certification: Exam 70-290
Managing and Maintaining a Microsoft Windows Server 2003 Environment

InsidersChoice to MCP / MCSE Certification: Exam 70-291
Managing, and Maintaining a Microsoft Windows Server 2003 Network Infrastructure

InsidersChoice to MCP / MCSE Certification: Exam 70-292
Managing and Maintaining a Microsoft Windows Server 2003
Environment for an MCSA Certified on Windows 2000

InsidersChoice to MCP / MCSE Certification: Exam 70-293
Planning and Maintaining a Microsoft Windows Server 2003 Network Infrastructure

InsidersChoice to MCP / MCSE Certification: Exam 70-294
Plan and Maintain a Microsoft Windows Server 2003 Active Directory Infrastructure

InsidersChoice to MCP / MCSE Certification: Exam 70-296
Planning, Implementing, and Maintaining a Microsoft Windows Server 2003
Environment for an MCSE Certified on Windows

InsidersChoice to MCP / MCSE Certification: Exam 70-297
Designing Microsoft Windows Server 2003 Active Directory and Network Infrastructure

InsidersChoice to MCP / MCSE Certification: Exam 70-298
Designing Security for a Microsoft Server 2003 Network

InsidersChoice to MCP / MCSE Certification: Exam 70-299
Implementing and Administering Security in a Microsoft Windows Server 2003 Network

ExamWise: TotalRecall IT Insight Certification Book Series:

ExamWise For MCP / MCSE Certification: **Exam 70-210**
Managing Microsoft Windows 2000 Professional

ExamWise For MCP / MCSE Certification: **Exam 70-216**
Implementing and Administering a Microsoft Windows 2000 Network Infrastructure

ExamWise For MCP / MCSE Certification: **Exam 70-217**
Managing a Microsoft Directory Services Infrastructure

ExamWise For MCP / MCSE Certification: **Exam 70-219**
Designing a Windows 2000 Directory Services Infrastructure

ExamWise For MCP / MCSE Certification: **Exam 70-220**
Designing Security for a Microsoft Windows 2000 Network

ExamWise For MCP / MCSE Certification: **Exam 70-221**
Designing a Microsoft Windows 2000 Network Infrastructure

ExamWise For MCP / MCSE Certification: **Exam 70-227**
Installing, Configuring, and Administering Microsoft Internet Security and Acceleration (ISA) Server 2000, Enterprise Edition

ExamWise For MCP / MCSE Certification: **Exam 70-270**
Installing, Configuring, and Administering Microsoft Windows XP Professional

ExamWise For MCP / MCSE Certification: **Exam 70-290**
Managing and Maintaining a Microsoft Windows Server 2003 Environment

ExamWise For MCP / MCSE Certification: **Exam 70-291**
Managing, and Maintaining a Microsoft Windows Server 2003 Network Infrastructure

ExamWise For MCP / MCSE Certification: **Exam 70-292**
Managing and Maintaining a Microsoft Windows Server 2003 Environment for an MCSA Certified on Windows 2000

ExamWise For MCP / MCSE Certification: **Exam 70-293**
Planning and Maintaining a Microsoft Windows Server 2003 Network Infrastructure

ExamWise For MCP / MCSE Certification: **Exam 70-294**
Plan and Maintain a Microsoft Windows Server 2003 Active Directory Infrastructure

ExamWise For MCP / MCSE Certification: **Exam 70-296**
Planning, Implementing, and Maintaining a Microsoft Windows Server 2003 Environment for an MCSE Certified on Windows

ExamWise For MCP / MCSE Certification: **Exam 70-297**
Designing Microsoft Windows Server 2003 Active Directory and Network Infrastructure

ExamWise For MCP / MCSE Certification: **Exam 70-298**
Designing Security for a Microsoft Server 2003 Network

ExamWise For MCP / MCSE Certification: **Exam 70-299**
Implementing and Administering Security in a Microsoft Windows Server 2003 Network

TotalRecall Certification Publications
CompTIA Titles

InsideScoop: TotalRecall's Complete Certification System Series:

InsideScoop to CompTIA A+ Hardware:	Exam 220-301
InsideScoop to CompTIA A+ OS:	Exam 220-302
InsideScoop to CompTIA Network+:	Exam N10-001
InsideScoop to CompTIA Security+ (Second Edition):	Exam SY0-101

InsidersChoice: TotalRecall IT Insight Certification Book Series:

InsidersChoice to CompTIA A+ Hardware:	Exam 220-301
InsidersChoice to CompTIA A+ OS:	Exam 220-302
InsidersChoice to CompTIA Network+:	Exam N10-001
InsidersChoice to CompTIA Security+: (Second Edition):	Exam SY0-001

ExamInsight: TotalRecall IT Insight Certification Book Series:

ExamInsight For CompTIA A+ Hardware:	Exam 220-301
ExamInsight For CompTIA A+ OS:	Exam 220-302
ExamInsight For CompTIA Network+:	Exam N10-001
ExamInsight For CompTIA Security+: (Second Edition):	Exam SY0-001

ExamWise: The TotalRecall Question Book Series:

ExamWise For CompTIA A+ Hardware:	Exam 220-301
ExamWise For CompTIA A+ OS:	Exam 220-302
ExamWise For CompTIA Network+:	Exam N10-001
ExamWise For CompTIA Security+ (Second Edition):	Exam SY0-101
ExamWise For CompTIA I-Net+ Certification:	Exam IK0-002
ExamWise For CompTIA Server+ Certification:	Exam SK0-001

Exam Saver™ Communication
Communicate with your Author/Instructor throughout your certification process
Asktheauthor@bfq.com $249.99 Membership

Money Back Book Guarantee

This guarantee applies only to books published by TotalRecall Publications, Inc.! We are so confident in our products that we are prepared to offer the following guarantee to YOU, our valued customer: If you do not pass your certification exam after two attempts, we will give money back!

Visit http://www.totalrecallpress.com/

Select "Money Back Book Guarantee" for details.

Registered book purchasers who qualify will receive:

1. 50% cash refund of purchase price
2. free TotalRecall book of equal value

NOTE: You must pay for shipping and handling.

To qualify for this TotalRecall Guarantee

you must meet these requirements and perform the following tasks:

1. Register your purchase at the TotalRecall web site
   http://www.totalrecallpress.com/
2. Fail the corresponding exam twice (No time Limit)
3. Contact TotalRecall for the RMA # and to claim this guarantee
   Send email to **mailto:Guarantee@totalrecallpress.com**
   Subject must contain your Membership # or Registration #

Ship the following to claim your refund:

1. RMA # from returned email
2. Documents of exam scores for both failed attempts
3. Return the Book to the following address:

TotalRecall Publications, Inc.

Attn: Corby Tate

1103 Middlecreek

Friendswood, TX 77546

888-992-3131 **bfquiz@swbell.net**

281-992-3131

281-482-5390 Fax http://www.bfq.com/ or http://www.bfqd.com

It's a Passing day here at the BeachFront.

Thank you for using the TotalRecall Certification Success Program.

Bruce Moran, President

ebooster limited

ebooster limited is the authorized distributor for TotalRecall Publications materials in Europe, the Middle East and Africa. We stock the full range of TRP products and charge at competitive prices, especially for volume orders. Come to us direct or order you're your favourite distributors and retailers including Amazon.co.uk, Waterstones, Borders, Books Etc., Gardners and Bertram Books.

e/booster limited	Office	email:
FAO: Chris MacNeil	+44 (0) 207 993 2253	office@ebooster.co.uk
P.O. Box 502 - 14		Web Site
Tottenham Court Rd		www.ebooster.co.uk
London, England		
W1T 1JY		

70-290 Download Instructions

BeachFront Quizzer (BFQ) version 4.0 Special Edition

System Requirements: Windows 95 & 98, NT, XP, 2000 and Server 2003 with a minimum of 6 MB hard disk space and 16 MB RAM.

The Center For Technology Certification, Inc. will help you accomplish your Microsoft Certifications. This state of art software program is designed to cut your study time in half, and get you to a passing level in the easiest and shortest amount of time possible. The program will adapt to you personally, and then lay out a prioritized study plan that will visually show you your progress on a day to day basis. When the software has recognized that you are at a passing level in each objective category, you're ready to sit for the exam. It's really that easy!

Installation Instructions: 70-290 Special Edition Practice Exam with eBook Visit http://www.technologyexams.com/download.php Download and Install the latest version of the BFQ Engine: File Name Quiz32.exe.

Visit http://snipurl.com/EI70290 and download the ExamInsight For 70-290 eBook Zip file to a folder on your hard drive.

This will install all software files:

Open the WinZip file and execute the 70-290SE.exe to install the testing software. Open the LicenseKey.txt file Copy and Insert the 12 digit number **License Key** when requested or type in the following License Key Numbers when requested.

TRP 70-290 SE Windows Server 2003 Environment Special Edition = 368671665867

The software is very user friendly.

After you get the program installed Open Click on the Help button menu Select contents for the on-screen manual. (You may want to print the Help File) You will follow a six step process that will lead you through the program efficiently. We are here to support you all the way. If you have any technical questions on the content, make sure you contact us. We are very proud of our pass rate, and we want you to contribute.

If you need additional assistance, visit our website http://www.totalrecallpress.com/ Please let me know that the download and installation worked properly.

Thank you for purchasing our product and Good Luck with your exam!

Sales: 877-654-2265, 727-450-0476 Technical Support: info@bfq.com 888-992-3131 or 281-992-3131 281-482-5390 Fax

Exclusive Money Back Book Guarantee

This guarantee applies only to books published by TotalRecall Press! We are so confident in our products, we are prepared to offer the following guarantee to YOU:
If you do not pass the real Microsoft 70-221 certification exam after two attempts, we will give money back!

Visit www.TotalRecallPress.com Select "Money Back Book Guarantee" for details.
Registered book purchasers will receive

1. Receive a 50% cash refund of purchase price

OR

2. Receive a free TotalRecall Press book of equal value.

To qualify for this TotalRecall Press Guarantee you must meet these requirements and perform the following tasks:

1. Register your purchase at the TotalRecall Press web site

   www.TotalRecallPress.com

2. Fail the corresponding exam twice (No time Limit)

3. Contact TotalRecall Press for the RMA # and to claim this guarantee

   Send email to **Guarantee@TotalRecallPress.com**

   Subject must contain your Membership # or Registration #

Ship the following, to the address listed below, to claim your refund.

1. RMA # from returned email

2. Documents of exam scores for both failed attempts

3. The 70-221 Book you have

TotalRecall Press

Attn: Corby Tate

1103 Middlecreek

Friendswood, TX 77546

888-992-3131 **bfquiz@swbell.net**

281-992-3131 **http://www.bfqonline.com**

281-482-5390 Fax **http://www.bfq.com**

It's a Passing day here at the BeachFront.

Thank you for using the TotalRecall Press Success Program.

Bruce Moran President

Made in United States
Cleveland, OH
05 November 2026

47670553R00192